Part One

The Writing Crisis

What Your English Teacher Didn't Tell You

Everything You Need to Know about Showcasing Yourself through Your Writing

Jean Reynolds, Ph.D.
Polk State College
Winter Haven, Florida

The Maple Leaf Press

WritewithJean.com

TABLE OF CONTENTS

Preface

So you want to be a better writer—congratulations! This book offers strategies for writing tasks in school and college, as well as your community, career, and personal life. You'll be learning the skills needed to showcase your personality, your ideas, and your accomplishments.

A new world opens up when you put your writing before the public—and computers have made it easier than ever before to reach a wide audience with blog posts, short stories, poetry, magazine articles—even a book. The only requirements are life experience (which you already have), determination, and writing skills.

But that is where too many people abandon their dreams. You may be a student right now, or you may already have completed required English courses in high school. Perhaps you took additional writing courses in college, and you may also have studied literature, absorbed the principles of composition, toiled night after night over your essays, and worked your way through a labyrinth of grammatical terminology. (I did all those things too.)

Despite all that effort, you may not be satisfied with your writing skills. It's true of many high school and college graduates (I used to feel that way too), and the problem is growing.

I'm an English teacher myself, and I've seen that kind of frustration again and again in the students I've taught during my long career. There were many late nights for me as I marked up thousands of student compositions. Although I worked as hard as my students did, the results were mixed, especially in my early years of teaching.

(If you're an English teacher, you can view a free PowerPoint about easing that paperwork load—while *improving* student performance—at this link: paperworkload.com. You can read an article about strategies for grading student papers at this link: paperworkrevolution.com.)

Many students enjoyed my classes, and I often saw real progress. But there were also students who continued to find writing confusing and difficult, and I used to wonder why. They completed the grammar drills, but usage mistakes continued to creep into their writing, and students couldn't spot them or fix them. Essays that were weak and disorganized continued to cross my desk. What, I wondered, was wrong? Teacher friends told me they faced the same problems.

Meanwhile I was facing new writing challenges myself. I became a prison teacher and learned a different kind of writing—incident and disciplinary reports for hearings that could determine an inmate's future. Businesses hired me as a writing consultant. I began publishing—a wonderful adventure that put me in touch with some of the best editors in the business.

What didn't your English teachers tell you? Answering that question led me to write this book. Quite simply, the curriculums, textbooks, and teaching software found in many school systems aren't always designed to prepare students for real-world writing. The reasons go back almost a thousand years, to the early days of the English language (see p. 8).

Writing is a tool—a powerful one—for communication, problem solving, and showcasing your personality, ideas, and knowledge. Here's a simple truth: If you aim to write like a professional, you need to know how to think like one. But some high school and college writing curriculums and teaching materials seem designed to teach you how to think like…a student.

For example, many composition textbooks have little to say about business and professional writing. Chances are you'll have to sign up for a technical writing course in college if you want to study business writing in depth. And what about submitting your work to magazines, journals, and commercial publishers? The first time I ever heard a professor talk about writing for publication was in my doctoral program.

This book will show you how professional writers think. (Hint: It doesn't involve diagramming sentences, labeling parts of speech, or circling adverbial clauses.) You'll learn quick fixes for usage problems, and you'll practice sound principles for organizing and presenting your information and ideas. There are practice activities, with answers provided so that you can check your understanding.

Why Write?

The answer is simple: When you write well, doors magically open. If you're still in school, your grades will go up. Your writing skills will help you succeed in science courses (which often require lab reports). You'll excel in courses that require research papers.

In the working world, good writing skills can help you get noticed and advance in your career. The higher up the career ladder you go, the more writing you're likely to do. High-paying positions often involve emails, memos, correspondence, reports, PowerPoints, and speeches.

If you're an innovator, you'll be able to present your ideas in professional newsletters, magazines, and journals. And the benefits of writing will spill over into other areas as well: You'll be able to help your children with their homework, take a leadership role in your community, and record your memories for friends and family. You can write articles for the newspaper in your town, launch an influential blog, write a novel...the opportunities are almost limitless.

What You'll Find inside This Book

My aim is to offer you a straightforward and practical pathway to better writing. In Parts One and Two I'll encourage you to discard some timeworn ideas about writing and replace them with a fresh approach that builds on what you already know (you may be surprised!). A pretest will help you evaluate your writing skills and design a personal writing plan.

Part Three deals with nuts-and-bolts writing issues: Organizing your ideas, writing effective sentences, and avoiding common mistakes. I'll show you a simple but powerful organizational system for putting together paragraphs, articles, and reports. (I use it myself for almost everything I write.)

Part Four is especially for students—although every writer can benefit from the information about modes of development, research, and Wikipedia.

Parts Five and Six deal with English usage. You'll discover that almost all writing employs four basic sentence patterns. Additional chapters cover punctuation and tips for avoiding common errors such as run-on sentences, comma splices, fragments, and parallelism.

Part Seven is for professionals (although students can also benefit from this information). You'll learn strategies that the pros use, as well as tips for self-publishing, creative writing, and business writing. There's information here about word-processing, copyright, and mistakes that even pros make.

At the end of this book you'll find a list of print and online resources. I especially encourage you to visit my website, WritewithJean.com, which offers free instruction, videos, and practice material on a host of writing issues. I hope you'll visit it often—and that you'll share your thoughts, questions, and suggestions with me: WritewithJean.com. Note: There are *no* paid endorsements in this book. I've recommended books, websites, and technology that have worked well for me for a long time. (There's no paid advertising on any of my websites either.)

Acknowledgments

Writers are made, not born. I owe my own success to a long line of great English teachers and professors, including William Testerman, Sara Deats, John Clark, and Richard Dietrich. I am forever indebted to a wonderful editor (now a successful mystery writer!), Maggie Barbieri. Colleagues at Polk State College were generous with their knowledge and experience, and my students helped me refine and broaden my ideas about language and writing. Members of Write Like a Pro in Winter Haven, Florida and the Literary Society at Polk Correctional Institution have been a sounding board for many of the ideas in this book, and their passion for writing helped shape this book.

I'm grateful to Tom Dowling for his expert help with my marketing materials, and to my reviewers Marcella Cooper and Wittaya Ongwiriyaphan for their helpful and generous feedback. A special thank-you goes to Natalie Bilokonsky for her superb copyediting. Her sharp eye and extensive writing background saved me from many errors.

My deepest gratitude goes to my husband, Charlie Reynolds, for...everything.

Free Resources

For students:

- PlanMyPaper.com (videos and PowerPoints about writing essays, articles, and reports)
- ResearchPaperSteps.com (videos and PowerPoints about research papers)
- WritewithJean.com (Jean's blog about a variety of writing topics)

For English instructors:

- PaperworkLoad.com (a PowerPoint about more responding more efficiently to student papers)
- PaperworkRevolution.com (an article that explores new approaches to grading papers)

Chapter 1

Why Writing Matters

There's a writing crisis in this country. Business and government leaders say their employees don't know how to handle technical writing and business correspondence. Overworked English teachers say they're seeing more usage errors and weaker essays. Students fear they're not ready for college and career writing tasks. Even the psychiatric profession is worried about writing: The *Diagnostic and Statistical Manual of Mental Disorders* now includes a category called the Disorder of Written Expression.

This epidemic of bad writing creates confusion and inefficiency that waste a great deal of time and money. Some sobering data came to light when the National Commission on Writing surveyed human resource directors who oversee nearly 2.7 million state government employees. According to the Commission's report, two-thirds of state managers complained that clerical and support staff had inadequate writing skills. The Commission estimated that the states spend $221 million each year on basic writing instruction, sometimes sending workers to $400-per-employee classes. In the end, of course, taxpayers and consumers underwrite these expenses.

Government officials have expressed concerns about the costs associated with these writing problems. "It's impossible to calculate the ultimate cost of lost productivity because people have to read things two and three times," said former Arkansas Governor and US Presidential candidate Mike Huckabee.

Former Senator Bob Kerrey described his own experiences with unintelligible memos, letters, and reports. "I read things that were absolutely incomprehensible," he said. Another hidden cost is the likelihood that good ideas are overlooked because readers miss their impact. "I see that all the time in writing and political speaking," Huckabee said. "There are some really bright people who can't communicate, and as a result their ideas probably aren't given the attention they deserve." Yet another problem is that writing problems may disqualify job seekers from landing jobs. Rachel Levy, director of marketing at Just Military Loans in Delaware, says she sees serious language flaws in many of the job applications that cross her desk.

Business leaders in the private sector share the same concerns. T. Rowe Price, for example, has a senior staff member—Garry Cosnett, head of global equity communications—who works full time helping employees with their writing. "It's amazing, the frequent disconnect," he said. "These are people who all did the very best at the best schools, probably since preschool, but they really have not developed their writing skills to the degree that they would have to in order to succeed in this organization."

In 2013, the Association of American Colleges and Universities published a survey of 318 employers conducted by Hart Research Associates. Eighty percent said colleges should focus more on written and oral communication. A recent Forbes study found that one of the skills employers most want to see in college graduates is the ability to create and edit written reports.

Colleges and universities—even topnotch schools—agree about the need for better writing skills. In a June 2013 article in the *New York Times*, Verlyn Klinkenborg described the writing deficiencies he encounters in the writing classes he teaches: "In the past few years, I've taught nonfiction writing to undergraduates and graduate students at Harvard, Yale, Bard, Pomona, Sarah Lawrence and Columbia's Graduate School of Journalism. Each semester I hope, and fear, that I will have nothing to teach my students because they already know how to write. And each semester I discover, again, that they don't."

Vast amounts of time, money, and expertise have been invested in the search for solutions without, however, reversing the trend. In California only ten percent of community college freshmen arrive with the writing skills needed for college: Remedial writing classes cost money and slow down students' progress towards a college degree. Other states report similar problems. Rachel L. Jablon, who teaches at the University of Maryland, says her students "barely write on a high-school level, let alone on the college level that is expected of them by their instructors."

Standardized testing, widely touted as the solution to our nationwide writing problem, has had little success. Florida abandoned its controversial standardized tests for college sophomores: Despite their enormous cost, the tests did not ensure that college graduates could write effectively. In 2005, responding to doubts about using multiple-choice questions to evaluate writing, the College Board added a writing sample to the SAT. Despite the added incentive for students to write better, English teachers are still waiting to see improvements.

Searching for Causes

Why, when so much time and money are expended on writing instruction, are writing problems so prevalent today? Experts have offered various reasons:

- Students don't try hard enough
- Schools are neglecting basic skills
- Classes are too large
- Teacher workloads are too large
- Homework has fallen out of favor
- PowerPoints and other innovations have replaced traditional assignments
- Tweeting and texting reinforce careless writing

But lately some experts have been pointing to another possible factor: English teachers are required to pass on an academic tradition that may have little to do with what really goes on inside a successful writer's brain. The purpose of this book is, very simply, to teach you how to think like a *writer*.

That probably sounds strange. After all, English teachers are the guardians of a long tradition that has produced some of the world's greatest literature. And English teachers are an inspiring lot (I've been one myself for over forty years), magically transforming the lives of countless students. (I owe my own career to the late William Testerman, an amazing teacher who had a powerful influence on me and many other students.) The brains of English teachers can do wonderful things, and one of the goals of this book is to teach you what we know.

But it's difficult to try to teach every skill in an overcrowded English 101 class that's designed around an equally overcrowded curriculum. A conventional

English class might have to cover such disparate topics as identifying compound and complex sentences, memorizing various categories of grammatical terms, and writing five-paragraph essays about poetry. (Another point is that students aren't always motivated to take advantage of the knowledge that's offered to them. I vividly remember my own resistance to learning.... If I had only listened harder to what Mr. Testerman was trying to tell me in my English classes!)

Please note that I'm not taking a stand against English usage, English literature, or any of the other topics in a typical curriculum. (For the record: I'm a stickler about good usage, I have a doctorate in English literature, I've written for a number of literary publications, and I'm on the editorial board for a scholarly journal.) But the fact is that huge numbers of English teachers share my frustration: We're not seeing the results we want from our students.

In Praise of English Teachers

As I said a moment ago, I've been an English teacher myself for over forty years, and it's not my intention to bash my dedicated and hard-working colleagues. No one outside the profession (with the possible exception of our long-suffering spouses) knows how hard we work. Here's just one example: One of my friends required surgery on both wrists to correct the carpal-tunnel problems created by years of grading papers.

And it's not just our hard work that commands respect. English teachers have a vast amount of useful information that we can call up in an instant. Here's something that happened in my classes all the time, to the astonishment of my students: As I walked to the chalkboard, I'd glance at a paper on a student's desk and spot a problem in, say, the second paragraph. It didn't matter that the paper was facing him, not me, or that I'd barely looked at it. I'd say, "Tim, I think there's a misspelled word in the third sentence of your second paragraph." Any English teacher can easily do the same thing.

Friends, family, and co-workers often ask for our help when they want to produce excellent writing—a school assignment, application letter, report. Our knowledge of English is deep and wide, and we're generous about sharing it.

But English teachers themselves will tell you that something is not right. Despite late-night grading sessions and oceans of red ink, students keep making the same usage errors and handing in disorganized and poorly developed papers. English teachers don't need a government study to tell us that America has a writing problem: We confront it every day.

Why I Wrote This Book

Years ago I began venturing outside my classroom to learn more about real-world writing. I became a consultant to agencies and corporations that were dissatisfied with their employees' writing skills. I went back to school myself for my doctorate and was blessed with a dissertation committee of superb writers who kindly but relentlessly pointed out my writing weaknesses. Most important, I became an author, publishing ten books and many articles for newspapers, magazines, and journals.

The more I wrote, the better I wrote, thanks to some sharp-eyed and demanding editors. And I wasn't the only writer who was improving. Soon I began to notice that my students were producing better papers. My new experiences gave me a better understanding of the difficulties they were grappling with and a larger arsenal of strategies for overcoming them.

Most important, I began to develop a writer's identity. Instead of lining up dry facts and ideas, my papers began to have a recognizable voice. (Can you hear it as you read these pages?)

I was thrilled, and gradually a new idea began to form: I would write a book—the one you're reading—for all the frustrated writers I've met. I vowed that I would focus on the most important skills of all—learning how writing can showcase yourself, your ideas, and your accomplishments.

What do I mean by "showcasing yourself"? Here's a story from my own career. Years ago, when I taught inmates in a Florida prison school, I noticed that the staff running the prison didn't always have the communication and problem-solving skills they needed. At workshops I heard other teachers saying the same thing, but no one knew what to do about it.

I decided to use my writing skills to call attention to the problem. I wrote an article about the importance of communication and problem-solving skills for a prison newsletter. My article was noticed by some important decision makers, and soon I was conducting workshops in a number of prisons.

Could you do the same? Very likely the answer is *yes*—if you're ready when the opportunity presents itself. Low-cost self-publishing opportunities and social media offer you unlimited possibilities to publicize your knowledge and accomplishments and—even more important—to influence other people.

Let me tell you a story about a famous person who *wasn't* prepared when the opportunity arrived. Jimmy Carter, who was elected President of the US in 1976, didn't appreciate the importance of public speaking until he arrived at the White House. In 1979 he decided to bring speech consultant Dorothy Sarnoff to help him speak more effectively to television audiences.

In her book *Speech Can Change Your Life*, Sarnoff described the busy weekend she spent working with President Carter. He worked hard, she remembered, but he was already President. Because there were so many demands on his time, he could spare only a few hours each day to work with her.

In her book, Dorothy Sarnoff had this advice for anyone with big dreams and large ambitions: "Speaking and communicating skills should be sharpened before you sit in the big leather chair, behind the big executive desk, in the big executive office. Once you get there, the demands of public and corporate life are so consuming that there's little time to develop those needed skills."

What about *you*? Will you be ready for the speaking and writing challenges that might lie ahead? Would you benefit from joining Toastmasters (a worldwide, nonprofit organization that has helped countless men and women improve their speaking skills)? Do you need to set aside time in your busy life for daily writing practice? And are you committed to start preparing for the future *right now*? If the answer is *yes* (and I hope it is!), read on.

Blame Julius Caesar

But to really understand why English studies are sometimes out of touch with real-world writing, we need to go back to the Roman Empire. Under the leadership of Julius Caesar, Rome extended its empire far across Asia, Africa, and Europe, bringing the Latin language along with it.

As the Roman Empire spread, local people were glad to replace their own languages with Latin in order to obtain high-paying jobs with the Roman government. (The link between money and language continues today: The better you can write, the more likely you are to hold a high-paying position.)

Another important influence was Christianity, which did much to spread the Latin language far and wide. For a time Latin became the preferred language of the upper classes in many places—including what we call the United Kingdom where, of course, the English language was born.

In 1066, when Norman the Conqueror triumphantly led his army into England, the same thing happened with French (a language that had its roots in Latin). Soon English was spoken only by the lower classes, while French was preferred by the wealthy and educated. As a result of this class split, centuries later we continue to use words derived from Latin and French in many professions. *Appellate*, *judiciary*, and *verdict* are familiar examples from the legal field; *operation*, *procedure*, and *cardio-pulmonary* are just a few of the many medical examples.

Meanwhile Latin lived in on schools and colleges, and educators tried to adapt their subjects to fit a Latin framework. Often Greek was offered as well. (William Shakespeare studied both languages intensively in school.) Residues of those days still live on in modern educational practice.

For example, many schools still seat students in rows of desks to write down what an instructor tells them—a throwback to the Dark Ages when books were scarce because the printing press hadn't been invented yet. By contrast, no business would waste valuable time that way. If your boss has information to share, it will be photocopied, faxed, or emailed to you, ready to read.

The academic traditions of the past still shape the way we teach English today. English is related to German, not Latin. It doesn't make sense to use Latin grammar to teach English—but that's exactly what happened in British schools. When the young Shakespeare went to school at Stratford-upon-Avon, he was taught in Latin, not English. And vestiges of that Latin tradition live on today.

For example, let's take a look at how English verbs are taught in modern schools. In English, unlike many other languages, verbs have few endings. *I dance, you dance, we dance, they dance, Fred and Ginger dance*—there's no need to change the word "dance" unless you use a singular subject: *Fred dances* or *he dances*. (Old English used to have many more noun and verb endings, but most of them disappeared more than a thousand years ago.)

On the other hand, present-tense Latin verbs have six endings, not two. Here are the endings for *amar*, the Latin verb "to love":

I love	**amo**	We love	**amamus**
You (sing.) love	**amas**	You (pl.) love	**amatis**
He, she, it loves	**amat**	They love	**amant**

Look inside any English textbook and you'll see the same six-part, Latin-based table:

I	**dance**	We	**dance**
You (sing.)	**dance**	You (pl.)	**dance**
He, she, it	**dances**	They	**dance**

Nobody seems to have noticed that our English verbs don't require this elaborate system. Only one verb category has a different ending: *He, she, it dances*. But the Latin system lives on, and children struggling with the difference between *he don't* and *he doesn't* are supposed to memorize a table with six parts and apply it when they write and speak.

It would be much simpler to teach children the rhyming phrase "1, 2, I, you," explaining that only "1" verbs get "s" endings: *He dances, she dances, Fred dances,* and so on. =

1 – S / He, she, it **dances**

2 / They **dance**

I / I **dance**

You / You **dance**

I used to tell my students to draw this little box on scratch paper before they tackled a writing task:

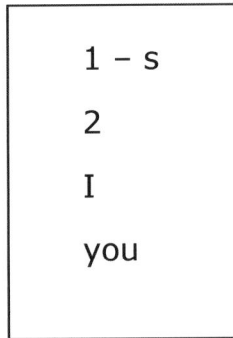

```
1 – s

2

I

you
```

But Latin-based instruction is so entrenched in our educational system that we're not likely to replace it anytime soon.

The classical tradition lives on in many other areas of academia, needlessly complicating the lives of everyone who wants to learn to write well. For example, some of the grammatical rules most revered by English teachers were invented by overenthusiastic Latinists who thought that English should be just like Latin.

The absurdity of what they were trying to do is obvious. For example, word order is almost irrelevant in Latin but very important in English: "A man bit a dog" is different from "A dog bit a man." In Latin, word order doesn't matter: The endings of the words tell you who did the biting and who was the victim. But the classical zealots in England's past ignored the huge differences between English and Latin, thereby discrediting some perfectly good English linguistic structures.

One example is the split infinitive. An infinitive is defined as "to" followed by a verb—for example, "to love." A "split" infinitive has a word between "to" and the verb—for example, "to deeply love." Some English teachers will still tell you that it's wrong to split an infinitive because infinitives can't be split in Latin.

Of course that's ridiculous: In Latin, you couldn't split an infinitive even if you tried, because all Latin infinitives are single words: *Amar* (to love). But it's both normal and useful to split infinitives in English. Think of Captain Kirk's powerful description of the mission of the Starship Enterprise on the original *Star Trek* TV show: "To boldly go where no man has gone before."

That's great writing—but traditionalist English teachers cringe when they hear it. They want you to say "To go boldly," even though that wording sounds awkward to us. Why? Because that's how Julius Caesar would have said it. (I used a split infinitive at the beginning of "Blame Julius Caesar" on p. 9: "But *to really understand* why English studies have lost touch with real-world writing, you need to go back more than 2000 years to the Roman Empire." Did that sentence cause problems for you? I doubt it.)

Contractions (*I'm*, *didn't*, *he's*) suffered the same fate. There are no contractions in Latin because many Latin words are so short already: The Latin word *sum*, meaning "I am," is only one syllable. But some worshippers of Latin decided that what can't be done in Latin shouldn't be done in English either. The result is piles of student essays full of stiff, unnatural prose: "I *am not* playing basketball this semester because I *do not* have time to go to all the practices and games." "I'm not" and "I don't" would sound much better—but the Ghost of Latin Past bars those useful words from many English classrooms.

Another damaging effect of our linguistic history is the widespread misconception that English words are somehow inferior to Latin-based words. Too many professional people today can't talk to lay people because they lack a common language. The fields of medicine, psychology, and law operate with a vocabulary derived from Latin or Greek that may be incomprehensible to the average man and woman. For example, the physician discussing your X-rays may use terms like "proximal to" and "anterior to" rather than "near" and "in back of."

Picture a woman with limited education holding a sick child and frantically searching for the children's clinic in a hospital—and not being able to find it because the sign says "Pediatrics Clinic"—from *paido*, the Greek word for "child." What's wrong with "Children's Clinic," and how much confusion is caused by our misplaced reverence for Greek and Latin? One goal of this book is to teach you how to produce thoughtful, intelligent writing without befuddling your readers.

Just last month I had a depressing reminder about our misplaced reverence for Latin. A government agency hired me to spend a morning encouraging employees to use clear, simple English in their written and spoken communications with citizens. To kick off the workshop, I asked participants to choose which of these requests they liked better:

a) Because of September's heavy rain, the picnic area will be closed until next Monday.

b) Due to an excessive amount of precipitation during the month of September, the area normally available for outdoor dining during the midday period will be unavailable for the remainder of this week.

Depressingly, *every participant* voted for option **b**—even though **a** is more clear and efficient. (By lunchtime I'd made real headway in my advocacy for normal English, but it wasn't easy.)

Perhaps the worst long-term effect of our classical heritage is the damage it does to students' confidence. Countless students who can't master Latinate terminology like *antecedents* and *conjunctive adverbs* give up trying to write well because they mistakenly believe that they have to know Latin grammar in order to write well in English.

The damage extends to our society at large, for we all pay the price when we fail to communicate effectively with one another. What if all the confusion between doctors and their patients could be wiped away? What if everyone who works for a business could write well? What if everyone in government knew how to communicate clearly and concisely?

Imagine how our health statistics, consumer confidence index, and gross national product data would look! There are encouraging signs that change is afoot, at least in government writing: In 2010 Congress passed the Plain Language Act, requiring greater clarity and simplicity in government writing, and President Obama signed the bill.

Here's a question I've often used to motivate my own students: How would your own life improve if you sharpened your writing skills? If you're in school, think about the impact on your grades; if you're in the working world, think about the effects on your career and income; in your personal life, think about the memoir you'd like to write or the short stories you long to create. The simple truth is that acquiring better writing skills can change your life for the better.

How Professional Writers Think

Professionals know that writing is primarily a *thinking* process. I can testify that professional writers rarely think in terms of "adverbial conjunctions" or "compound predicates." When I sit down to write, I ask myself how to:

- balance my need to sound sophisticated and professional with my readers' need for clarity and simplicity
- showcase myself, my ideas, and my accomplishments most effectively
- write more efficiently
- make my information convincing
- make a personal connection with my readers

Professional writers use all kinds of tricks to engage readers. One you're going to learn is called "arrive late, leave early" (p. 93). On p. 116 in this book you'll learn about "hot spots," such as the first and last sentences in a paragraph, that help you add interest and emphasis to your writing. You'll master four sentence patterns that add sophistication and polish to your writing without befuddling your readers. If you find yourself worrying about making mistakes, Part Six features a complete review of English usage, with practice exercises and answers.

One area that I think urgently needs a fresh approach is *modes of development*. Most writing courses require students to use various organizational tools including comparison/contrast, process, classification, narrative, and cause/effect. Sadly, the examples in writing textbooks tend to be little more than lists of facts, and the papers that students turn in are just as dull.

But professional writers know that these modes of development are powerful thinking tools and problem solvers. Why not teach them that way? The writing textbook I published with Prentice Hall some years ago did exactly that—and both instructors and students found it helpful. In this book I use same approach. (See Chapter 18 beginning on p 125.)

I hope you'll be surprised and delighted to learn how simple these principles are. While I was organizing ideas for this book, a thought kept popping into my head: *If only someone had told me these things back when I was a freshman....* (Or if only I had listened when my teachers *did* tell me about them! Ah, youth.)

Here's an easy trick that can instantly make your writing sound more professional: Occasionally change a period to a semicolon. This is easy to do; just remember to lower-case the word after the semicolon. (I just did it! Here's how that sentence would read with conventional punctuation: *This is easy to do. Just remember to lower-case the word after the semicolon.*)

But most conventional English textbooks complicate semicolons by offering a long explanation couched in Latinate terminology: *Use a semicolon to combine two independent clauses that are closely related in thought, especially if they're joined by a conjunctive adverb or a transitional phrase.* Yikes! Semicolons aren't that hard—honest.

Here's another issue that preoccupies professional writers: Efficiency. Someone who's working hard to finish a 300-page book on a deadline doesn't have time to diagram sentences or label parts of speech. Professional writers need quick strategies for getting English usage and punctuation right the first time. There isn't time to tangle with the Latin grammar we talked about a few pages ago. Here are some professional tricks that anyone can use:

- A simple rule that for placing possessive apostrophes correctly, so that there's no confusion about "before the *s* or after the *s*" (p. 180)

- How an inexpensive highlighter can help with commas (p. 102)
- Two categories for word-groups that eliminate the need to learn confusing grammatical terminology (p. 164)
- An easy way to distinguish between restrictive and non-restrictive clauses (p. 164.) Surprise: You do it already when you're speaking!
- Tips to overcome procrastination (see p. 86)
- A foolproof way to use semicolons (you already read how on p. 14)
- A trick for simplifying complicated sentences (p. 115)

Most important are the strategies and tips that the pros use:

- Techniques to make writing sound more sophisticated without sacrificing clarity and simplicity
- A strategy called building to a climax (p. 98—I've used it several times in the pages you've just read—did you notice it?)
- A template for organizing writing projects in school and the workplace (p. 47)
- Ways to use modes of development as thinking and problem-solving tools (p. 125)
- Information about real-world writing topics like copyright, word-processing (p. 276), blogging (pp. 240-1), and images (pp. 243-4)

Throughout this book I've also provided links to my website, WritewithJean.com, where you can find more practice activities, additional instruction, and lively examples to enhance what you're learning—all free.

Unlike more traditional books that start with a review of abstract grammar, this book aims to build on what you already know. Here are the four principles that guided me as I was writing this book:

1. You are already a language expert.

Whether your native tongue is English or some other language, you already know a great deal about how language works.

2. You can train your ear and eye to help you write correctly.

Simple guidelines like the Thumb Rule (p. 188) and "finish the sentence" (p.

189) can clear up confusion instantly without long grammatical discourses about *subjects*, *objects*, *agreement*, and *case*.

3. Good models are invaluable.

Old-time language instruction wasn't always bad: One excellent practice, largely forgotten in today's schools, was having students imitate the writing of famous authors from the past. You can do the same.

4. Writing is communal.

If you read biographies of famous authors, you'll learn they met to share their writing. C.S. Lewis, author of the Narnia books, belonged to informal group called the Inklings; another member was J.R.R. Tolkien, author of *The Hobbit* and *The Lord of the Rings* trilogy.

Even if you're shy, you can benefit from feedback from others. (No, they won't shred your writing or your ego if you know what to ask for.) This book will show you how sharing your writing can build your confidence and competence.

5. Anyone can learn to write well.

Writing requires expertise in language, which you've been using all your life, and with thinking, which you've been doing since you were born. There's nothing mystical or mysterious about writing well. I hope you're excited about the adventures that lie ahead!

Chapter 2

What You Need to Know—and What You Know Already

Your brain is a living computer that specializes in language—even if you've never spent a single minute thinking about formal grammar. Linguistics experts say that we're born with the hard wiring for language already installed in our brains. By the time we're two or three years old, we've learned most of the grammar we need to know, without even thinking about it. That's how powerful our brains are.

And that's only the beginning. As the years go by, our days of full of language experiences that stimulate our brains to develop additional neurons and connections. In Chapter 3, "Your Amazing Brain," I'm going to show you that you know much more about language, grammar, and usage than you think.

One important goal for this book is to *build on what you already know*. For example, did you realize that you automatically lower and raise your voice for certain constructions when you're speaking? Listen to yourself read this sentence aloud to see what I mean:

Caroline who did such a good job on the budget report should be on the financial committee. EXAMPLE

Changes are you lowered your voice slightly for "who did such a good job on the budget report." (Try it again—you'll hear it!) That voice change is the basis for Comma Rule 3, which you'll learn more about on p. 172. Here's how to punctuate the sentence you just read:

Caroline, who did such a good job on the budget report, should be on the financial committee. CORRECT

Solving English Usage Problems

Because I've spent so many years teaching writing courses, I know what students are likely to know and where most of the usage problems lie. For example, many people—and perhaps you—write "women" when they mean "woman": *My Aunt Betty is an amazing* **women**. (Here's how the sentence should read: *My Aunt Betty is an amazing* **woman**.) Similarly, many people:

- aren't quite sure about the difference between *it's* and *its*
- sometimes put an apostrophe after the *s* in *its*
- are afraid to use semicolons
- are frightened by hyphens (I used to be afraid of them myself)
- aren't sure when to capitalize words like *mother* and *father*
- struggle with everyday word pairs like *good/well* and *I/me*
- sometimes write *there* instead of *they're*

The good news is that most usage problems are surprisingly easy to solve. You've learned more than you think in both school and your daily language experiences, and you can easily build on that knowledge:

1. Most professional sentences are based on just three comma rules (p. 163).

2. You can stop worrying about fancy grammatical terminology: Every group of words is either a *sentence* or an *extra idea*, and those two categories are the building blocks of everything you write (p. 102).

3. You can solve most pronoun problems with just four rules (p. 187).

4. You can solve most subject-verb agreement issues with just five rules (p. 195).

5. There are two ways to use apostrophes, and you already know one of them—contractions (p. 180).

6. A few simple tricks will ensure you're using capital and lower-case letters correctly (p. 216).

7. You can easily train your brain to sort out confusing words like *good/well, I/me, it's/its,* and *they're/there/their* (Chapter 36, p. 208).

8. There are only two rules for using hyphens (p. 231).

9. Problems with misplaced modifiers (p. 224) and parallelism (p. 225) are easier to solve than you might think.

Mastering English usage requires focusing on these nine issues. How long do you think it would take you to work your way through that list? The answer: Probably not as long as you think. Remember: You already know much of this content. Here's the *real* question: Are you willing to make that commitment? The ability to write well gives you a tremendous advantage in school, college, and almost any career. Who *wouldn't* be willing to work on these skills?

Tackling Writing Tasks

Once you're finished with school, there are no more spelling quizzes or usage tests. You'll need to focus on various kinds of writing tasks, such as emails, business correspondence, and reports. Perhaps you're also interested in writing short stories, creating a memoir, or some other kind of personal writing.

Every type of writing requires you to generate ideas, organize them, and put them into sentences. Not everyone masters these skills in school. You may have unpleasant memories of struggling to write an essay or research paper, rushing to finish it at the last minute, and then wincing when your work was returned full of corrections. *I tried hard*, you're thinking. *What went wrong?*

Writing can seem like a hit-or-miss proposition. (I often felt that way myself in school.) Sometimes teachers loved my work; other times it seemed I couldn't do anything right. *If only someone would show me a surefire way to do this*, I would think every time an essay was returned covered with arrows, circles, and scribbled remarks in red ink. The good news is that someone has done it (and you might be surprised to hear that I'm not claiming credit). Professional writers have known for a long time (more than a thousand years) how to present their ideas, knowledge, and personalities to best advantage. What they know—and have passed on—is the basis for this book.

Dealing with Brain Freeze

If you've ever been assigned an essay or research paper, you've probably experienced the dreaded *brain freeze* phenomenon. You sit there looking at a blank piece of paper or an empty computer screen, and NOTHING HAPPENS. You can't think of anything to write. The words just won't come...and you conclude that you're just not cut out to be a writer.

Brain freeze is the reason many students wait until the last minute to tackle writing assignments, causing more problems. Because time is so short, there's no time to call upon the brainpower I talked about at the beginning of this chapter. The result is wails from teachers that *Nobody knows how to write any more* and *My students can't even put a sentence together*.

The good news is no one has to struggle with brain freeze...*ever*. I've published ten books and many articles (plus a doctoral dissertation and numerous research papers). I started out the same way many students did, putting the assignments off and handing in work that did not please my teachers. (That's an understatement!) But I was lucky enough to have instructors and editors who showed me some strategies that worked amazingly well, and I'm sharing them with you in this book.

How the Pros Do It

Pros don't see a blank piece of paper or an empty computer screen. What they see are *shapes*. The problem, of course, is that these shapes are invisible. Pros are familiar with them, but new writers have to learn how to see them. Once you've figured that out, you can write like a pro. (Have you ever heard a sculptor described as a person who frees a statue that's trapped in a block of stone? The same idea is true of writers.)

Are you curious about what these shapes looks like? Here are typical shapes that a writer might use for an article, essay, research paper, or business report:

Introduction

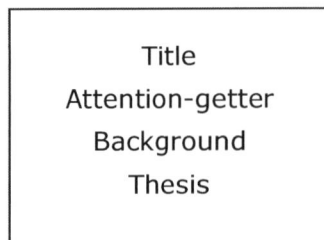

Title
Attention-getter
Background
Thesis

Body paragraph

```
┌─────────────────────────┐
│     Topic sentence      │
│   Ideas and examples    │
│                         │
└─────────────────────────┘
```

Body paragraph

```
┌─────────────────────────┐
│     Topic sentence      │
│   Ideas and examples    │
│                         │
└─────────────────────────┘
```

The pro keeps writing body paragraphs this way until the piece comes to the end:

Conclusion

```
┌─────────────────────────┐
│ Wrap up your essay      │
│ with an example,        │
│ an idea, or a           │
│ prediction. Don't       │
│ introduce anything      │
│ new. Repeat your        │
│ main point.             │
│                         │
└─────────────────────────┘
```

You'll see an actual essay organized this way on p. 50.

When I work on a writing task, I imagine these boxes in front of me. If I follow the instructions, I will end up with a professional article, report, or book. (If this imaginary box sounds strange to you, think of all the times you follow an invisible set of instructions for everyday tasks like tying your shoelaces, making a sandwich, and fixing a technology glitch.)

You'll be learning how to do all this as you read this book. If you'd like to get a head start, you can watch several short, free PowerPoints and videos about organizing an essay at PlanMyPaper.com.

Part Two

Getting Started

Chapter 3

Your Amazing Brain

In 1993 a pair of psychologists named Nalini Ambady and Robert Rosenthal experimented with an unusual way to evaluate teachers. They asked students to watch three short videotapes—less than 10 seconds each—with the sound turned off. The students were able to rate the teachers as accurately as other students who sat through an entire course. Ambady and Rosenthal repeated the experiment with even shorter videotapes—just *two* seconds long. The results were the same.

I learned about this unusual experiment in Malcolm Gladwell's *Blink*, a fascinating book about our ability to do many types of fast, accurate, and complex thinking in only a few seconds. The human brain, Gladwell says, is like "a giant computer that quietly processes a lot of the data we need in order to keep functioning as human beings." What's even more interesting, Gladwell says, is that much of this thinking happens "entirely below the surface of consciousness."

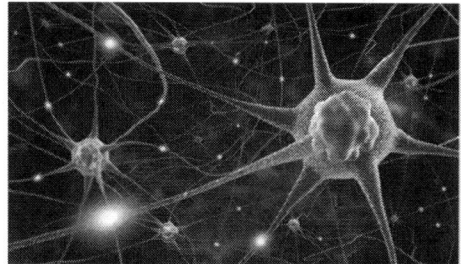

If you watch yourself go through a typical day, you'll quickly come to the conclusion that Gladwell is right. While you're maneuvering your car through a complicated maze of streets in rapidly changing traffic, you can sing a popular song that's playing on your iPod, settle an argument with your children in the back seat, and plan what you'll serve for dinner—never noticing how many tasks you're processing, smoothly and competently, while your hands are on the steering wheel and your eyes are focused on the road ahead.

Could that brainpower be used to help you become a better writer? *Yes.* Unfortunately many would-be writers take a detour into traditional grammar terminology when they set out to improve their skills. It's sad but true: Many people who could be wonderful writers give up on that dream because they find

23

Latinate grammar so boring and confusing. What's even worse is that no one ever tells those hopeful writers that they've already mastered a surprising amount of information about how the brain processes language. *Building on what you already know* is the fast track to becoming a better writer.

To get you started, here are four examples of the hidden language processes your brain uses again and again. I figured these out myself over many years. As time went by, I became my own teacher—something you can do yourself as your awareness grows. After all, language is all around you: All you need to do is start noticing. Later we will use these four processes as building blocks for expanding your writing skills.

1. Your brain is already programmed to expect a new sentence every time a sentence ends with the word *and* followed by a comma.

I know what you're thinking: "Not my brain! I'm not good at commas. I don't think that way." Yes, you do, and I can prove it.

Imagine that you're reading a story about a family picnic at a beautiful state park. While you're reading, you come across a sentence that starts like this:

We roasted marshmallows and a squirrel…

Poor squirrel. That was a pretty nasty picnic! But now suppose the same words had been written with one change—a comma, like this:

We roasted marshmallows, and a squirrel…

You know without even stopping to think about it that the squirrel (hallelujah!) is ok. The sentence is saying that the squirrel *did* something:

We roasted marshmallows, and a squirrel grabbed one.

And there you have it: Proof that your brain automatically reads a sentence differently when there's a comma. To put it another way: Comma rules aren't arbitrary annoyances invented by grammar experts. Your brain automatically knows how to interpret them.

So here's a useful rule: Whenever you write an *and*, check to see if there's a new sentence coming. If so, use a comma. Compare these two examples:

I invited Bob and Mary...
I invited Bob, and Mary...

I would bet the farm that you instantly recognized that there's a big difference between these two examples. In the first, I invited two people: Bob and Mary. In the second, Mary probably issued her own invitation: I invited Bob, and Mary invited someone else. (Incidentally, *but* works the same way, and so do five other words: *nor*, *or*, *yet*, *so*, *for*. You'll learn more about these words in the chapter beginning on p. 167.)

2. Often your brain can use a single clue word to automatically complete an idea.

I know this is another one that sounds crazy: In an instant, your brain expands a single word into a whole idea? Yes, it does, and again I can prove it.

Imagine this scenario: It's Friday afternoon, you've spent most of the week sitting at a desk, and you want to do something more active after work. Bowling! You call a friend who enjoys bowling as much as you do to suggest meeting at Cypress Lanes tonight at seven. Your friend says, "I'd love to, but..." and his phone goes dead—he forgot to charge the battery.

Is your friend going bowling with you? Probably not. When you heard "but," your brain automatically finished the sentence: "I can't tonight."

Now try a slightly different scenario: Your friend says, "I'd love to, and..." before his phone shuts off. Your brain automatically finishes the sentence: He's probably going to be there at seven.

Clue words are powerful tools. When readers know where you're taking them, your ideas are easier to read and understand. And because your audience is having a good reading experience, they think you're a good writer. Good writers frequently use clue words like *but*, *therefore*, *because*, and *however*—and so should you.

3. A couple of commas can convey a lot of information.

This is a vital skill that all of us learned years ago, when we were growing up and beginning to master language. If you've been around small children for any length of time, you know that they tend to run ideas together in long, breathless strings of ideas. You may need to listen patiently in order to figure out what *really* happened on the playground or at the birthday party.

But most adults know how to construct sentences that convey information concisely and efficiently. For example, the two sentences below are almost the same. If you were the person responsible for running off copies of the budget report, which sentence would require *more* copies of the report? (If this question sounds strange to you, try reading the sentences aloud. You'll notice the difference immediately!)

Committee members, who were away last week, will need budget reports.
Committee members who were away last week will need budget reports.

In the first sentence, *everyone* on the committee was away and will need a copy. In the second sentence, only *some* of the members were away and will need copies, and you will have less work to do. How do you know? The commas (or the lack of them) tell you what you need to know. (You'll learn more about these commas when you read about Comma Rule 3 beginning on p. 172. Many English teachers refer to this construction as an *interrupter*.)

4. Building to a climax adds power to your ideas and examples.

Arranging ideas for effect is another skill that most of us developed as we were growing up, without ever noticing that we were learning something important. Small children tend to blurt out information in any order, but most adults automatically perform a surprisingly sophisticated sorting process—and they do it rapidly and unconsciously.

Picture yourself telling a friend about a recent meeting with your boss for your job evaluation. Put the phrases *complimented me on my efficiency,* *promoted me to assistant manager,* and *praised my problem-solving skills* into the blanks below, in the order you think best:

My evaluation with Mr. Chinowski went really well. He
_____, _____, and
_____.

Did you put *promoted me to assistant manager* into the last blank? Most people do—and properly so—because the promotion was the best news you received during your evaluation. Good writers constantly think about *climaxes*— saving the best item in a list for last, putting the best example at the end of a paragraph, and making the final point in an argument as strong as you can.

Beginnings are just as important: You can use them to pique your readers' interest or to make a complicated subject easier by explaining where your readers will be going and how they'll get there. Later we'll explore how thinking about beginnings can help you write a better report for your job, get a higher grade on a research paper, or market a book.

For now, though, let's celebrate something important you've already accomplished: Your brain has created the beginnings of a template for sorting and organizing ideas. You can easily build on that foundation to learn how to shape a writing task. (You'll learn more about templates beginning on p. 46.)

Chapter 4

Make a Writing Plan

Of course you can improve your writing without a writing plan. If you simply read this book and apply the strategies you're learning, your writing will definitely get better. But your progress will almost certainly be better if you do an assessment and follow it up with a plan that will:

- encourage you to make systematic progress
- keep you focused
- motivate you
- address the writing issues most important to you
- build writing habits that meet your special needs

This book offers you several tools for designing a plan tailor-made to the strengths you already have and the skills you'd like to improve. The Pre-Test on pp. 29-31 will help you identify the areas you need to work on. It's a short test, designed for efficiency, and the answers follow immediately. Many student writers say that the Pre-Test provides a great brush-up on some skills that were getting rusty.

The next step is to answer the questions beginning on p. 35: Your Writing Profile. They will help you identify your priorities and develop a personal plan for achieving your writing goals, and you'll set up a system for evaluating (and celebrating!) your progress. Most important, you'll see results quickly.

Pre-Test

Instructions: Answer the questions below. When you're finished, check your answers on p. 32.

Part I Organizing Your Ideas

Instructions: Choose the correct answer to each question.

1. The first sentence of an essay or article should

    a) capture readers' interest

    b) state your main point

    c) introduce yourself to your readers

    d) a, b, and c

2. The first sentence of a paragraph should

    a) state a fact

    b) state the main point of the paragraph

    c) offer additional evidence about the topic in the previous paragraph

    d) summarize what you've already said

3. A student is writing an essay with a thesis and three supporting ideas. Which of the following transitions could he use before supporting idea #3?

    a) third

    b) last

    c) most important

    d) a, b, and c

4. A student is writing a paragraph about the presents she received on her ninth birthday. Her favorite was a bicycle. She should mention the bicycle

a) in the first sentence

b) in the last sentence

c) in the middle of the paragraph

d) at any point that feels comfortable to her

5. The main point (thesis) of an essay or article should appear

a) in the first sentence

b) in the first or second paragraph

c) not until the end of the essay or article

d) anywhere that feels comfortable to the writer

Part II English Usage

Instructions: Put a √ in front of each correct sentence. Put an X if the sentence is incorrect.

_____6. Ray helped Ben lift the carton, it was too heavy for one person.

_____7. I'll let Janet and he know that the house they want is no longer on the market.

_____8. Misuse of prescription drugs are a growing problem with young people today.

_____9. It was wonderful to see the joy on the childrens' faces when we told them about the party.

_____10. The proposal is no problem for my assistant and I, but you should ask the managers for their opinion.

_____11. After a long training program that involved many evening and weekend hours; Raquel earned her teaching certification.

_____12. Driving home from work this evening, the radio had an interesting report about tax reform.

_____13. The Patel's want to know if we can join them for dinner.

_____14. The resort was wonderful and I want to go back there.

_____15. I bought everything on your shopping list, but the grapefruit.

_____16. You should ask your Doctor if the new antibiotic has any risky side effects.

_____17. Parents who visit our daycare center always say, "My child is going to be happy here".

_____18. Acme Corporation surprised everyone with the announcement about closing it's factory in Tennessee.

_____19. There's three people waiting to talk to you about the position advertised in today's paper.

_____20. I think grandpa will really enjoy the fishing trip we've planned for next month.

_____21. Marilyn told me that "she would pick me up in time for the show tonight."

_____22. City Hall, an old building needing many repairs will be closed for renovations next month.

_____23. I'm sure I can do a better report than her.

_____24. The location is perfect for us, however, the house has only one bathroom.

_____25. Going back to school was a difficult decision although, I'm doing better than I expected in both my classes.

Part III Spelling

Instructions: Put a √ in front of each word that's spelled correctly. Put an X if the word is incorrect.

recieve   potatoe   seperate   truely   occassion

priviledge   alright   definate   miniscule   arguement

Pre-Test Answer Key

Instructions: Check your answers here. Then make a list of topics you need to review and the corresponding page numbers to use. You'll refer to this list when you draft your Writing Plan, pp. 39-40.

Part I Organizing Your Ideas

1. The first sentence of an essay or article should:

    a) capture readers' interest (p. 91)

2. The first sentence of a paragraph should:

    b) state the main point of the paragraph

3. A student is writing an essay with a thesis and three supporting ideas. Which of the following transitions could he use before supporting idea #3?

    c) most important (pp. 99-100)

4. A student is writing a paragraph about the presents she received on her ninth birthday. Her favorite gift was a bicycle. She should mention the bicycle:

    b) in the last sentence (pp. 99)

5. The main point (thesis) of an essay or article should appear:

    b) in the first or second paragraph (p. 48)

Part II English Usage

Every sentence is incorrect. The corrected sentences appear below, along with page numbers where you can find explanations.

X 6. Ray helped Ben lift the carton. It was too heavy for one person. (Periods and Semicolons: pp. 176)

X 7. I'll let Janet and him know that the house they want is no longer on the market. (Thumb Rule: p. 188)

X 8. Misuse of prescription drugs is a growing problem with young people today. (Subject-Verb Agreement Rule 4: p. 196)

X 9. It was wonderful to see the joy on the children's faces when we told them about the party. (Apostrophes: p. 181)

X 10. The proposal is no problem for my assistant and me, but you should ask the managers for their opinion. (Thumb Rule: p. 188)

X 11. After a long training program that involved many evening and weekend hours, Raquel earned her teaching certification. (Comma Rule 1: p. 165)

X 12. While I was driving home from work this evening, the radio had an interesting report about tax reform. (Misplaced Modifier: pp. 224-5)

X 13. The Patels want to know if we can join them for dinner Saturday night. (Apostrophe: pp. 180-1)

X 14. The resort was wonderful, and I want to go back there. (Comma Rule 2: p. 168)

X 15. I bought everything on your shopping list but the grapefruit. (Comma Rule 2: p. 168)

X 16. You should ask your doctor if the new antibiotic has any risky side effects. (Capital Letters: p. 205)

X 17. Parents who visit our daycare center always say, "My child is going to be happy here." (Quotation Marks: p. 185)

X 18. Acme Corporation surprised everyone with the announcement about closing its factory in Tennessee. (Pronoun Rule 2: p. 188)

X 19. There are three people waiting to talk to you about the position advertised in today's paper. (Subject-Verb Agreement Rule 1: p. 195)

X 20. I think Grandpa will really enjoy the fishing trip we've planned for next month. (Capital Letters: p. 205)

X 21. Marilyn told me that she would pick me up in time for the show tonight. (Quotation Marks: p. 185)

X 22. City Hall, an old building needing many repairs, will be closed for renovations next month. (Comma Rule 3: p. 172)

X 23. I'm sure I can do a better report than she. (Pronoun Rule 4: p. 189)

X 24. The location is perfect for us. However, the house has only one bathroom. (Periods and Semicolons: p. 178)

X 25. Going back to school was a difficult decision although I'm doing better than I expected in both my classes. (Comma Rule 1: p. 165)

Part III Spelling

Every word is incorrect. The correct spellings appear below.

receive	potato	separate	truly	occasion
privilege	all right	definite	minuscule	argument

Your Writing Profile

Instructions: Answer the questions below. When you're finished, complete "How to Write Your Plan" on p. 39. You'll also need your list of topics to work on from pp. 32-34.

1. What typically happens when you tackle a writing task? Check all that apply.

____a) put it off as long as possible

____b) write it once and submit it

____c) rewrite it several times

____d) make it as perfect as you can the first time

2. Do you seek help when you're working on a writing task? Check all that apply.

____a) feedback from family, friends, or coworkers

____b) assistance from a software program

____c) tutoring (in person, online, or both)

____d) professional editing

3. What kinds of writing do you regularly do? Check all that apply.

____a) business writing

____b) school assignments

____c) emails, Tweets, and Twitters to friends, family, or both

____d) one or more blogs

____e) creative writing, such as poems, songs, or stories

____f) writing related to citizenship, such as letters to the editor

____g) writing related to friends and family, such as annual holiday letters

____h) other (describe:_____)

4. What motivates you to want to write better? Check all that apply.

_____a) succeeding in school

_____b) succeeding in a career

_____c) becoming a role model for family or friends

_____d) impressing or influencing others

_____e) getting published

_____f) increased self-confidence

_____g) other (describe:_____)

5. How many days in a typical week do you plan to spend at least 30 minutes working on your writing skills?

6. How much time in a typical day do you plan to spend on your writing skills?

7. How much time are you willing to spend reading during a typical day?

8. What challenges do you expect to face as you work on your writing? Check all that apply.

_____a) time pressure

_____b) fatigue

_____c) low motivation

_____d) conflicts with family or friends

_____e) interruptions or distractions

_____f) other (describe:_____)

9. What resources can you draw upon to help you improve your writing skills? Check all that apply.

_____a) support from family or friends

_____b) word-processing skills

_____c) Internet skills

____d) good study habits

____e) love of reading

____f) excellent writing instruction (past or present)

____g) other (describe:_____)

10. What changes are you ready to make *immediately* to help you reach your writing goals? Check all that apply to you.

____a) set aside a regular time each day for writing practice

____b) ask someone you know to help you with your writing

____c) organize an attractive and comfortable place to write

____d) purchase needed supplies (such as paper, pens, a computer, word-processing software, a dictionary, a folder to store your work, etc.)

____e) set aside a regular time each day to read about writing

____f) apply for a library card

____g) ask a friend or family member to become a writing buddy (such as writing together or reading and commenting on what you've written)

____h) improve your computer skills on your own or by taking a course

____i) use the spellchecker on everything you write

____j) regularly visit a website devoted to writing

____k) subscribe to a writer's magazine (or read one at the library)

____l) blog or start a journal about your writing challenges and accomplishments

____m) meet with your instructor to talk about your writing

____n) make a list of writing issues you want to work on

____o) other (describe:_____)

How to Make a Writing Plan

Congratulations! The work you've done on pp. 29-37 is about to pay off. You're ready to design a writing plan personalized for your needs—and you're about to see your writing skills improve dramatically.

Here's an example of what a plan might look like. (Remember, however, that your plan will be *yours alone*—don't try to sound like someone else!)

My Writing Plan

Writing well has always been a dream for me. My fourth grade teacher invited a friend to visit our class and tell us about a book he had written about growing up in Michigan. Ever since then I've wanted to write my own book.

First, though, I need to graduate from college. I'm a freshman and having a hard time with my Composition I class. Friends tell me that I'll have to write research papers in other courses. I never did very well in high school English, so I'm worried about college writing.

My career goal is business management. Corinne, my older sister, is director of a human resources department. She tells me that most business jobs require extensive writing.

So I have many reasons for wanting to write well. The problem is how to get there. Here are my plans:

- *spend a few moments each day picturing myself holding a book I've written*
- *go to the learning center at least once a week to work on a writing program*
- *learn all three comma rules, and learn how to use apostrophes (the weak spots that showed up in my Pretest)*
- *introduce myself to the tutors in the Learning Center*
- *visit a tutor at least once for each writing assignment*
- *ask my sister or a friend to read over each paper before I hand it in*
- *carefully read over all the comments my professors write on my papers*
- *visit the professor's office if I don't understand the comments*
- *reward myself with a movie or a trip to Starbucks for each A or B paper*

I know there will be obstacles. Sometimes I put off studying. Writing is especially hard for me because it makes me feel lonely. I'm going to read this contract at least once a week to keep me motivated. I'm also going to look for a writing buddy in my English class. Maybe we can get together to do our papers. Writing in the learning lab might also help me feel less lonely.

I'm confident about my goals and excited (as well as nervous) about getting started. At the end of this semester I plan to reread this contract, think about what worked for me, and then revise it for the new semester. By graduation I plan to be ready for the working world, and I might even start writing a book.

Drafting Your Plan

Now you're ready to draft your writing plan. You should already have a list of ideas:

- Your reasons for wanting to write better
- Your present and future goals
- The challenges you'll be facing
- The strategies you plan to use

Congratulations! You've already done the most difficult part—generating ideas to write about. All that remains now is to write a sentence about each idea. Don't stop to fix spelling and usage: Just keep writing. You can always make corrections and changes later. If you get stuck, reread the sample writing plan on pp. 29-30.

When you've finished drafting your ideas, take a moment to congratulate yourself. You're almost finished! All that remains is revising what you've written to ensure it clearly states what you want it to say. Reread each sentence to see what corrections and changes are needed. Keep revising until your plan is finished. Be sure to use the spellchecker and grammar checker to make corrections.

Finally, make your writing plan as attractive as possible. If you wish, add pictures or symbols to your plan: A book cover you've designed with your name on it, a college diploma, a dollar sign. Make your writing plan personal, exciting, and real.

When you're finished, display your plan in a place where you'll see it frequently and be reminded about the plans you've made. Take time to reread it, slowly and thoughtfully, any time you feel your motivation sinking. You'll find that this writing plan is a powerful tool as you strive for success in all your writing goals.

Chapter 5

The Writing Process

In Chapter 10, "The Secrets of Good Writing" (p. 74), I'm going to explain ten principles that will help you excel every time you sit down at a keyboard or pick up a pen. But there's another principle that's so important that it deserves its own chapter, so here it is. There is one special habit that sets superior writers apart from average ones: *Good writers use a three-step process for almost everything they write.* Average writers, on the other hand, generally use just one step.

To put it another way: The difference between good writers and poor writers is the amount of crossing-out they do. Average writers complete a draft, hand it in, and go on to another task. Good writers go through several drafts—sometimes many of them. You don't need talent to be a superb writer: You need *persistence*.

Here's a famous example. In 1958 George Plimpton interviewed novelist Ernest Hemingway for the *Paris Review*. Plimpton asked Hemingway how much rewriting he did. "It depends," Hemingway replied. "I rewrote the ending to *Farewell to Arms* thirty-nine times before I was satisfied." Surprised, Plimpton asked Hemingway what the problem was. "Getting the words right" was Hemingway's terse answer.

How much do *you* care about "getting the words right?"

Introducing the Writing Process

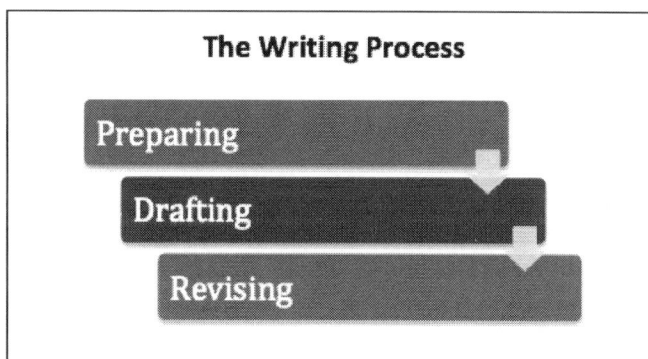

Good writers work in three stages: Preparing, drafting, and revising. They do a lot of planning and experimenting before they've written a single sentence. When they get to the sentences-and-paragraph step, they make many changes, cross-outs, and deletions. I used to say that average writers have one or two crumpled pieces of paper in their wastebaskets; superior writers have hundreds. Nowadays, with computers, the difference is that the superior writer's delete key is worn out.

The first stage is **preparing to write**. This is when you gather information to write about, and you give your unconscious mind time to work. A good rule of thumb is that the more preparation you do, the easier the other stages will be. Your unconscious mind—the hidden part of your brain—will do a lot of the work for you if you a) give it plenty of material to work with and b) give it plenty of time. (But your unconscious mind won't be much help if you start a paper at eleven o'clock the night before it's due!)

Here are some preparation tasks you might find helpful:

- Reading
- Looking at old pictures if you're writing about a personal memory
- Discussing the topic with a friend
- Looking up the topic on the World Wide Web
- Listening to a podcast about the topic

Here's the most important rule for the preparation stage: *Turn off the editor inside your head*. Don't worry about spelling, logic, vocabulary choices, or punctuation. It's fine to scribble ideas and play with them. At this stage you're trying to warm up your brain and discover facts and ideas to write about.

Here's a planning sheet I did for **Chapter 15, Writing Effective Sentences**:

> *Four tips:*
> - *begin with a person, place, thing (sentence, extra idea)*
> - *it is a thing*
> - *look at the beginning of a sentence to fix usage*
> - *be careful starting with -ing word (dangling modifier, fragment)*
>
> *Thinking about meaning rather than grammatical categories. Not just punctuation. Assemble a sentence toolbox for yourself.*
>
> *Starting with There is/There are - but Jane's sentence is a good one*
>
> *"There was no library in Lake Alfred in 1961."*
>
> *loud/soft (subordinate conjunctions, interrupters)*
>
> *ideas are equal/cancel each other out (lack of thinking, priorities) coordinate conjunctions psychologists and but don't use in a thesis*
>
> *don't start a paper with a "not" sentence*
>
> *sophistication: semicolons*
>
> *sentence variety*
>
> *his" rather than "the" - brain picks up subtleties (Chapter 3, Your Amazing Brain)*
>
> *William Zinsser - don't do readers' work for them*
>
> *some redundancy is necessary*

Notice that most of my planning sheet is a list of notes. I didn't bother with sentences or punctuation. The planning sheet isn't logically organized. My goal was to write down my ideas for the chapter. The preparation stage is important to me for two reasons: It fires up my internal writing engine, and my notes ensure that I won't forget any points I want to make.

The second stage is **drafting**. At this stage you think of a thesis (main point) and decide how you're going to develop it. You'll organize your ideas and examples into paragraphs, and you'll start writing complete sentences.

At this stage you still want to silence your internal editor. Your sentences can be sloppy and childish, and so can your spelling. You can forget about ,punctuation if you want to. The only rules are: 1. Put your ideas into some kind of order and 2. Fill your computer screen or piece of paper.

A moment ago I mentioned that you'll need to think of a thesis and how you'll develop it. Here's a preview of what you'll be learning in the next chapter, Writing Paragraphs and Essays. This is a typical outline:

Outline

Ballroom dancing has enriched my life in ways I couldn't have imagined. THESIS

One unexpected change has been increased confidence. SUPPORTING IDEA

Another surprise was learning to appreciate music on a new level. SUPPORTING IDEA

The greatest gift that dancing has given me is *fun*. SUPPORTING IDEA

(I've met students—and some instructors too—who worry that an outline might stifle creativity. I used to feel that way too, and I was proud that I never tried to stuff my ideas into an outline...until my doctoral committee said "Do it that way or else!" I did what they said—of course—and was amazed at the improvement in my writing.)

The last stage is **revising**. It's cleanup time! You search for errors and correct them. You make your sentences sharper and more professional. You move ideas around and expand them when necessary. (This is when Hemingway revised the last page of his novel thirty-nine times.) There's a simple rule for revising: Don't stop until you're sure you've done your best with the writing task at hand.

A Few More Pointers

Every writer's working process is slightly different. For example, I often blend the drafting and revising process, even though that's not a good practice for most writers. My problem is that I'm such a stickler that I can't write a word unless it's spelled correctly. The result: I stop writing to check spellings at Dictionary.com far more often than I should.

Another habit—a good one—is dropping back to the preparation stage frequently to get more information about a point I want to develop. Friends tell me they have their similar quirks and preferences.

Feel free to be yourself as you move through the writing process. Just remember two points: Do plenty of preparation before you start drafting, and allow time for thorough revising before you submit your final draft to your instructor (or your supervisor, if you're completing a workplace project).

Chapter 6

Writing Paragraphs and Essays

If you've always thought that writing well is complicated, think again. Effective writing requires expertise in just two basic areas: organizing ideas and writing sentences (which you'll learn about in Chapter 15, beginning on p. 110).

In this chapter we're going to focus on *organization*. We'll begin with two simple templates (step-by-step patterns) that anyone can easily learn. You already met the essay template on pp. 20-21.

The Paragraph Template

Paragraphs are the basic building blocks for almost everything you write. Here's a step-by-step guide to writing effective paragraphs:

Paragraph Template

Start with the point you want to make, and stay with it until the paragraph is finished. State your point in the first sentence. Follow up with an explanation. Then write more sentences, supporting your point with examples. Readers especially enjoy stories, so try to include at least one if you can. If you have several examples, save the biggest one for last. Consider using a closing sentence, like a bow on a package, to wrap up your paragraph with a powerful ending.

The following excerpt from *Spirit Dances* by professional writer Melaney Sreenan is an example of an effective paragraph. As you read it, look for answers to these three questions:

1. What point is Melaney Sreenan making?

2. Which sentence explains her point?

3. Can you find the story that illustrates her point?

---

from *Spirit Dances* by Melaney Sreenan, Ph.D.

From early childhood until we went off to different colleges, I tagged along with my older brother Greg. Greg believed in himself and set a good example. He always believed in the truth of things and held fast to the idea that he could make his dreams become a reality simply by believing in them. More than anything, he loved to fly planes, and to everyone's amazement except his, Greg had his pilot's license before he had his driver's license. You see, he believed.

Here are the answers:

1. Sreenan's main point: "I tagged along with my older brother Greg."

2. Her explanation: "Greg believed in himself and set a good example."

3. The story: "He earned his pilot's license before he had his driver's license."

There's something else you can learn from this paragraph. In her closing sentence Sreenan used a professional technique called *closure*: "You see, he believed." Professional writers often end their paragraphs this way—and you can too. You'll learn more about closure in Chapter 13.

How did you do? This template will ensure that your paragraphs are well organized and fully developed. You're on your way to better writing skills!

The Essay Template

The second type of organization is the *essay template* that you can also use to write articles, business reports, research papers, and books. Did you ever build a tower or castle by stacking up blocks when you were younger? That "stacking" idea is the basic principle for most writing tasks: You stack up paragraphs in an orderly way to write your essay.

Begin with an introductory paragraph that catches readers' interest and makes your main point, called a *thesis*. It's the most important sentence in your paper. After you've written your introduction, add as many supporting paragraphs as you need. When you get close to the end, write a climax paragraph. Finish with one more paragraph—a conclusion that wraps up your essay. Here's a template:

Essay Template

First paragraph: Catch your readers' interest, perhaps with a story. Provide background to help your readers understand your topic. State your main point, idea, or position (*thesis*).

Second paragraph: Begin with a *topic sentence* that supports your thesis. Then develop your topic sentence with explanations and examples.

Third paragraph: Begin with a topic sentence, and develop it with explanations and examples.

Write as many supporting paragraphs as you need.

Climax paragraph: Put your strongest supporting idea here and develop it.

Conclusion: Restate your thesis and wrap up your paper. Don't add anything new. State why your topic will be important in the future or call your readers to action—or both.

About the Thesis

The most important part of any essay, report, article, research paper, or book is the *thesis* (main point). I like to say that the thesis does the "heavy lifting" because it shapes every sentence you write. It is your main point, and you need to state it early, probably in your first paragraph, so that readers know where you'll be taking them.

In the sample essay beginning on p. 50, the thesis is *Ballroom dancing has enriched my life in ways I couldn't have imagined.* Once I've written my thesis, the rest of my paper has a shape: I will be writing several paragraphs about ways my life has been enriched. What I *can't* write about (even though it's true!) are ways that ballroom dancing has complicated my life. I can't mention the expense, the time, or the frustration that sometimes come with ballroom dancing. I'm limited to ways it has *enriched* my life because that's the keyword in my thesis.

Sometimes students want to explore two sides of an issue and then put the thesis—their final opinion—at the end. This type of organization is called *inductive reasoning*, and it's difficult to do well. (I almost never use it.) You'll get your point across most successfully if you state it early and support it strongly. Resist the temptation to waver back and forth, for and against.

About Topic Sentences

Many professional writers (including me) start most of their paragraphs with a *topic sentence*. These are also hard-working sentences because they have two jobs to do. One is supporting the thesis. So, for example, my essay has three topic sentences about ways that ballroom dancing has *enriched my life*. Remember, that's my thesis, or main point:

- One unexpected change has been increased confidence.
- Another surprise was learning to appreciate music on a new level.
- The greatest gift that dancing has given me is fun.

What's the other job that topic sentences do? They predict what the paragraph will be about. So, for example, I'll write a paragraph about my new confidence, another about appreciating music, and another about having fun. Always, though, I'll keep an eye on my thesis: *Ballroom dancing has enriched my life in ways I couldn't have imagined.*

See a Completed Essay

I've written an essay about my passion for ballroom dancing. As you read, notice how I followed the instructions in the template. On p. 51 you can read this essay again, with the parts labeled. I encourage you to go to PlanMyPaper.com to watch several short, free PowerPoints and videos that show you in detail how this essay is organized—and how to organize an essay of your own.

Ballroom Dancing

I'm swirling around a beautiful ballroom in the arms of a handsome man. He expertly guides me through one complex dance pattern after another, perfectly matched to the music playing in the background. At the end of the day I go up to the judges' table, where I'm given a handful of blue and gold ribbons—awards for my dancing skills. I've been a ballroom dancer for over twenty years, and what began as a casual pastime has become a passion. Ballroom dancing has enriched my life in ways I couldn't have imagined.

One unexpected change has been increased confidence. I'm an English teacher who's always been more comfortable in a classroom or library than at a party. When I started taking ballroom lessons, my teacher told me that I needed to go to the studio parties to practice dancing with other partners. I was terrified: Who would want to dance with an absolute beginner like me? What would we talk about? Would I fit in? What I discovered was that dancers are gracious people who encourage one another and aren't bothered at all by an occasional mistake. Our shared interest in dancing meant that there was always something to talk about, and I began to expand my world beyond the academic little box where I usually spent my time. Twenty years later, I have rich friendships with a diverse group of men and women who love dancing as much as I do.

Another surprise was learning to appreciate music on a new level. I've always loved music, I have a huge CD collection, and I often stream songs on my computer when I'm writing. But I had never thought about phrasing, breaks, tempo changes, and other features of popular songs. After a few years of lessons and dance parties, I began to listen more closely to how songs are orchestrated and sung. For example, I used to think that most of Frank Sinatra's songs were pretty much alike. But now I know that his music can be romantic, sassy, tender, brash, or elegant. My favorite discovery is that I can perform right along with Sinatra by improvising an arm movement or tossing my head at an exciting moment in a song.

The greatest gift that dancing has given me is *fun*. I love dressing up, experimenting with makeup and hairdos, and wearing fancy shoes decorated with rhinestones. Dance parties are always full of laughter, and often we play games on the dance floor. I used to be afraid of competitions and showcases because I thought the dancers would be stuffy and arrogant. The truth is very different: Dancing attracts people who want to squeeze the most enjoyment out of their lives. Ballroom dancing is surprisingly playful, with lots of teasing and joking on the dance floor. I'm always glowing at the end of an evening of dancing. The biggest surprise of all is that the lessons are just as much fun. It's a totally different kind of learning that's good for my body and soul.

It took courage for me to walk into a dance studio the first time, and even more courage to come back for the next lesson. It was scary to watch the other students gliding confidently with their teachers. Would I ever be able to dance the way they did? "The first steps are the hardest," my teacher reassured me—and he was right. I'm so glad I decided to try ballroom dancing, and I can't wait to put on my dance shoes again for another evening of sheer delight.

Labeling the Parts of an Essay

Here's the essay again, this time with the *thesis* and *topic sentences* labeled so that you can see how they work together:

Ballroom Dancing

I'm swirling around a beautiful ballroom in the arms of a

handsome man. He expertly guides me through one complex dance pattern after another, perfectly matched to the music playing in the background. At the end of the day I go up to the judges' table, where I'm given a handful of blue and gold ribbons—awards for my dancing skills.] I've been a ballroom dancer for over twenty years, and what began as a casual pastime has become a passion. [**Ballroom dancing has enriched my life in ways I couldn't have imagined**. [Thesis – the keyword is *enriched*]

One unexpected change has been increased confidence. [**Topic sentence – the keyword is *confidence*]** I'm an English teacher who's always been more comfortable in a classroom or library than at a party. When I started taking ballroom lessons, my teacher told me that I needed to go to the studio parties to practice dancing with other partners. I was terrified: Who would want to dance with an absolute beginner like me? What would we talk about? Would I fit in? What I discovered was that dancers are gracious people who encourage one another and aren't bothered at all by an occasional mistake. Our shared interest in dancing meant that there was always something to talk about, and I began to expand my world beyond the academic little box where I usually spent my time. Twenty years later, I have rich friendships with a diverse group of men and women who love dancing as much as I do.

Another surprise was learning to appreciate music on a new level. [Topic sentence – the keyword is *music*] I've always loved music, I have a huge CD collection, and I often stream songs on my computer when I'm writing. But I had never thought about phrasing, breaks, tempo changes, and other features of popular songs. After a few years of lessons and dance parties, I began to listen more closely to how songs are orchestrated and sung. For example, I used to think that most of Frank Sinatra's songs were pretty much alike. But now I know that his music can be romantic, sassy, tender, brash, or elegant. My favorite discovery is that I can perform right along with Sinatra by improvising an arm movement or tossing my head at an exciting moment in a song.

The greatest gift that dancing has given me is fun. [Topic sentence – the keyword is *fun*] I love dressing up, experimenting with makeup and hairdos, and wearing fancy shoes decorated with rhinestones. Dance parties are always full of laughter, and often we play games on the dance floor. I used to be afraid of competitions and showcases because I thought the dancers would be stuffy and arrogant. The truth is very different: Dancing attracts people who want to squeeze the most enjoyment out of their lives. Ballroom dancing is surprisingly playful, with lots of teasing and surprising on the dance floor. I'm always glowing at the end of an evening of dancing. The biggest surprise of all is that the lessons are just as much fun. It's a totally different kind of learning that's good for my body and soul.

It took courage for me to walk into a dance studio the first time, and even more courage to come back for the next lesson. It was scary to watch the other students gliding confidently with their teachers. Would I ever be able to dance the way they did? "The first steps are the hardest," my teacher reassured me—and he was right. I'm so glad I decided to try ballroom dancing, and I can't wait to put on my dance shoes again for another evening of sheer delight.

Looking Ahead

Students sometimes worry about getting stuck in this template forever. What fun is that? Don't worry! As you gain experience, you can try other ways to organize your ideas. Chapters 13 and 18 will have suggestions for you.

Always remember, though, that the template in this chapter will work for most writing tasks. I use it myself, with variations, for all of my professional publications. You can even stretch the template into a business report, magazine article, or book. In Chapter 19, Writing a Research Paper (p. 137), you'll see it again, expanded into the template for a research paper. *The essay template you're learning is a writer's best friend.*

Chapter 7

Think Like a Writer

Want to watch a husband and wife working smoothly as a writing team? Don't come to our house. My husband is a garden writer who drafts his newspaper columns in longhand. I'm an excellent typist, so it makes sense for him to read his handwritten columns aloud to me while I type them. Except that we argue—or at least we used to. A lot.

Here's a habit of mine that used to infuriate him. When he reads the word *and*, I stop typing. For example:

> Many gardeners already appreciate the value of mulch and

If you recall what I said about *and* on pp. 24-25, you already know why I always stop typing: If another sentence is coming, I have to put a comma after *mulch*. I don't want to type the rest of the sentence and then have to backspace to insert that comma:

> Many gardeners already appreciate the value of mulch, and regular applications can make an amazing difference in a landscape.

On the other hand, maybe another sentence *isn't* coming, and I won't need that comma:

> Many gardeners appreciate the value of mulch and regular applications of time-release fertilizer.

So I always wait until my husband finishes reading the whole sentence, and then I type like mad to catch up with him. (If all this fuss about *and* seems confusing, please don't worry about it yet. On p. 169 you'll have a chance to do some practice exercises that will clear up any doubts.) My husband, you'll be happy to know, eventually caught on to what I was doing, and now our typing sessions go much more smoothly.

But this chapter isn't about marital advice for husband-and-wife writing teams. What I want to focus on here is how a professional writer's brain—mine, for example—works.

A professional writer's brain is always running a complex software program that efficiently spots common language problems (using *your* instead of *you're*, for example), and it also notices instantly when someone uses language well.

Here's an example from my experience: Some years ago I toured a cooperative farm with a remarkable activist named Margarita. Although she'd never been to college, she knew how to work with community leaders to solve problems and get things done. Plainspoken and down-to-earth, Margarita had instant rapport with the farm workers we were visiting. I was impressed.

And it wasn't just her organizational skills. While we were all talking during lunch, I heard her use an unusual grammatical construction called a "possessive with a gerundive." *Probably an accident,* I thought. But a short time later Margarita did it again. And then I heard it a third time. Here's an example: "John's leaving the farm upset everyone for a few weeks." Most people would say, "John leaving the farm upset everyone...."

It's a construction I'm careful with when I'm writing, but I rarely use it in conversation. Margarita did, every time. And her pronouns were always right. And she never made a single subject-verb agreement error. In fact she was pretty much a walking grammar textbook.

I was the only academic who visited the farm that day, and I could tell that Margarita was a little uncomfortable around me. When we said our good-byes, she took a moment to apologize for the pain that her broken English must have inflicted on my professorial ears.

I shook my head. "You're not as earthy as you like to appear," I told her, and then I explained about the sophisticated grammar I kept hearing in her conversation. "Obviously you attended a private school," I said. "Those constructions aren't taught in public schools." (I'm a public-school product myself.)

And then the story tumbled out. Margarita had lost her mother when she was young, her family was large, and there wasn't much money. But a man at her church was so impressed with her personality and brains, even when she was little, that he talked her father into sending her to a Catholic boarding school, even paying her tuition himself. Margarita lived among nuns for years, having her grammar corrected from morning till night. Although she assumed she'd forgotten most of what she'd learned, she was still using it decades later, when I met her.

Margarita was fortunate to have received such an excellent education. But what can *you* do to expand your language skills? The answer is to do the same things I did. Remember—I didn't attend a private school either!

1. Read.

Many writers (I'm one) have learned most of what they know about writing from reading. In addition to expanding your knowledge, reading will enhance your writing in at least four ways:

- sharpen your analytical thinking
- increase your vocabulary
- improve your ability to spell and punctuate
- supply ideas and examples to use in your writing

If you're serious about improving your writing, you should spend at least 30 minutes a day reading. Reading almost anything is going to help you: It doesn't have to be Shakespeare or Plato. Read the Harry Potter books, *People* magazine, a best-selling novel. Read e-books, paperbacks, and newspapers. Start today if you don't already have the reading habit.

2. Ask a friend or family member for feedback.

You'd be surprised how many writing problems can be cleared up by a non-expert—your sister, your next-door neighbor, the person at the next desk. If you know someone who's a voracious reader, that's even better—you'll get great suggestions.

Our own brains are likely to miss many mistakes. I'm remembering countless mornings when I reread, aghast, something that seemed brilliant when I wrote it the night before! A friend or co-worker is more likely to notice a word that's been left out, an awkward phrase, or an unclear point. The book you're reading benefited immensely from feedback from Natalie Bilokonsky, a wise and sharp-eyed copyeditor who corrected many mistakes that had slipped past me.

I've often thought that many D and C students in my classes could have earned B's and A's if they had simply asked someone else to read over their essays before I graded them. (If you're taking a writing course in high school or college, check with your instructor to make sure you're permitted to get feedback on your writing. Many instructors will happily say yes.)

3. Write.

Write letters, emails, and postcards. Write comments on your Facebook page. Keep a journal. Create a blog. Tweet. Write letters to the editors of the magazines and newspapers you read. (You do read newspapers and magazines, right? See #2.) Leave comments on websites. Volunteer for writing tasks at your job. Write stories and poems. Reflect. Observe. You don't have to be self-critical or submit what you've written for a grade. Just keep writing. Over time you'll find it easier to express and organize your thoughts, and your writing will acquire more sophistication.

4. Improve your vocabulary.

Buy a word-a-day calendar. Visit a vocabulary website regularly. Carry a dictionary with you, or make frequent visits to Dictionary.com. Write down interesting new words in a notebook, and review them often.

5. Use a spellchecker.

Almost everything you write on a computer can be spellchecked. But remember that spellcheckers aren't infallible: They may not pick up a word that's spelled correctly but used in the wrong place, like *there* instead of *their*.

6. Use the grammar checker in your word processor.

Grammar checkers are wonderful if you remember to use your common sense: Even the most sophisticated software program can make mistakes. If your computer suggests a change that sounds wrong to you, seek a second opinion from a friend or family member.

7. Educate yourself about writing.

To get over the idea that writing is a dull subject, read a lively book like *The Elements of Style* (Strunk and White), *Watch Your Language* (Theodore Bernstein), or *Naked, Drunk and Writing* (Adair Lara). Better yet, read all three books—and then go to the library and look for more. (My own website, WritewithJean.com, has many free resources to help you learn about writing.)

8. Awaken your curiosity.

Start noticing the words you read and hear in your daily life. Pay attention when a word intrigues or amuses you, and ask yourself why—you may pick up a trick or two to use in your own writing. Think about word choices: Effective? Too folksy? Too formal? Pick apart books, magazines, Tweets, and emails. (But don't share your critiques of friends' writing or speaking habits unless they ask you for feedback!)

9. Experiment.

Substitute a semicolon for a period. They're pretty much the same thing, except that a period is automatically followed by a capital letter, but a semicolon isn't. Use your new words whenever you can; it's fun to explore new ways to express your ideas. (Did you notice the semicolon?)

10. Make a plan and carry it out.

Do an assessment to find out what skills you need to strengthen, explore some strategies for addressing them, and set aside time every day to work on those areas. If you haven't already taken the Pre-test in Chapter 4, try it now. And for best results, spend some time making a Writing Plan (you learned how in Chapter 4). Although detailed planning takes time, you'll achieve your goals much faster. Get started now!

Chapter 8

Myths about Writing

Myths and misunderstandings about writing can cause you to lose your way on the road to success as a writer. Although I had wonderful writing teachers in high school and college, I was exposed to some misinformation. Perhaps you've heard these myths too. If so, it's time to get rid of them! It's never too soon to start thinking like a professional writer.

Myth #1 You have to use good English all the time.

The truth is that there's no such thing as "good" or "bad" English. Language is a tool; the real question is whether the words we're using will help us get the job done. *Ain't* is a risky word to use at a job interview, but your friends or family might feel perfectly comfortable with it. What's essential is acquiring the vocabulary, usage patterns, and pronunciation that suit your career and the friends you want to have around you. It's perfectly normal—and ok—to follow usage rules carefully at school and work but let yourself be more relaxed with your friends. That practice is called code-switching, and it's universal. (Listen to teenagers speak to each other, and notice the difference when they talk to their grandmothers: That's a perfect example of code-switching.)

Myth #2 Language should be logical.

Because language and logic occupy different parts of the human brain, it's a mistake to insist that language constructions stand up to the demands of logic. "How do you do?" is a completely illogical form of greeting—but it's a useful question when you're meeting someone new.

Many of the expressions we use all the time aren't logical—and don't need to be. Countless English teachers have preached against the double negative construction ("I don't have none" is an example) on the grounds that two negatives cancel each other out. But double negatives are a common and correct feature in Spanish and many other languages. You might be surprised that the earliest form of English (called Old English by scholars) had double negatives too.

The real problem with "I don't have none" is that professional people don't talk or write this way. If you're in the habit of using double negatives, you may have trouble landing or keeping a job.

Bottom line: When you're thinking about language, don't ask what's logical. Instead strive to find out what other educated people are saying and writing, and do the same.

Myth #3 You can't start a sentence with *but* (or *and* or *because*).

Open today's *New York Times*, or whatever newspaper you read, to the first page and scan a few columns, noting the beginnings of sentences. I guarantee you won't get far before you find a sentence starting with *but*. Keep looking, and you'll soon find another one starting with *and*—and another one starting with *because*. Look at a magazine. Pull your favorite book off the shelf. Yes, it's true even if the author was a Nobel prizewinner! You'll see countless sentences starting with *but*, *and*, *because*. Try the King James Bible. Try Shakespeare, the Gettysburg Address, and famous writers old and new. You'll find sentences beginning with *but*, *and*, and *because* in all of them.

Still not convinced? Start looking at classic books about good writing: Strunk and White's *Elements of Style*, Fowler's *Modern English Usage*, Bernstein's *Watch Your Language*, Lynn Truss's *Eats, Shoots, and Leaves*, and *Warriner's English Usage and Composition*, the standard grammar text when I was in high school. None of them warn you about starting sentences with *but*—and all of them contain sentences that start with *but*, *and*, and *because*.

A friend of mine once worked for a newspaper editor who thought *because* was a bad word. The editor used to call him every time he used it, insisting that he substitute another word. She never noticed that *because* appeared in almost everything she read—or bothered to check the dictionary, where she would have discovered that *because* is a perfectly respectable word. Did she look foolish? Yes. Don't repeat her mistake.

For years I told my students I would pay $100 in cash to anyone who could bring me a reputable book saying you can't start a sentence with *but* (or *and* or *because*). Nobody has ever collected a penny from me. There's no such rule: It's a myth!

Myth #4 Don't use a word that isn't in the dictionary.

A few years ago I served on a committee that was drawing up a contract for mentors. We ran into an unexpected difficulty when we began listing the expectations for mentees: Several committee members objected that *mentee* isn't a word because it's not in the dictionary. I'm happy to report that we argued them down, and *mentee* remained in the contract even though it was too new to be in the dictionary we were using.

Because every living language is always adding and discarding words, dictionaries are always a little behind in this process. Such useful words as *software*, *graffiti*, and *burrito* took a while to make their way into modern English dictionaries. Eventually *mentee* found its way there. (I'm expecting *binky*—a children's word for "pacifier"—to make its way there before long.)

You should also know that some words disappear from the dictionary because there isn't room to include everything. I still dance the *Peabody* (it was comedian Jack Gleason's favorite dance), but it doesn't appear in any of the dictionaries I just checked.

If a word comes out of someone's mouth, pen, or computer keyboard, it's a word. Whether it's a useful word for a particular situation is a different question. Unless you're being very informal in the company of family and close friends, or you're making a joke, substandard words like *ain't* and *irregardless* are best avoided. But don't try to claim that they're not words!

Myth #5 It's bad to repeat a word.

One particularly insidious myth is the belief that you can't use a word more than once. If you believe this one and try writing a research paper about, say, symbolic dogs in depth psychology, you'll soon find yourself going crazy looking for academic synonyms for the word *dog*. There's *canine* and…. I'm sorry to tell you that there aren't any more.

But the good news is that you don't need synonyms: Nobody is going to notice that you're repeating the word *dog*. If your paper is well written, they'll be too interested in what you're saying to notice.

Sometimes repetition can add rhythm and emphasis to what you're writing. For example, Charles Dickens started his novel *A Tale of Two Cities* with a wonderful (and repetitious) sentence: "It was the best of times, it was the worst of times...." And then there's this memorable sentence from Abraham Lincoln's Gettysburg Address: "But, in a larger sense, we cannot dedicate—we cannot consecrate—we cannot hallow this ground." (I can't resist adding a question: Did you notice that this famous sentence starts with *but*?)

Pick up a newspaper and look for the words *say* and *says*. You'll find them again and again, dozens of times. Journalists aren't permitted to use synonyms like *declare, state, utter, verbalize*. They have to keep using *say* and *says*. And the repetition doesn't bother anyone; nobody even notices.

What you want to avoid is repeating descriptive words that quickly get tiresome, such as *wonderful, beautiful, amazing*. But those words aren't particularly useful anyway. Instead of saying that it was a wonderful vacation, describe what you especially enjoyed. What did you see that made the scenery so beautiful, and what happened that amazed you? Give your readers specific details, and you won't have to worry about overusing words like *terrific* or *great*.

Myth #6 Don't use *I* or *you*.

This is at best a half-truth. Yes—in some formal writing, it's inappropriate to refer to yourself and your personal experiences. For example, I used *I* to refer to myself in only once place in my book *Pygmalion's Wordplay*: the Preface. Other formal writing, however, uses *I* and *you* all the time. You can verify this yourself! Look at presidential speeches, professional articles, business correspondence, autobiographies, and other published works.

Myth #7 The English language is deteriorating.

All languages change over time. What we call Standard English or "good English" today is so different from Old English (spoken in England between the

5th and the 12th centuries) that its speakers would probably faint if they had to listen to us today. Here, for example, is the beginning of the Lord's Prayer in Old English (c. 1100):

> Fæder ūre þū þe eart on heofonum
> Our father, who art in heaven

Modern English has lost most of its complex genders, conjugations, and declensions—but that doesn't mean that it's bad: It's just different. The only languages that don't change are the dead ones—Latin, for example. So we can all stop wringing our hands as words mutate and usage evolves.

Myth #8 Good spelling is the same as good writing.

False! The ability to spell has nothing to do with the ability to write effectively. English is a notoriously difficult language to spell—so much so that many famous writers (such as Samuel Johnson, Mark Twain, Theodore Roosevelt, and Bernard Shaw) have advocated spelling reform.

Luckily you don't need to be a good speller in order to write well. There's a simple solution to your spelling problems: Turning on the spellchecker in your computer. Another good practice is to make a list of words that give you trouble (mine are words with double letters) and study it diligently.

Myth #9 Don't use contractions.

Did you notice that I just used one? (See also p. 11.)

Myth #10 Talent is essential.

I saved this one—the most devastating myth of all—for last. Good writing is about persistence and determination, not talent. What distinguishes good writers from poor ones is what's in their wastebaskets. Poor writers spend only a few minutes revising—or don't revise at all. Good writers have overflowing wastebaskets (or worn-out delete keys!) because they keep making changes until they've produced something they're proud of.

Most writers have issues with certain aspects of language. (As I noted a moment ago, one of mine is words with double letters—I struggle when I have to spell words like *appellate*, *commitment*, and *occasion*.) The solution is to find strategies to help you with the problems that are unique to you. Use technology, lean on your friends and family, and hire an expert if you have to. *Never* allow anything you write to go forward until you're sure it's right.

Myths about Grammar and Usage

While we're at it, let's look at some grammar myths that can cause confusion. All of the following widespread beliefs about writing are false.

1. A comma takes the place of *and*.

No, it doesn't. You won't find this useless rule in any grammar book. Often, in fact, you do need a comma with *and*—with Comma Rule 2 sentences, for example (Chapter 25, p. 168). Here's an example:

My boss told us to take next Monday off, and I'm going to spend the day on the beach. CORRECT

What if you have a list of three items—do you use an "Oxford comma" (also called a "serial comma") before *and* in a list)?

I'm serving spaghetti, garlic bread, and a big salad tonight. CORRECT
I'm serving spaghetti, garlic bread and a big salad tonight. ALSO CORRECT

The answer: Maybe. If you're writing for a newspaper or magazine, you probably shouldn't use the Oxford comma. Note, though, that the *New Yorker* magazine does use it. If you're writing a book, most publishers want you to use it. The rest of the time it's your choice, unless your instructor has a strong preference one way or the other.

Many writers, including me, have found that the Oxford comma makes sentences easier to read. Just remember to be consistent: Use the Oxford comma all the time or not at all.

2. Use a comma with a person's name.

Not always. Use a comma with a name only when you write a Comma Rule 3 sentence, like this one:

Dorothy Hamill, one of America's great figure skaters, was a contestant on *Dancing with the Stars*. CORRECT

Don't use a comma with a person's name in other situations:

Dorothy Hamill is one of America's great figure skaters. CORRECT

You can learn more about Comma Rule 3 beginning on p. 172.

3. Use a comma when you pause.

Because people pause at different times and in different places while they're speaking, this supposed rule doesn't work. What's needed is a consistent, easy-to-use system for placing commas. You'll learn more about commas beginning on p. 165.

4. *Ain't* ain't in the dictionary.

Yes, it is. (Look it up!) *Ain't* is a word. Admittedly it's slang, but nevertheless it's a real word with a long history.

5. Any really long sentence is a run-on.

Not true. A run-on sentence is simply a sentence that needs a period or semicolon. Some run-ons are very short, like this one:

He likes wrestling, Joe doesn't. RUN-ON
He likes wrestling. Joe doesn't. CORRECT
He likes wrestling; Joe doesn't. CORRECT

Sentences can be as long as you like if you get the punctuation right. In general, though, many writers—including me—prefer shorter sentences that are easier to read. Turn to p. 159 to learn more about run-on sentences. (Sometimes they're called *fused* sentences or *run-together* sentences. The problem is the same.)

6. Use *a* before words that start with consonants and *an* before words that start with vowels.

Not exactly. Read the following words aloud, and you'll quickly see what's wrong with this system. Although these word pairs begin with the same letter, they sound different:

uncle   uniform
house   hour

Let the sound, guide you, not the spelling: *an uncle, a uniform, a house, an hour.*

7. Never end a sentence with a preposition.

Winston Churchill, an excellent writer as well as a great statesman, reportedly had a wonderful tongue-in-cheek response to this myth: "That is something up with which I will not put." Ignore this silly rule.

8. Don't mix verb tenses in a sentence.

It's both normal and correct to write sentences with mixed tenses (meaning sentences that have both present and past actions) like this one:

Martha wants to buy the dress she saw in the store window yesterday (*wants* is present; *saw* is past). CORRECT

9. *I* is more elegant than *me*.

Many people mistakenly think that *I* is a better word than *me*, resulting in usage errors like this one:

The Browns invited Linda and I to stay in their beach house next month. INCORRECT

To see why *me* is the correct choice here, shorten the sentence:

The Browns invited me to stay in their beach house next month. CORRECT

When you put "Linda and" back, *me* is still the correct word:

The Browns invited Linda and me to stay in their beach house next month. CORRECT

Of course *I* is correct in many sentences. Just don't try to use *I* all the time! For example, here are two sentences in which *I* is used correctly (the same "shorten the sentence" strategy works here as well):

Next month I will stay in the Browns' beach house. CORRECT
Next month Linda and I will stay in the Browns' beach house. CORRECT

To learn more, go to p. 188 and read about Pronoun Rule 3, "The Thumb Rule."

10. Possessive words need apostrophes.

This one is partially true. Apostrophes are required in most possessive ("of" phrases):

John's car (car of John)

A day's pay (pay of a day)

The Johnsons' party (party of the Johnsons)

You can learn more about apostrophes beginning on p. 181.

But there's an important exception to the rule that apostrophes show possession: pronouns. Of course you don't use an apostrophe in *his*. But are you careful not to use the apostrophe in other possessive pronouns? Here they are:

his   hers   ours   yours   theirs   its   CORRECT

None of these possessive pronouns use apostrophes. (If you put an apostrophe into *it's*, the meaning changes to "it is.") Here are some examples:

Anita's dress is nicer than hers.   CORRECT

Their vacation cost twice as much as ours. CORRECT

My coat is missing one of its buttons. CORRECT

It's time to pick up Jeff from school. CORRECT

To learn more about these pronouns, go to p. 188.

Chapter 9

Seize Your Power

A friend told me this charming story, and it still makes me smile. A middle-aged couple she knew decided to put their house up for sale. First, though, they took a long-planned vacation. While they were away, their adult son secretly rounded up some friends who knew the couple from church, and they set to work on a wonderful surprise: giving the house a facelift (repairs, fresh paint, new landscaping) to make it more attractive to buyers. When the couple returned from their vacation, they were so delighted with the results that they decided not to move after all!

It's a wonderful story about love and generosity—and, I would argue, *power*. That couple didn't realize they had the power to transform their house into the kind of home they wanted; they were ready to leave it behind. There's an important lesson about life here—always make the most out of what you have.

But I want to relate the story specifically to writing. You—like the couple who were dissatisfied with their house—have the power to make your writing better *if* (like the son and his friends) you have the right tools and know-how.

Think of this chapter as a toolbox, and don't be surprised if some of these ideas are new to you, even if you took four years of English in high school and survived freshman comp in college. I did well in English all through my school years, and the pixie dust that made me a good writer followed me into graduate school. I was thrilled when a professor used one of my essays as a model paper for a class.

And yet I had a lot to learn. The writing instruction I grew up with and imitated when I started teaching was long on inspiration and corrections but short on practical advice. Teachers urged me to write better but couldn't always tell me how to do it. The red scribbles that often appeared in the margins (*weak! off the subject! awkward!*) told me something was wrong, but the advice I got was little more than a plea to "do better next time." Sometimes my next paper really was better, but often nothing seemed to help.

Light began to dawn in graduate school, and my knowledge grew still greater when I began writing for publication. The shocker was that the new tools I acquired from professors and editors were easy to learn. I took them back to the students I was teaching, and many of my students gobbled them up. The improvement in their writing was a delight to them and to me.

Taking the First Step

It's an old joke: "How many psychiatrists does it take to change a light bulb? One—but the light bulb has to *really* want to change." That desire to change is no joke when your goal is to become a better writer. If you combine that desire with the concept of power, you're truly on your way.

If all of this sounds obvious, think again. I've already told you that most of my C and D students (and yes, many of the F students) could have earned A's and B's if they had believed in their power to change. Notice that I *didn't* say, "if they had been willing to work harder." Some of those students were like the couple who were planning to sell their house. It never occurred to them that they could do something *themselves* to make the house more to their liking.

Many average writers think they're finished when they've written the final word and laid down their pen or turned off the computer. They don't try to rework their sentences, reorganize their ideas, and make a few deletions and additions in order produce a really fine piece of writing. Like the couple who wanted to sell their house, some students lack the imagination (or courage) to envision something different—something better—for their writing.

Let's say you've decided to stop procrastinating and get to work on a long-delayed writing project. You sit down with pen and paper (or position yourself at your computer) and start writing. When you're finished, you read over your work and realize that it is…appalling. Absolutely awful. What should you say to yourself?

Congratulations! In the chapter on Time Management for Writers (beginning on p. 83), I'm going to explain why writing a bad first draft is the best way to overcome procrastination. For now, I'm going to limit myself to three observations. (The first is actually a confession.)

1. My first drafts are awful.

I always darken the computer screen when my husband comes into our home office so he can't see how terrible my stuff is.

2. You can learn many useful things from a bad first draft.

New ideas often pop into your head when you sit down to tackle a writing project for the first time. They may not be developed very well, and the organization may need to be redone, but you have something to work with. The next step is to read over what you've written and start making changes.

3. No matter how bad your first draft is, you can always make it better.

What's amazing is that this "make it better" step is always easy! You already have a draft to work with. Tinkering and making changes are the fun part of writing for many people (I'm one of them).

Step One: Make It Interesting

I know what you're thinking: "Yeah, right!" The advice about making it interesting is like telling someone to invest only in stocks that are going to go up in price, not down. Or advising a friend not to get married unless he's sure it's going to work. If only it were that simple!

It's not always easy, but it's certainly doable. Experienced writers have an arsenal of strategies they use to increase the chances that their writing will, indeed, be interesting to read. One is writing the first draft that we just discussed. Here's a vital principle for you to live by: *Writing badly is always better than writing nothing.* (And here again is the second principle, just as important as the first: *You can always make it better.*)

Why sit down to write if you don't think you have anything interesting to say? Here's why: Writing is a complex mental activity that can stimulate your thinking in amazing ways. Psychologists say that when you're stuck in a stubborn situation and can't think of a solution, writing about it will often stimulate your brain to come up with new possibilities. So if you're looking for something interesting to say, just sit down with a piece of paper and start moving your pen across the paper. Or pull up a chair in front of your computer—your choice.

You don't have to write complete sentences. I like to warm up by listing ideas and details that pop into my head. Sometimes I draw stick figures and get them talking. You don't need capital letters, correct spelling, or punctuation. Just start writing and see what happens.

Another strategy is to use your imagination. If you're working on a school assignment about a vacation with your family, take a break to look at the pictures you took during your trip. Talk to someone who was there with you—a brother or sister, or one of your parents; if your family has a video from the trip, sit down and watch it again. This strategy can be applied to almost any topic you're writing about. Take some time to look for additional ideas via the Internet, a phone call, a trip to the library—anything that might stimulate your thinking.

A third strategy is to *react* to something—a remark, a wrong-headed idea, a mistaken viewpoint you heard on a TV show. Some of my strongest writing began when I disagreed with something I'd heard or read.

What you want to avoid at all costs is telling your readers what they already know. Have you ever heard a teacher tell students that they need to be more responsible, or work harder, or take school more seriously? Boring. What about motivational speakers who talk about the importance of love, or loyalty, or friendship? You've heard it before. And how about parents who lecture repeatedly about being more respectful or helping out more at home? Their kids immediately tune them out.

That doesn't mean you have to avoid familiar ideas. The trick is to find a way to make them fresh—something that clever parents have been doing as long as there have been families. Instead of delivering a sermon about why lying is wrong, tell your children a story about a time a lie got you in trouble. The same technique can work beautifully in an article or essay you're writing. Tell a story—from an unusual angle, if possible—and use it to make your point.

Here's a wonderful example from the book *Mama's Bank Account* by Kathryn Forbes. The Hansens are a Norwegian-American family living in San Francisco. Katrin, the teenaged daughter, has just been fired from a part-time job for a horrible mistake. Mama is trying to teach her that mistakes can be overcome. Instead of a lecture, Mama tells a story:

---

from *Mama's Bank Account* by Kathryn Forbes

Before her marriage, Mama lived with her Aunt Lena, a woman who baked superb cakes. One time, after Aunt Lena had made one of her famous cakes, Mama sneaked into the kitchen and ate all the frosting. Aunt Lena went ahead and served the bald cake to her guests, who included the man Mama was dating, and she explained why there was no frosting. "What happened when he found out what you'd done?" asked Katrin. "He married me anyway," said Mama.

Make It about *You*

Everything you write is shaped by your personality, values, and experience. Let's say you decide to write a research paper about vocational education programs in prisons—an impartial report based on information from criminal justice experts. No matter how hard you try to be objective, the paper is going to end up reflecting your interests and your point of view. You're the one who chose the topic, right? Right there you've injected yourself into your writing, even if you never use the words *I*, *me*, or *my*.

Your personality can bring zest and energy to your writing, making it sound as if only you could have written it. *That strong voice is the hallmark of good writing*. And you don't have to limit yourself to writing about your personal experiences. What you have to do is find a topic—or a point of view about a topic—that stimulates and empowers you.

During a recent trip to England, my sister and I toured Windsor Castle, about 17 miles from London. I had misgivings about going there because it required changing trains, I wasn't sure I wanted to spend a whole day walking around an old castle (I'd visited castles before), and I don't like crowds. But Windsor was hosting a picture exhibition we wanted to see, so we decided it was worth a visit.

The day started much as I expected. The exhibition was wonderful, the crowds were large, and there was much more old armor and antique furniture than I really wanted to see. But then I noticed a kind of tingling inside me, and I started getting excited as we walked from room to room. What was going on?

And then it hit me. A favorite book that I reread every year is Marion Crawford's *The Little Princesses*, about Crawford's years as governess to Queen Elizabeth and her sister Princess Margaret when they were children. Much of the book takes place at Windsor Castle, where Crawford and the two princesses lived during World War II and the bombing of Britain. I was recognizing parts of the castle that Crawford had talked about and things she had seen.

Most startling were two beautiful dolls that Crawford had described in her book—gifts for the princesses from France, with miniature Cartier jewelry and designer clothing. I'd never expected to see the dolls up close, and I found myself searching for evidence that the little girls had actually played with them—a scratch, perhaps, or a missing button in a dress or jacket. Crawford said that the two princesses used to take the dolls down to a bomb shelter in the basement of the castle. Did the girls cuddle them while the bombs exploded overhead?

That day at Windsor turned out to be the most vivid part of our trip—one I'm sure I could turn into an interesting essay if I had to write a school essay about What I Did Last Summer.

Who are *you*? What excites you, angers you, makes you quiet and dreamy? What thoughts are hidden inside you that only *you* can put into words?

Chapter 10

The Secrets of Good Writing

When I began my teaching career, long before computers and the Internet, students wrote their essays by hand or typed them on cranky typewriters that required messy correction fluid or correction strips. Because there were no spellcheckers, many students carried well-worn dictionaries everywhere they went. Almost all of us were relieved when computers came along.

Despite the changes in technology, however, one thing has stayed constant over the years: The principles of good writing. Whether you're working on a short story, a love letter, a magazine article, a blog, or a scholarly book, you're going to need some essential concepts. And no, I'm not talking about comma rules and capitalization.

This is the most important chapter in this book. I suggest inserting a bookmark on this page so that you can come back and reread it—several times, if possible. Copy the most important points onto a piece of paper or index card and carry them with you to study. The principles here will take you a long way towards effective writing, and the corollary is also true: If you skip over any of these principles, you may fall short of the success you're dreaming of.

1. Content has to be *worked*.

Many of the students in my writing classes and workshops have had remarkable lives. *Great*, I always think: *I'm going to get an up-close-and-personal look at events I've never experienced myself, places I've never seen.* And then their writing lands on my desk, and I start reading…a description of packing, driving to the airport, getting on the plane, arriving at the airport, taking a cab to the hotel, checking in, unpacking. Dull. Dull.

Whenever I rifle hopefully through a pile of student papers waiting to be read, at least half are written the same way. When I began editing for pay, I found myself stumbling over the same dullness. I've worked with writers who have had unusual jobs, or grew up in amazing families, or lived in exotic places, or experienced something else that intrigues me. But too often their writing is just a list of events. It hasn't been *worked*.

How do you *work* an idea, a memory, or an experience? You have to dig into your thoughts to find a meaning: a strong emotion, an important lesson, an unexpected message. What you have to avoid at all cost is what I like to call the Wikipedia approach to writing: All facts, no human voice—no writer's identity. (Don't get me wrong: I use Wikipedia all the time when I need information for a writing task. But I always provide the *meaning* myself.)

I recall a student who wrote about how she'd prepared for first-time motherhood (her son was six months old). She described choosing a color for the nursery, buying a layette, and picking the baby's name. It was one of the flattest papers I'd ever read, and I asked for a conference.

She was surprised that I expected more depth and scope in her paper. It had never occurred to her to think about the kind of mother she wanted to be. The choices that many new parents obsess over had never crossed her mind. Are toy guns ok? What about spanking? Would she be taking her son to church? Should she breastfeed or bottle-feed? Would she get him a dog? Her easygoing approach seemed to work well for her son, but it made a disastrous essay. She hadn't *worked* the experience of new motherhood. There was no voice and no living person behind the words on the paper.

Another disappointing paper came from a first-year student who wrote about her favorite singer—a talented young man who was known for his tough-guy-from-the-streets image. Her paper (largely lifted from Wikipedia) mentioned that he'd been criticized for lyrics that demeaned women. When we sat down to talk, she struggled to understand what I was asking for: It had never occurred to her to examine her own responses to his songs, or to ask her friends for their reactions. Again, she hadn't *worked* her subject.

Ann E. Berthoff, an authority on the teaching of writing, says that writing is about "making meaning." That doesn't mean you have to be a know-it-all or take a stand on every issue, but it does require a point of view. I often write about controversial topics without stating my own opinion—but I do point out that the issues are complex, and I explain what experts are arguing about.

I recently published an article about a legal policy called "automatic arrest": Any time police are called to an argument between a couple, someone has to go to jail. I did some research first and found that experts disagree about what should be done—and I knew then I had the makings of a good article.

Some experts say that it's a good idea to arrest one of the partners: A violent spouse might exercise more self-control next time. Other experts say that automatic arrest policies can make police look ridiculous. A woman throws a doughnut at her husband, and an officer arrests her...is that necessary?

The tension between the two viewpoints made for an interesting article. Digging into a topic to "make meaning" this way is essential to good writing. If, on the other hand, I'd simply explained what an automatic arrest policy was, I'd have ended up with a dull article that no one would want to read.

2. A list is not an essay.

This seems like a simple point: We all know what a grocery list or to-do list looks like. It seems obvious that anything written in sentences and paragraphs is not a list. But over the years I've read many essays that were actually lists in disguise (and earned failing grades, I'm sorry to say). This organizational problem also shows up from time to time in the two writing groups I facilitate.

So what's the difference between a list and an essay? A list is a series of facts. An essay is a series of ideas and examples that *make a point.*

Here's a quick exercise that will help you see the difference between a list and a true essay. You're about to read the introductory paragraphs to two essays about a visit to New York City. The first essay was written by a student named Carol, who visited her aunt and uncle in New York. The second essay was written by Brett, who visited his brother in the city. Which student do you think went on to write a list—and which one wrote an essay that made a point?

Here's the first paragraph of Carol's essay:

A Trip into New York's Past

Last summer my aunt and uncle invited me to visit them in New York City for two weeks. I was wildly excited about going shopping and seeing Broadway plays, but Aunt Mamie and Uncle Grant had other ideas. On my first morning in the city, Aunt Mamie insisted on taking me on a two-hour history cruise around Manhattan. My mother had drilled me on being a gracious guest, so I pasted a big smile on my face and headed for the boat. The cruise turned out to be a fascinating mini-course in New York history that added another dimension to my visit to the city. For the rest of the two weeks, I kept connecting the places I saw to what I had learned on that boat.

And here's the first paragraph of Brett's essay:

A New York Adventure

Last summer my older brother invited me to spend two weeks visiting him in New York City. Even though it's been a year since the trip, I keep thinking about the places we visited, the things I learned, and the good time I had. Joe took me on a history cruise around Manhattan, and we visited several museums, so I learned a lot. We also crammed a lot of fun into those two weeks. I saw two Broadway plays, and Joe treated me to dinner in some great restaurants. After the first week I learned my way around the city and felt confident doing some exploring on my own. It was a wonderful trip, and I can't wait to go back.

Which essay do you think will focus on a single point? Carol's. Instead of listing an assortment of things she did—shopping, museums, plays, restaurants—she organized her essay around one feature of her trip: What she learned about New York history. Brett, on the other hand, wrote a series of disconnected sentences about what he did in New York: He took a boat cruise, visited the American Museum of Natural History, saw his first Broadway play, and so on.

Be aware that your point doesn't have to be intellectual, serious, or heavy.

Carol and Brett could have made any of a number of points about a trip to New York. For example, Brett could have written about developing new self-confidence as he began to discover the city on his own. He learned how to hail a taxi, navigate the subway system, and ask strangers for help when he needed it.

Don't be surprised if you find it challenging to stick to a single point. It's easy to start writing a string of sentences about first-I-did-this-and-then-I-did-that. When you notice yourself doing that, stop! Remind yourself about the point you're making, and focus your energies there.

3. An anecdote is not an essay.

An anecdote is a little story (also called a *narrative*). You probably have countless stories about funny, surprising, painful, or important happenings in your life. Those stories can enrich your essays (I use lots of them myself)—but always remember that a great story is only one ingredient in a good essay.

For example, over the years I've entertained friends with the story of a dispute I had with a taxi driver in a small city in Mexico. I refused to pay the fare he was asking because I thought he was trying to cheat me—and he drove off with my suitcase in his trunk. Eventually a police officer came, the taxi driver returned, I paid the fare, and I got my suitcase back.

It's a funny story—but it doesn't make a point. On the other hand, I could use it as an example about the things I've learned on my travels, such as asking taxi drivers to write down the fare for a long trip *before* I put my suitcase into their trunk.

4. Avoid personal topics that you're still wrestling with.

It's true that the best writing is honest and real. But it also has to be thoroughly *worked* (there's that idea again). Over the years I've had students write long, painful essays about life issues they were still struggling with. Writing can be great therapy, allowing you to explore an experience or feeling from many angles. But that's personal writing, and you shouldn't confuse it with a polished essay for a school or college assignment.

Here's an example: I assigned students to write an essay about an experience that revealed a quality in someone they knew. A student wrote about a camping trip with her father and two brothers. When I read her paper, the trip sounded like fun, but her father was only a shadowy figure. When we talked about the paper, she told me that he had left her, her brothers, and their mother years before. This trip was supposed to be the start of a new relationship with them. She was still trying to figure out why he suddenly wanted to be part of their lives again after being away so long.

I could hear the pain and confusion she was expressing, and I felt for her—but a writing class requires polished, finished work. I asked her to start over and write about something less raw and someone she knew better. She finally selected her grandmother and earned an A on the paper. Bottom line: Choose a subject you feel comfortable exploring and sharing.

5. Allow enough time to write several drafts.

Your first attempt will usually be a for-your-eyes-only *discovery draft*. Use it to explore your topic and experiment with ways to shape your ideas. Often—and this is the magical part of writing—the movement of your pen, or your fingers on the keyboard, or your vocal muscles as you dictate, will awaken new ideas.

Here's the biggest mistake writers make: Confusing that exhilarating flow of ideas—your discovery draft—with a finished piece. You need to select a viewpoint, organize your ideas into paragraphs, and write an attention-getting introduction. Revision and proofreading will be necessary. All these tasks (and more!) go into the writing of a good essay, article, research paper, or report.

My doctoral dissertation is a great example of the benefits of a discovery draft—and the necessity for rewriting it. My committee was pleased with my dissertation, a pioneering look at postmodern features of Bernard Shaw's writing. "Publish it!" was their advice. I was ecstatic.

Exhausted after my doctoral program, I put the dissertation aside for several months. When I pulled it out to read again, I was aghast. Sure, the ideas, information, and writing were good. (I'd worked like a maniac for years to write it!) But the ideas rambled all over the place. I'd learned as I went, so the last chapter ended up in a completely different place from the first one. There was no overall plan. (How could there have been? I started from scratch knowing almost nothing about the topic.)

The experience I had with my dissertation is typical of discovery drafts. They create momentum and help you gather the information and ideas you need for a fine piece of writing. But you're headed for disaster if you confuse a discovery draft with a polished final piece. Always treat your first attempt at any writing task as a discovery draft, and always allow time to revise it. (Eventually I organized my ideas about Bernard Shaw and published my book.)

6. Have a keyword in mind.

Focusing on one word helps you avoid the problem of *writer's sprawl* that afflicts so many aspiring authors. The human brain is not a disciplined organ. Most of the time, this is good news. The billions of cells in our brains can range far and wide in just an instant, a boon when we want to be creative.

But this capacity for wandering and discovery is a disadvantage when you're writing for an audience. Your readers want to know where you're taking them, and they need to be able to follow the path from idea to idea and from point to point.

Do you remember Carol's and Brett's essays about visiting New York? Carol's keyword could be *history*, and Brett's could be *confidence*. In my essay about ballroom dancing, my keyword was *enriching*, and my focus was what dancing had done for my life.

Don't pressure yourself to find your keyword right away. When Carol was working on her New York essay, she did a great deal of freewriting before she decided to focus on the history-themed boat write. So feel free to do some wandering in the beginning, when you're writing the discovery draft that we discussed a moment ago. Then, when you're ready to start planning your essay, choose your keyword and hang on to it. (Think of dangling a sock in front of a dog. He's going to pull on it as hard as he can, never letting go.) Work your keyword into your piece as often as you can. Make sure every sentence relates to it. Check every example to be sure it's relevant. *This one principle is the key to professional-quality writing.*

7. Have a consistent tone.

Even advanced writers sometimes struggle with this requirement. If you're writing about a happy memory, you can't suddenly insert something dark and gloomy ("Six weeks after that wonderful birthday party, we heard that Grandpa needed major surgery"). Similarly you can't inject slang, humor, or sarcasm into a straightforward discussion of a serious topic. Choose a tone for your piece, and stick to it. To put it differently: It's fine to be folksy, snarky, or funny—but you have to carry that feeling through your *entire* piece.

8. Expand your world.

You're probably familiar with the saying that "It takes a village to raise a child"—the principle that children need the support and wisdom of a whole community to grow up into responsible and happy adults. In the same way, it takes a life to make a writer. The more you know, and the more experience you have, the more powerful your writing will be.

If you're a dynamic personality with piles of money and a lot of free time, it's easy to pursue interests and experiences that will enrich your writing. But what if you're trying to juggle a demanding job, a family, and several additional responsibilities on a paycheck that never goes far enough?

Nobody ever said that becoming a successful writer is easy—but here are a few suggestions to get you started:

a) Read. You have a library card, right? And you read a newspaper daily?

b) Cultivate diverse friendships. Get to know stimulating people from different backgrounds and age groups.

c) Make wise entertainment choices. I've been subscribing to the monthly newsletter from my local public TV station for many years. At the beginning of each month I highlight the shows I want to watch and post their program schedule onto my refrigerator door. I listen to NPR in my car, along with talk shows from other parts of the political spectrum. My Netflix queue features a long list of interesting movies that I've heard about and want to watch.

d) Use the Internet. I regularly write news articles and commentary for a law enforcement website, and coming up with ideas is tough because I don't work in the field. To find topics, I use Google Alerts and visit newspaper websites: the *Washington Post*, *LA Times*, and *New York Times*. The comments at the ends of published articles often help me come up with an angle to write about.

9. Ask a friend or family member to read what you've written.

It's worth repeating: Getting feedback on your writing is the best way to improve. You don't need to look for a language expert. You'll be surprised at the useful suggestions you receive from friends and family members. It's so easy for writers to miss small errors, or to think what we've written is crystal clear when it really isn't.

10. Respect the feedback you're given.

I've already mentioned that I often ask friends and family members for feedback. If even one person seems confused about a sentence or an idea, I revise it for clarity. A wise teacher once told me that writers always overestimate their ability to be clear and precise. If even one person misses the point—*fix it*!

And there you have it—advice based on my experiences as a teacher, editor, and—most important—*a writer*. Take them to heart, and you'll soon see dramatic improvement in your own writing.

Chapter 11

Time Management for Writers

I almost gave this chapter a different title: The Putting-It-Off Problem. We writers are such a varied group of people that it's almost impossible to generalize about us. But there's one thing many of us have in common: We hate sitting down to start a writing task.

It's certainly true of me. When a writing project looms, I suddenly start getting excited about activities that have nothing to do with writing: Cleaning the attic. Painting the bathroom. Shopping for holiday presents (even if it's only July). A lifetime of struggling with procrastination inspired me to write a book about it—*Five Minutes a Day: Time Management for People Who Love to Put Things Off*.

But you don't have to read a whole book about procrastination (and you probably shouldn't, since your priority right now is to get busy *writing*). We're going to explore why it's so hard to get started on a writing task—and what you can do about it. Luckily there are plenty of simple strategies to help you overcome that inertia.

Is writing hard? The answer is *no*. It's worth repeating: *Anyone with normal intelligence can be a writer*. You've been using language all your life. Resources are available to help you with any rough spots you encounter. For most people, it's only the early stages that are hard. We dread sitting down and getting started.

So let's switch gears for a moment and think about something positive: What your life would be like if you didn't complicate it by putting off writing tasks until the last minute. If you're a student, picture yourself relaxed and calm the night before a paper is due. While your classmates are tearing out their hair in big handfuls, you're watching TV or hanging out with your friends.

If you're facing a deadline for a writing project at your job, picture yourself puttering around doing routine tasks at work the day before it's due. Stress-free living is wonderful!

If putting off a writing task causes so many headaches, why do so many of us keep doing it? You might think that laziness is the culprit, but that's usually not true. Often when you're putting off a dreaded task, you'll notice that you have plenty of energy for other things. The problem is that writing isn't one of them.

There are two major reasons why we put off writing tasks:

1. We're afraid of failure. Nobody likes to feel inferior. If you're researching a topic that's new to you, either at school or at work, of course you're going to feel intimidated. If an assignment calls for you to use a new skill—writing a process paper, for example, if you've never done that before—you might have a hard time getting started.

2. We're overwhelmed. If a mountain is looming, it's natural to put off climbing it until another day when you might feel more energetic, ambitious, or courageous—or when the mountain has magically shrunk to a more manageable size. Writing an essay or a business report can feel like climbing a mountain, and the same magical thinking ("I'll wait till I feel like writing" or "It won't seem so scary if I wait until tomorrow") can stop us cold.

Once you know why you're tempted to procrastinate, you can start looking for strategies for getting yourself moving. If you're afraid of the task that lies ahead, get help—and start looking for it early. Go to the writing lab, look for a solution online, pair up with a friend or co-worker, talk with your instructor—there are many ways to get the information you need to overcome your fears.

The best antidote to the "I'm overwhelmed!" problem is to start early. Take baby steps at first, do a little every day, make a plan—all of these strategies will get you warmed up and moving, well before your deadline.

 It's impossible to overemphasize the necessity for doing something— anything—to get yourself warmed up and moving.

Years ago I heard a wonderful story about Winston Churchill, Great Britain's prime minister during World War II, that teaches an important lesson about overcoming your fears. Churchill decided that he wanted to become a painter. But when he actually sat down to paint, all he could do was stare at the empty canvas. Luckily a friend came to his rescue:

---

from *Painting as a Pastime* (1932) by Winston S. Churchill

At that moment the loud approaching sound of a motor car was heard in the drive. From this chariot there stepped swiftly and lightly none other than the gifted wife of Sir John Lavery. "Painting! But what are you hesitating about? Let me have a brush - the big one." Splash into the turpentine, wallop into the blue and the white, frantic flourish on the palette—clean no longer—and then several large, fierce strokes and slashes of blue on the absolutely cowering canvas. Anyone could see that it could not hit back. No evil fate avenged the jaunty violence. The canvas grinned in helplessness before me. The spell was broken. The sickly inhibitions rolled away. I seized the largest brush and fell upon my victim with berserk fury. I have never felt any awe of a canvas since.

The fear of making a mistake is the number-one reason for procrastination. We writers are putting ourselves on the line every time we pick up a pen or start pounding a keyboard. Will our readers understand? Will they like what we've written? Will they like *us*?

Those fears can be particularly paralyzing when there's a lot at stake—writing for an editor, for example, or for an instructor. I started coming to grips with my own fears during my last semester of graduate school. In *Five Minutes a Day*, I told this true story:

from Five Minutes a Day

I had misgivings about my final course, and the first class meeting confirmed my worst fears. I returned home, shoulders slumping, and told my husband that the required paper was out of my league. I'd earned straight A's in my graduate program, and now it was all going to come crashing down around me.

Charlie asked what would happen if I wrote a bad paper. "He'll give me a B," I said.

"He'll give you a B?" asked my husband. "You're worried about a *B*, for heaven's sake?"

"Well, I'm a good writer," I said. "I'm sure I could pull off a B."

"So do it," he urged. "Relax. Nobody's ever going to know what grade he gives you. This is your last semester. Just get through it."

And that's exactly what I did—except that after I wrote a mediocre first draft, I started to see some things I could easily improve. I decided to read another article, add a couple of details, sharpen a few ideas….

The paper earned an A. I couldn't wait to tell Charlie and thank him for helping get me past that rough spot the first day.

He wasn't at all surprised. "Do you realize," he said, "that you've pulled that I-can't-do-this routine in every course?"

I gasped. "Do you mean," I said, "that you've been giving me that go-for-a-B advice all through my graduate program?"

"Of course," he said, and returned to his newspaper.

Overcoming Procrastination

Here are eight strategies to try:

1. Do it badly.

When you were growing up, you probably heard this bit of wisdom from your mother: "If it's worth doing, it's worth doing right." (My mother used to tell me that too.) It's great advice for many situations (if you're a surgeon, for example), but it's a terrible way to approach a writing task.

It's much better to start out badly (sorry, Mom!). You can always make improvements later (and you probably will). Your goal is to get something—*anything*—on paper. (And remember to darken the screen if anyone walks past your computer!)

2. Give your unconscious mind plenty of time to get things rolling.

Given a chance, your unconscious mind (the hidden part of your brain that operates beneath your awareness) will do much of the work for you— *if* you give it something to work with. Let's say it's Friday afternoon, and your instructor assigned you to analyze a short story in a 500-word paper that's due next Wednesday.

If you're smart, you'll read the short story immediately—several times, if possible—so that your brain can start working on the assignment. Then you can forget about it and do other things until it's time to sit down and write.

Your brain will get to work analyzing the story and developing ideas for your paper while you're texting your friends, washing your car—whatever you typically do when you're not in school. When you do sit down to write the paper, you'll be surprised to find out that many of your ideas have already been worked out, even though you thought you had forgotten about the story.

Always do research and other preparation for writing early. As you saw on p. 19, your brain is a complex thinking machine that can easily work on several tasks while you're busy with other things. When it's time to create, organize, and develop your ideas, you'll find much of the work is already done for you.

3. Do a leading task.

A "leading task" is an action that gets you moving. It should be something quick and easy. For example, I despise paperwork. Sometimes when I'm faced with a letter I don't want to write or a form I don't want to fill out, I get the envelope ready. Once that's done, I'll start thinking about spending five minutes on the actual paperwork. And presto—before I know it, the job is done.

A "leading task" for a writing assignment might be typing a title, looking up an article, making a list of ideas, writing a sentence, correcting some writing mistakes—anything to get you warmed up. Try it the next time you feel stuck: Instead of starting big, think small—and watch your energy level start to soar.

4. Use the 80-20 Rule.

The 80-20 Rule is a time management principle that says that 80% of the benefits are found in 20% of the possibilities. If you have a list of 10 tasks, 8 are a waste of time, and 2 have tremendous potential.

You can use the 80-20 Rule to turn a looming mountain into a small and manageable hill. Instead of groaning about everything you have to do, choose the 20% with the most potential. Do those right away. (You can always add more later.) This is a great way to build momentum. A bonus is that often you'll discover that the other items on your list really were unnecessary.

5. Use Alan Lakein's "Swiss Cheese Method."

Alan Lakein is the author of a bestselling book called *How to Get Control of Your Time and Your Life*. One of his best tools is the "Swiss cheese method"—"poking holes" in a task rather than forcing yourself to do the whole thing at once.

The "Swiss Cheese Method" is a boon to writers facing complex tasks like reports and research papers. Do a little every day. Sit down whenever you have a free moment and see if you can add something else to your project. Before you know it, you'll be well on your way to completion and success.

6. Enlist a friend.

Have a friend come over for a morning or evening of writing, or make plans to meet in the library or a coffee shop. If you can't get together, make a plan to update each other about your writing process via email or (better yet) Skype. Writing with a friend—even when you're working on totally different projects—has huge benefits. You'll be making each other accountable and counteracting the loneliness that so many writers endure. (Hint: It's ok to start your session with conversation over a cup of coffee!) Often you can give one another valuable feedback. Find a writing buddy and cultivate that friendship!

7. Build a habit.

Develop the habit of sitting down in the same place at the same time every day to write. Get your pen moving, even if it's only "The quick brown fox jumps over the lazy dog." After a while your unconscious mind will automatically energize you when writing time is near. (This strategy also works great for research projects: Head to the library at the same time every day, even if all you do at first is walk around and look at the bookshelves.)

8. Make it pleasurable.

I don't enjoy working. (That's an understatement. Sigh.) I don't like desks. I don't like To Do lists. In order to get anything done, I have to look for ways to fool myself into thinking I'm not really working. Our home has a wireless Internet connection so that I can use my laptop in bed or in front of the TV. (It's amazing what I can get done during commercial breaks!)

I do like to work in coffee shops, and when I'm at home, I usually have music playing. (I listened to a lot of Abba when I was writing my book on Shaw.) Give yourself a break whenever you can—you'll be easier to live with, and you'll be surprised by what you can accomplish.

These suggestions really work! Choose one and make it part of your life. Then choose another suggestion. As you work your way through this list, you'll find yourself moving steadily towards achieving your writing goals. Be sure to celebrate every step of your progress!

Part Three

Taking Your Writing to the Next Level

Chapter 12

How to Write an Introduction

Whether they're writing an essay, a research paper, or a report for a corporation, many writers struggle with introductions. As I noted on p. 20, one problem is the "blank piece of paper" or "empty computer screen" problem that freezes many writers into immobility.

Like many writers, I used to get stuck there myself. Luckily I've learned how to avoid that problem altogether. Instead of fretting about how to get started, I can start filling in the parts of the template for writing the beginning of *any* writing task:

> Get your readers' attention. (A brief story often works well.) Next, give readers some background information that's new to them. Then make the point (thesis) that you're going to develop with ideas and examples.

None of this has to be elegantly written. The main goal is to get my pen to move across the paper or to make the computer keys start clicking.

Another possibility is to postpone writing my introduction until I've worked up some momentum—an idea that probably sounds odd but really works for me. Instead of staring at the empty computer screen, I try to come up with something—anything—that I'll be using. I don't worry about mistakes, awkwardness, or disjointed ideas. My only goal is to write or type some words.

What's most important is to stay focused on Time Management Strategy #1, which you met on p. 86: *Do it badly*. I remind myself that I can always make improvements later on.

I faced that stuck feeling when I started writing the chapter you're reading right now. I didn't have a clue about how to begin it—but I did know I'd be using the opening from Louisa May Alcott's novel *Little Women* at some point. (It will be coming along soon.) I found a full-text version of *Little Women* online, copied and pasted the beginning dialogue into this document, and added some ideas about how I would use it. By the time I'd finished, my thoughts were starting to hum, my fingers were moving, and I was able to tackle the beginning of this chapter.

The second principle to remember about writing an introduction is that you don't have to invent a way to do it. Familiarize yourself with introductory strategies that other writers have used, and choose one. Here's a list that many writers have found helpful:

Introductory Strategies

- A story
- A contrast
- A quotation
- An opinion
- A surprising fact
- A question
- A problem
- An analogy
- A definition
- An explanation

Did you notice that there are *ten* strategies? If you recall the 80-20 Rule (Time Management Strategy #4), you already know what I'm about to say: You'll probably use two of those strategies most of the time. My favorites are #1, a story, and #2, a contrast. I like to begin a writing project with a story (see pp. 17 and 41 for examples) because it's a great way to engage and involve readers.

And I like contrasts because they challenge readers to do some critical thinking on their own. In fact I used contrasts in the first paragraph of a wring project I'm working on: An article about Bernard Shaw's thoughts on education that I wrote for a book that a friend was putting together.

Notice that my introduction explains how Shaw was different from modern education experts. In a way, I'm challenging readers of the book to choose between Shaw's approach to education and what today's educators are doing:

---

from "Shaw and Education"

"Cognitive domain," "measurable objectives," "quantitative methods": These clinical terms are the hallmarks of much contemporary educational theory, research, and practice. By comparison, Bernard Shaw's far-ranging ideas about education might seem irrelevant—almost quaint. An autodidact with a revolutionist's soul and a mystic's idealism, Shaw had no training in classroom management or school administration, and no interest in the numbers-driven outcomes that so often drive decisions about education in our time.

I also like to use #7, a problem—in fact that's the strategy I used to open this book (see p. 2). And I use all of the other strategies in various writing tasks. During my writing career I've probably used every one of them multiple times.   .

And here's one more that's a favorite of the pros: *Arrive late, leave early*. When you watch a TV show or movie, notice how often you land in the middle of a situation—and how often the scene ends before it's finished. Screenwriters call this strategy "arrive late, leave early." It's a great way to catch viewers' interest and keep involved with the story, and you should do the same whenever you can.

Conventional advice to begin at the beginning doesn't work well for most writing tasks. Walk into any elementary school where children are writing papers about a historical figure, and invariably you'll find this dull sentence pattern right at the beginning: *[Famous person] was born in [fill in the date]*. "Abraham Lincoln was born in 1809." "Rosa Parks was born in 1913." Similarly, most employees begin a site visit report with a weak sentence like this one: "I arrived in San Antonio at 9:30 AM on Monday, April 12." Who cares?

Better openings might be:

Abraham Lincoln didn't set out to be the Great Emancipator. BETTER
Rosa Parks made history when she stepped onto a Birmingham bus on a Thursday evening in 1955. BETTER
Last week's trip to the distribution center in San Antonio alerted me to several inventory and chain supply problems. BETTER

If you're writing about an event—a site visit connected with your job, a family trip for a school essay—jump right to the most interesting part. Don't spend too much time on what professional writers call the *backstory* (background events). Skillful writers can weave that background into the unfolding events.

See How a Pro Did It

Here's an activity that will help you deepen your understanding of what an introduction is supposed to accomplish. Although this example is fictional, the principles apply to almost any writing task.

The opening lines from Louisa May Alcott's *Little Women* are reprinted below. (Note that Alcott uses Strategy #1, a story, to get her novel going.) This is a classic book that was first published after the Civil War. It's never been out of print, and you're about to see why.

Take a few moments to read the excerpt below, and then write down everything it tells you about the characters and their situation. Don't try to get too clever or psychological: Stick to simple facts, and don't cheat if you've already read *Little Women* or seen one of the movie versions! (By the way, this is an exercise I do with my writing groups—it's a great way to sharpen your skills if you yearn to write fiction.)

Here's my list:

- It's just before Christmas in the home of a poor family on a cold day
- The story takes place at an earlier time when fireplaces provided heat
- Four sisters are facing a bleak holiday: Jo, Meg, Beth, and Amy
- Past Christmases were happier
- The family has had a change in fortune recently
- Jo isn't afraid to be unladylike
- The girls' parents probably aren't in earshot
- The girls' father is away at war and in danger
- Beth is less materialistic than her three sisters
- Amy is the youngest
- The girls love their father and miss him
- The girls are close to one another

Not bad for only 121 words!

There's a reason why people continue to read *Little Women*: This is *good writing*. In a few lines you're drawn into the story, introduced to *six* characters, their personalities, and the challenges they're facing. The backstory (Father is away at the war, the family is facing money problems, and the girls have been told there will be no Christmas presents this year) is woven into the dialogue.

Is there anything an effective introduction should *never* do? Yes, of course. Your introduction should not announce what's coming or what you're planning to do. "My paper will explain why…" "I plan to show you how…" "This article is about…" No. Never.

Let's return to Meg, Jo, Beth, and Amy again for a moment. What would have *Little Women* have been like if Alcott had not been such a skillful writer? Here's how the opening might have read:

> I'm about to tell you the story of a loving and lively family consisting of four sisters, their mother, and their father. He is away at war, money is scarce, and the family is facing a bleak Christmas.

Dreary, isn't it? So let's return to what the introduction *should* do. In addition to getting you involved and engaged, it should set the stage for what's going to follow. If you're writing a paper about your cruise to the Bahamas, make sure there's a taste of the tropics somewhere in your introduction: Don't get sidetracked into too many details about trip preparations. If you're writing a novel, inject your theme early. (Did you notice that Alcott quickly inserts the ideas of **family** and **poverty** that are so central to *Little Women*?)

In a research project about a timely issue (such as voter rights or child abuse), you should quickly demonstrate that your subject is important. It's a good idea to use a quotation from an expert or some statistical data to back up your point. (If you take another look at p. 2 of this book, you'll see that I lined up several experts to try to convince you that writing skills are important.)

Armed with these strategies, you should feel confident tackling the introduction to almost any writing task. Now you're ready to move on to other issues related to essays, articles, workplace reports, and other projects.

Chapter 13

Strategies for Better Essays

In Chapter 5, Writing Paragraphs and Essays (p. 41), you learned how to use a basic template for an essay, article, or workplace report. In this chapter I'm going to show you several advanced principles and strategies that can be incorporated into your essays. You can use them in almost anything you write, and the results will be well worth the effort: Everything you write will stand out.

1. Tell stories.

Other names for stories are *examples* and *narratives*, and they are the heart and soul of writing. I've just reread this manuscript to see how many stories I've used so far, and I stopped counting at 25. That's a story every two or three pages in a book about a rather impersonal topic—writing instruction.

Why have I included so many of them? Stories are *solid gold*. They bring your ideas to life, entertain your readers, and keep them interested. If a point isn't clear, a story can drive it home. Readers will remember your stories and the point they were making long after they've forgotten the explanation you took such a long time to write.

Stories can be unusual (such as my story about Margarita, p. 55) or ordinary (my husband's grumbling when I type his columns, p. 54). A story can drive home a point you're making (the editor who was afraid of the word *because*, p. 60) or poke fun at yourself (my struggles to spell words with double letters, p. 63).

Here's some advice about using stories:

- Keep them short. Sometimes a sentence or two is all you need.
- A story can be a great way to begin a chapter in a book, a research paper, or an essay.
- If you're writing about a personal topic (for a school essay, for example), try to include a story in every paragraph.

You'll learn more about stories (also called *narratives*) in Chapter 18, Modes of Development.

2. Plan your essays to build to a climax.

This is where you take a giant step toward professional-quality writing. This is also one of the principles that shape the template—the "invisible shape"—that I just told you about in Chapter 6. Professional writers often aim to end with something big, and you can try this too. In a paragraph, put your best example near the end. In an essay, save your best supporting idea for last.

Let's say you're writing an essay about your eighth birthday party. Your main point will go in the first paragraph: It was a wonderful birthday. You're going to write three body paragraphs describing what made that birthday special: One about playing games with your friends, another about gifts, and another one about the birthday cake.

What was the *best* thing about that eighth birthday? The gifts! Save that idea for your *third* body paragraph, and use a climactic transition to make sure your readers get the point: *Best of all, most of all,* or *most important.* I'll return to transitions later in this chapter.

I built a climax into my essay about ballroom dancing. Here's the outline. Notice that I saved my best supporting idea—the fun I'm having—for last:

Outline

Ballroom dancing has enriched my life in ways I couldn't have imagined. THESIS
- One unexpected change has been increased confidence.
- Another surprise was learning to appreciate music on a new level.
- **The greatest gift that dancing has given me is fun.** CLIMAX

---

3. Consider using closure to end a paragraph.

Closure means "closing" or "ending." Closure is a professional trick that I wish more writers would use: When you come to the end of a paragraph, add one more sentence to finish it and close it down. You can think of closure as a *bow* on a package—an extra touch. Closure isn't necessary for every paragraph, and you don't want to overdo it. But you'll be surprised how useful it is.

Because I didn't learn this trick in school, I was puzzled when an editor told me about it. If it's not taught in English classes, how was I supposed to learn how to do it? She suggested that I start looking at the ends of paragraphs in articles and books. And she was right—I soon figured it out. That simple trick has added polish to my paragraphs for years now.

(Did you notice how I closed down the previous paragraph? I used closure— an extra sentence to close down the paragraph: *That simple trick has added polish to my paragraphs for years now.*)

Here are some effective paragraph "wrap-ups" I've seen recently:

I've loved that song ever since.
She turned her head and smiled at him.
That remark stung.

3. Use paragraph transitions.

Transitions are another tool that professionals use often. Transitions are like bridges, helping you get from one idea to the next. To explain how they work, I'm going to use the example from the previous page—your eighth birthday.

The most basic transitions are numbers. In the essay about your eighth birthday, you could use number as transitions, like this:

> **First**, the games were fun.
> **Second**, the party food was wonderful.
> **Third**, I loved all my gifts.

But that can sound a little impersonal and mechanical. Many students try to make their writing sound more human by getting away from a numerical list, like this:

> **First**, the games were fun.
> **Next**, the party food was wonderful.
> **Last**, I loved all my gifts.

If you want to write like a pro, however, use the "build to a climax" trick we discussed earlier. Professional writers never use *last, finally,* or *last but not least.* (I used to ask my students to promise they would never use "last but not least" again for the rest of their lives!) Here's what a professional writer would do with our outline:

> **First**, the games were fun.
> **Next**, the party food was wonderful.
> **Best of all** were my gifts.

4. Plan some of your *paragraphs* so that they build to a climax.

Earlier you learned how to make your essay build to a climax by putting your best supporting paragraph last. You can do the same *inside* a paragraph. Here's a paragraph about a student's eighth birthday, with the climax highlighted. Notice that she saved her favorite party game for last.

First, the games were fun. One silly one was taking turns kneeling on a chair and trying to drop clothespins into a bottle. My cousins Bill and Dan made fun of some of the girls because their clothespins kept missing the bottle. They found out it wasn't as easy as it looked when their turns came, and we all had a good laugh about that. Another game I always loved was pin-the-tail-on-the-donkey. I liked the feeling of being blindfolded and trying to figure out where the donkey was. It was a little bit of an adventure, and I loved the moment when the blindfold came off, even though I didn't win the game that year. My favorite game was musical chairs. We scrambled and giggled and raced to get to a chair when the music stopped. I didn't win that one either, but I couldn't stop laughing even when my friend Laura got the prize instead of me.

Now that you've seen the strategies that advanced writers use, please go to PlanMyPaper.com to watch several short, free PowerPoints and videos that will bring these ideas to life.

And here's one more thing to remember: These strategies will work in many types of writing tasks—from letters to the editor to essay assignments to workplace reports.

Chapter 14

Understanding Sentences

If you've ever worried about sentence errors, this chapter is for you. You're about to learn how an inexpensive highlighter—something you probably already own—can help you spot and fix most sentence problems. (If you don't have a highlighter, a pen or pencil will work fine.)

And there's a bonus: You'll also learn Comma Rule 1 a handy guide to punctuating many sentences correctly. (There's a short chapter on Comma Rule 1 beginning on p. 165—but you can easily learn it right now.)

Sentences and Extra Ideas

To understand sentences, all you need are two basic concepts:

1. Anything you say, think, or write is either a *sentence* or an *extra idea*. There are no other possibilities.

2. An extra idea can't stand on its own and must be attached to a sentence.

That's it. With these two facts you can write effective sentences almost *every time*, and you'll quickly be able to find and fix many sentence errors that creep into your writing.

Here is the key to understanding sentences and extra ideas: Sentences start with a person, place, or thing. Extra ideas don't. Mind you, extra ideas are fine things—as long as you don't start treating them like real sentences. (That mistake is called a *fragment* (p. 211).

Think of a garage: It's something extra added to a house. You wouldn't want to live in a garage, but it's a great place to protect your car from the weather and store your lawn mower. Extra ideas are just like that: They're nice to have as long as you don't start thinking they're real sentences.

A Closer Look at Sentences

Let's compare some sentences and extra ideas. Remember: Looking at the beginning is the key. Is there a person, place, or thing? If the answer is *yes*, you probably have a sentence. Here are some examples:

Person, Place, or Thing

I

my favorite book

last year's budget

Joe

We

It

A fat, friendly poodle

Savannah

Ballroom dancing

That snazzy Corvette

Music

Lincoln Road

Here are some sentences with the person, place, or thing highlighted:

I agree with Candace.

My favorite book is *Gone Girl*, by Gillian Flynn.

Last year's budget worked well for me.

Joe is late again.

We stayed for the whole game even though it lasted for fifteen innings.

It needs a fresh coat of paint and some landscaping.

A fat, friendly poodle entertained all of us at the park.

Savannah is one of my favorite places to visit.

Ballroom dancing is my passion.

That snazzy Corvette caught my eye right away.

Lincoln Road will be closed for traffic tomorrow morning.

(Were you surprised that *it* counts as a thing? A group of words beginning with *it* counts as a sentence: *It needs a fresh coat of paint and some landscaping.*)

A Closer Look at Extra Ideas

A moment ago you learned that any group of words is either a sentence or an extra idea. The difference is that a sentence usually begins with a person, place, or thing; extra ideas don't.

> I plan to go to the Cycle Shop tomorrow. SENTENCE

Now you're going to look at a group of words that's not a sentence:

> Since my bicycle needs a new front tire. EXTRA IDEA

How do you know this is an extra idea? The first word is *since*—not a person, place, or thing. (Do you know anyone named *Since*? Have you ever visited *Since*, or owned a *since*?)

> Since my bicycle needs a new front tire. EXTRA IDEA

You can make this extra idea into a sentence in either of two ways. One is to omit the word *Since*:

> ~~Since~~ My bicycle needs a new front tire. SENTENCE

A second possibility is to add on a sentence (italicized in this example):

> Since my bicycle needs a new front tire, *I plan to go to the Cycle Shop tomorrow.* SENTENCE

(Did you notice the comma? An extra idea is usually followed by a comma. You've just been introduced to Comma Rule 1!)

Let's try another example:

> When the Prowlers won last night's game. EXTRA IDEA

One way to fix it is by removing the word *when*:

> ~~When~~ The Prowlers won last night's game. SENTENCE

Another way to fix it is by adding a complete sentence (*italicized* in this example):

> When the Prowlers won last night's game, *the whole college celebrated*.
> SENTENCE

You can use a highlighter to ensure that you're writing complete sentences. Just highlight the beginning of each sentence, and check to make sure it starts with a person, place or thing.

Practice Activity: Look for Sentences

Instructions: Highlight the beginning of each sentence, and look for a person, place or thing. Put a check √ in front of each sentence; mark each extra idea with an X. The correct answers follow.

- ____ Paula learned to speak Russian as a child.
- ____ I plan to study Spanish in Mexico next summer.
- ____ Because I want to work with Hispanic children.
- ____ If my plans work out.
- ____ A friendly tutor has been helping me with my Spanish homework.
- ____ When my roommate signed up for French.
- ____ Winnie tutored her every weekend.
- ____ Although the textbook looked difficult.
- ____ My roommate learned to speak French well.
- ____ Many people want to speak at least two languages.

ANSWERS Practice Activity: Look for Sentences

1. √ Paula learned to speak Russian as a child.

2. √ I plan to study Spanish in Mexico next summer.

3. X Because I want to work with Hispanic children.

4. X If my plans work out.

5. √ A friendly tutor has been helping me with my Spanish homework.

6. X When my roommate signed up for French.

7. √ Winnie tutored her every weekend.

8. X Although the textbook looked difficult.

9. √ My roommate learned to speak French well.

10. √ Many people want to speak at least two languages.

Practice Activity: More Practice with Sentences

Instructions: Look at (or highlight) the beginning of each item below. Put a check (√) if you think the item is a sentence. (Reminder: A sentence generally begins with a person, place, or thing.) Put an X if the item is an extra idea.

1. ____My blue dress needs to be dry cleaned.

2. ____Although the test wasn't difficult.

3. ____Jane called me.

4. ____At the end of yesterday's meeting.

5. ____The dance ended at midnight.

6. ____We left.

7. ____Before I make a decision about graduate school next year.

8. ____It probably needs a new battery.

9. ____The Empire State Building used to be the tallest building in the world.

10. ____Falling in love is an amazing experience.

ANSWERS Practice Activity: More Practice with Sentences

4. √ My blue dress needs to be dry cleaned. [*My blue dress* is a thing.]

5. X Although the test wasn't difficult. [*Although* is not a person, place, or thing]

6. √ Jane called me. [*Jane* is a person.]

7. X At the end of yesterday's meeting. [*At* is not a person, place, or

thing]

8. √ The dance ended at midnight. [*The dance* is a thing.]

9. √ We left. [*We* are people.]

10. X Before I make a decision about graduate school next year. [*Before* is not a person, place, or thing]

11. √ It probably needs a new battery. [*It* is a thing.]

12. √ The Empire State Building used to be the tallest building in the world. [*The Empire State Building* is a thing.]

13. √ Falling in love is an amazing experience. [*Falling in love* is a thing.]

A Closer Look

Did any of the answers to the previous Activity surprise you? Students often wonder why *We left* is a sentence. Who are *we*, and what did we leave? You may also have wondered about *It needs a new battery*. What is *it*?

Here's what you need to know: Sentences don't need to be clear or logical. They simply need to begin with a person, place, or thing (and remember that *it* is a thing). In the context of a conversation or a story, these word-groups would make perfect sense:

My car won't start. It probably needs a new battery. CORRECT
The server never came to our table to take our order. We left. CORRECT

Even something that's total nonsense can be a complete sentence, like this sentence from John Lennon's book *In His Own Write*:

"I'm partly Dave" he would growm in the morning which was half the battle.

I don't know what Lennon meant (and I suspect he didn't either), but because he used *I* (a person) at the beginning, what he wrote is indeed a sentence.

Now let's take another look at a principle I just mentioned: If it starts with *it*, it's a sentence. Memorize this principle. It's going to come in handy.

Unfortunately many students use a comma with sentences starting with *it*, like this:

Memorize this principle, it's going to come in handy. INCORRECT
Memorize this principle. It's going to come in handy. CORRECT

I gave you a similar example on the previous page:

My car won't start. It probably needs a new battery. CORRECT

You can avoid many comma mistakes by remembering this rule of thumb: *If it starts with "it," it's a sentence.*

Working with Sentences and Extra Ideas

Earlier you learned that extra ideas are useful as long as they're attached to complete sentences (like a garage attached to a house). You can put an extra idea at the beginning or the end of a sentence—your choice.

If you put the extra idea in front of a sentence, use a comma after it. In the example below, *because algebra is difficult for me* is the extra idea. (*Because* is not a person, place, or thing.) You'll learn more about these commas beginning on p. 165 (Comma Rule 1).

Because algebra is difficult for me, I'm working with a tutor. CORRECT

You can also attach the extra idea to the back without a comma:

I'm working with a tutor because algebra is difficult for me. CORRECT

Activity: More Practice with Sentences and Extra Ideas

Instructions: Highlight the beginning of each item below. Label the sentences √ and the extra ideas X. When you're finished, check your answers below.

14. ____When I looked at the clock.

15. ____His cat meowed.

16. ____On the top shelf in the storage room.

17. ____Although I've always liked that color.

18. ____Because Shoshanna has always wanted a career in law

enforcement.

19. ____It fascinates her.

20.____Our passports will expire next month.

21. ____A red Mustang convertible is guaranteed to turn heads.

22. ____I agree.

23. ____Until the hotel confirms our reservations.

ANSWERS Activity: More Practice with Sentences and Extra Ideas

- X When I looked at the clock.
- √. His cat meowed.
- X On the top shelf in the storage room.
- X Although I've always liked that color.
- X Because Shoshanna has always wanted a career in law enforcement.
- √ It fascinates her. [Remember that *it* is a thing.]
- √ Our passports will expire next month.
- √ A red Mustang convertible is guaranteed to turn heads.
- √ I agree.
- X Until the hotel confirms our reservations.

Activity: Add Sentences to Extra Ideas

Instructions: Here are the extra ideas you just saw. Add a sentence to each to make it complete. The first one is done for you. (No answers are provided.)

1. When I looked at the clock, *I saw that I'd missed my first class*. CORRECT

2. On the top shelf in the storage room,_____.

3. Although I've always liked that color,_____.

4. Because Shoshanna has always wanted a career in law enforcement,_____.

5. Until the hotel confirms our reservations,_____.

Chapter 15

Writing Effective Sentences

Earlier in this book I promised that you would be building on what you already know. Now that you understand how sentences work, you're ready to start learning how to solve common sentence problems.

First let's look at three tricks professional writers use to spot problems and fix them.

- Look at the beginning of the sentence. Many mistakes start there.
- Shorten a sentence to isolate an error so that you can fix it.
- Make a sentence slightly longer to help yourself hear the mistake.

In this chapter we'll be using the first trick: Look at the beginning of the sentence. Later in this book you'll learn how to use the other two.

Tips for Effective Sentences

Here are four tips you'll use again and again:

1. Anything that begins with a person, place, or thing is probably a real sentence and should end with a period.

Elaine wanted to leave the party early. SENTENCE

You learned all about this in the last chapter. If a group of words doesn't begin with a person, place, or thing, it's probably an extra idea that should a) end with a comma and b) be attached to a real sentence.

Because Elaine wanted to leave the party early, EXTRA IDEA
Because Elaine wanted to leave the party early, I parked the car across the street. SENTENCE

(Go to p. 165 to read about Comma Rule 1.)

2. Remember that *it* is a thing. Here's a handy rule of thumb: If it starts

with *it*, it's a sentence. (You already met this principle on p. 108.)

> Larry stared at the gift, it took him by surprise. INCORRECT
> Larry stared at the gift. It took him by surprise. CORRECT

3. Checking the beginning of the sentence can often solve usage problems.

Take a look at this sentence. Which verb would you choose—*is* or *are*?

> Focusing on our priorities (is, are) especially important this year.

If you think about the word *focusing*, you'll know immediately that the verb should be *is*. [Focusing...is]

> Focusing on our priorities is especially important this year. CORRECT

(Go to p. 196 to read about Subject-Verb Agreement Rule 4.)

4. Be especially careful about starting sentences with *-ing* words.

Of course it's correct to start a sentence with a word ending in *–ing*, but you risk writing a sentence fragment or a misplaced modifier. (Go to pp. 224-5 to learn more.)

> Combing his hair as he pulled on his jacket. FRAGMENT
> He was combing his hair as he pulled on his jacket. CORRECT
> Combing his hair, his cell phone rang. MISPLACED MODIFIER
> While he was combing his hair, his cell phone rang. CORRECT

Writing Professional Sentences

Now let's focus on some ways to make good sentences *better*. I'm going to be discussing ideas about sentences that I learned as a graduate student and a professional writer. This is your chance to move into the realm of professional writing. Take your time, reread when necessary, and—most important—look for opportunities to practice what you're learning.

Here's a point we're going to be returning to again and again: Sentences can be broken down into parts. Some parts are "loud," in a sense, while other parts are "soft." For example, listen to yourself read the following sentence aloud:

Charles Schulz, who created the *Peanuts* comic strip, was inducted into the US

Hockey Hall of Fame for his outstanding contributions to hockey.

Very likely you changed your voice—dropped it slightly to make it "soft"—when you read "who created the *Peanuts* comic strip." Here's the sentence again, with the "loud" part in **bold**:

Charles Schulz, who created the *Peanuts* comic strip, **was inducted into the US Hockey Hall of Fame for his outstanding contributions to hockey.**

Using your voice this way allows you to emphasize the most interesting part of your sentence: A cartoonist was inducted into the hall of fame for a sport.

Let's try another example. Listen to yourself read this sentence aloud:

Fort Wood, a star-shaped military fort constructed in 1809, eventually became the base for the Statue of Liberty.

What's the most interesting part of this sentence? The Statue of Liberty was built on the remains of a fort—so you'll want to make that part "loud." (The year the fort was built isn't as interesting, so that will be the "soft" part of the sentence.)

Fort Wood, a star-shaped military fort constructed in 1809, **eventually became the base for the Statue of Liberty.**

Did you notice that the commas tell you where to change your voice.? You'll be learning more about these commas in Chapter 26, Comma Rule 3 (p. 172).

This "loud" and "soft" idea is one of the most useful strategies in your writer's toolbox.

Sentences with *But*

You already know that it's perfectly all right to start sentences with *but* (p. 60) and that you need a comma when you join two sentences with *but*:

I bought a ticket for the show, but bad weather kept me from going. CORRECT

So let's see what else there is to learn. Professional writers know that *but* can be a tricky word because it sets up equality between two opposite ideas—and sometimes that's exactly what you *don't* want. *But* can cause the two sentences to cancel each other out, so you're left with...nothing. In fact some psychologists won't allow their patients to use *but* in a therapy session for that very reason.

I don't completely agree with the psychologists. However, I think they have a point. Imagine that you're in a romantic relationship. One evening your beloved starts a sentence like this: "I love you very much, but...." You don't even have to hear the rest, right? The relationship is *over*. The word *but* cancels the "I love you" sentiment.

So here's some advice about sentences with *but*: Always double-check to make sure the two sides don't cancel each other out.

Writing a Thesis

At this point you might be thinking that this is interesting enough—but is it going to help you with your writing? The answer is *yes*. Here's an important rule: You can never use *but* in a thesis. You will remember that a thesis is the "heavy-lifting" sentence in an essay, research paper, or report. You state your thesis early, and everything else supports it.

Here's the problem: *But* sets up two opposite and equal ideas that cancel each other out. You can't develop a thesis that's been set up that way. It would be like driving a car down two roads at the same time. You have to pick *one* direction.

For example, suppose you were writing a research paper about Richard Nixon, the 36th President. He had some significant achievements (ending the Vietnam War, opening relations with China, desegregating Southern schools, and establishing the Environmental Protection Agency). But he also lied about the Watergate break-in and eventually had to resign from the Presidency.

So there are two truths about President Nixon that contradict each other: He did some great things, and he was dishonest.

Here's a thesis statement that *won't* work because it takes two contradictory positions:

Richard Nixon changed America for the better, but he also brought shame to the Presidency. TWO OPPOSING POSITIONS

Your thesis needs to choose *one* position:

Although Richard Nixon had some farsighted ideas, his criminal activities brought shame to the Presidency. EFFECTIVE THESIS

OR

Although his criminal activities tarnished his reputation, Richard Nixon had farsighted ideas that made America a better country. EFFECTIVE THESIS

The word *although* tells you that an idea is "soft" and won't be your main point. You can write about Nixon's achievements or his mistakes, but you can't go in both directions at once.

Sentences with *And*

Years ago, one of my graduate school professors complained that I joined too many of my sentences with *and*. I was puzzled: *And* is a useful word that everyone uses all the time. What was he talking about? I finally figured it out.

And (like *but*) is a useful joining word that makes sentences equal. Here's the problem: Many times one sentence is more important than another, so they shouldn't be written in a way that makes them equal. (If you're starting to think about the *loud* and *soft* principle, congratulations! That's exactly the point.)

Here's an example of what I'm talking about:

Bears are hungry after hibernation, and they can be particularly dangerous in the early spring.

That sentence is grammatically correct, but no scientist would write it that way. Can you see what's wrong?

Here's the problem: The sentence makes *hungry* equal to *dangerous*, but that's not actually the case. There's a cause-effect relationship: Bears wake up hungry in the early spring, and that's why it's a risky time to encounter them.

Here's how the sentence could be rewritten, with the "loud" part of the sentence in **bold**:

Because bears are hungry after hibernation, **they're especially dangerous in the early spring**. BETTER

Or the sentence could be written this way:

Bears, which are hungry after hibernation, **are particularly dangerous in the early spring.**

More Tips for Better Sentences

1. Simplify sentences with the Rule of Three.

When you're revising, look for sentences with more than three commas. Often you'll discover that they're tangled and confusing. Breaking complicated sentences into two sentences (being careful to ensure that they still make sense) might make them more readable. (Please note that there's nothing inherently wrong with using four or five commas in a sentence! The Rule of Three is just a tool for spotting and simplifying sentences that need more clarity.)

2. Use semicolons for sophistication.

It's easy to take your writing to a higher level without sacrificing meaning. All you do is change an occasional period to a semicolon (but no more than once on a page). Remember to lower-case the word after the semicolon. Don't be intimidated by semicolons. They're easy! (Don't be intimidated by semicolons; they're easy!)

3. Look for small ways to add interest to your sentences.

Sometimes changing just one word can make a sentence more interesting. Here's why: The human brain works faster than we could ever imagine. While our eyes are darting from one word to the next, our brains are busy making connections, forming pictures, and asking questions. It's almost like there's a movie theater in your head. Professional writers know this, and they look for subtle ways to spark responses in readers' brains.

For example, compare these two sentences:

> Mrs. Salo planted milkweed to attract butterflies to the garden.
> Mrs. Salo planted milkweed to attract butterflies to her garden. BETTER

Did you catch it? The second sentence has only one tiny change: *her* garden instead of *the* garden. It goes by so quickly that you might not have noticed it—

but your brain did. *Her* causes your brain to picture—just for a millisecond—a woman. It humanizes your sentence. When I'm revising something I've written, I'm always looking for ways to make small improvements.

4. Pay particular attention to sentences in "hot spots."

The first sentence in a paragraph is particularly important because it has two jobs to do: Supporting your main point and introducing the rest of the paragraph. So, for example, an essay about a miserable place where you lived when you were first married might have a paragraph that begins, "I was embarrassed that we couldn't afford a single decent piece of furniture." The rest of the paragraph will develop that sentence, discussing your strained finances and the shabby furniture you were stuck with.

Remember too that the last sentence of a paragraph can be used for climax (your strongest example) or closure (a wrap-up sentence). So you can end your paragraph with a sentence about the piece of furniture that embarrassed you most—perhaps a couch that was so worn and lumpy that you were ashamed to invite friends over.

When a friend (Jane Brumbaugh) wrote a history of the library in her town, she began with a strong first sentence: "There was no library in Lake Alfred in 1962." Notice how the sentence works: You immediately know what's going to follow—how the town acquired a library.

Some self-proclaimed "experts" would say that Jane's sentence breaks a writing rule: Never begin a sentence with *there is, there are, there was,* or *there were.* Nonsense! If you try to revise Jane's sentence without "There was," it doesn't work as well:

Lake Alfred had no library in 1962. WEAK

Suddenly the emphasis has shifted from "no library"—Jane's real point—to "Lake Alfred." The sentence loses something.

Start experimenting with small changes in your sentences, and you'll soon find yourself writing with more confidence and power.

Part Four

If You're a Student

The word cloud contains the words: student, writer, pronoun, revise, grammar, conjunction, grade, corrections, sentence, essay, capitalize, research, plan, literature, concentrate, read, study, edit, feedback, question, think, focus, critique, dictionary, composition, report, spellcheck, draft, tutor, librarian, computer, library

Chapter 16

Tips for Student Writers

Written assignments in high school and college present special challenges. Your instructor is going to be hunting for errors, the required length may seem impossibly long, the instructions can be hopelessly complicated, and often you don't get to choose the subject you're going to write about. Daunting, isn't it?

But there's good news as well. In high school and college, your instructors often give you specific guidelines to help you produce a good product—useful information that you probably won't get from your boss when you tackle writing tasks on the job. Another good feature of school assignments is that often you're allowed to seek help along the way.

Free tutoring is probably available, both in person and on line, and very likely you'll have access to excellent writing software. Many instructors have office hours when you're welcome to drop in for extra help, along with email and voicemail in case you have a question after you leave the classroom.

During my teaching career I've seen many nervous students, including some who started out with weak writing skills, reach a level of success that surprised and delighted both them and me.

Strategies for Student Writers

1. Aim to give your instructors exactly what they're asking for.

Obvious, isn't it? If your teacher is giving you a grade, of course you should follow the instructions *exactly*. But the truth (and I'm speaking from years of teaching experience) is that many students don't bother to do that. Young people taking high school or college courses don't always have the maturity and self-discipline to follow directions precisely. (I didn't either at that age!)

And there may be other reasons why students don't complete a task correctly: They didn't understand the assignment, didn't allow enough time, didn't have the materials needed, or—sadly—just don't care. Those are easy problems to solve, and you shouldn't allow them to get in your way. Prepare carefully for each assignment, make a realistic schedule for completing it, and ask for clarification if you have a question. Resolve never to let a foolish mistake hold you back or, heaven forbid, end your schooling prematurely.

Back when I was teaching in a police academy (long before computers), I once saw a cadet dismissed from the program because he wrote all his assignments with a ballpoint pen that kept skipping. He didn't care enough to buy or borrow another pen, and that was the end of his dream of a law enforcement career. The first rule of success is to *give your instructors what they want* (a principle that will be useful again later when you're writing for a boss).

2. Engage your unconscious mind.

You already heard this advice on p. 87. Believe in it: It works! In graduate school I spent hours and hours doing research for my doctoral dissertation with no idea how I would organize the information I was reading. One morning I woke up much earlier than usual with a picture of the entire first page of my dissertation in my head. I ran to my computer and starting typing before I'd even brushed my teeth—and received glowing compliments later when my committee read what I'd written.

3. Allow enough time for excellence.

If you're a typical student, you sometimes put off assignments because a) you don't feel like doing them and b) you think you're going to do them poorly. (I've done that too.)

A paper you write at the last minute is going to be full of the kinds of problems that drive English teachers crazy: Usage errors, sloppy thinking, clumsy sentences, and weak writing. All of those are problems you can solve yourself if you allow time to do your best work. (My early drafts have those problems too— which is why I always start my writing projects long before the deadline.)

You don't need a degree in English to write well. (Honest!) But you do need to invest time in your writing. Going over your work several times is the only way to ensure that your teacher will be pleased with the final product. (You might want to reread Chapter 11, Time Management for Writers, beginning on p. 83.)

4. Ask someone to look over your work before your instructor reads it.

Here's another reason to get started early on an assignment. Even a non-specialist can often give you excellent feedback on what you've written. When I wrote my first scholarly article years ago, I asked another scholar to critique it—and I also gave it to my husband (a garden writer for a newspaper) to read. Amazingly, some of the feedback I received from them was exactly the same.

Another benefit from sharing your work is that talking about what you've written is a great way to strengthen the connectors in your brain that deal with language. Over time you magically become a much better writer. (One caution: Make sure your instructor allows you to ask others for help. Most welcome this kind of outside help—I always did!)

5. Ask your instructor for feedback *before* the final draft is due.

Many instructors are glad to look at your outline, first draft, research notes, or anything else you're working on while you're completing an assignment. College instructors usually have office hours when they're available for this kind of help, and high school teachers will often meet with you during a planning period or before or after school. You might also be able use email or voicemail to get in touch with your instructor when you need extra help.

6. Use your school's resources.

When I started teaching, there were no faculty phones, computers, or tutors. Times have changed! Many instructors post assignments, lectures, and other learning aids on line, and personal tutoring is available both in person and via the Internet. Librarians can give you expert help in person, online, and by phone if you have questions about a research paper. Use every resource available to make sure your writing represents your best work and meets your instructor's requirements. (One warning: Don't ask a tutor to do your work for you. That kind of laziness will keep you from developing a positive relationship with a tutor who's in a position to provide you with excellent help.)

Ensuring Your Success

Here are some practical tips that have worked for countless students. Which ones will work for you?

- Plan for success. Set aside time (at least an hour a day) to work on your writing. Don't figure you'll write during your leftover time.
- Set up a comfortable place and assemble the tools you'll need.
- If your room is noisy, or your family keeps interrupting you, go somewhere else. Author Jean Kerr found that she couldn't write at home when her four children were small. Her solution was to get into her car, drive to a quiet spot, park, and sit there to write. The result was a bestselling book, *Please Don't Eat the Daisies*.
- Don't let anything stop you.
- Celebrate your progress.
- Learn how to concentrate in less-than-perfect surroundings.

Now take a moment to review the suggestions in this chapter. Are you noticing how simple and sensible they are? Not only that—they can help you bypass some of the confusion and frustration that students often experience when they sign up for a writing course. These suggestions are easy to implement, and they can make a huge (and positive) difference in your life. Start putting them to work for you right now!

Chapter 17

Writing Papers That Earn A's

Do you remember *Blink* (p. 23), the book about complex mental tasks that our brains can process in only a few seconds? Author Malcolm Gladwell says hidden parts of our brain are at work.

Smart students use that information to earn A's in English. When an instructor picks up an assignment to grade, an impression is automatically (and unconsciously) generated, for better or for worse. Do you honestly think that impression isn't going to affect your grade? (Remember the students who evaluated a professor based on *two seconds* of a videotaped lecture?)

A+

Happy instructors give higher grades. Your instructor might grade more than a hundred papers during a typical weekend. (That describes my life for many years.) The process slows down if a few students staple their papers in the wrong corner, put their names in the wrong place, or use a tiny typeface that's hard to read.

So here's Rule #1: *Follow your teacher or professor's instructions exactly,* even if they seem foolish to you. If your instructor wants your name on the right, a staple on the left, and the course number in the middle, *do it that way.* Your instructor is probably going to be reading a big pile of papers, and anything you do to make the grading process easier will earn a silent *thank you.*

And think about this: Your instructor cares about good writing. That's why people like me major in English: We love it so much that we're willing to spend years learning about it. How can you demonstrate that you're a person who also respects good writing (and thereby win your instructor's goodwill)? By *caring about the details.*

That means doing your best possible work before you ask your teacher to read it. Typos, spelling errors, omitted words, tangled sentences, and other obvious errors should be fixed before you submit your writing for a grade. Don't expect your instructor to fix mistakes: That's *your* job.

This weekend a former student asked me to look over some writing samples he would be submitting with a job application. When I downloaded his samples, my spellchecker found a dozen misspelled words, and my grammar checker underlined several missing and repeated words, along with four or five other careless mistakes.

Back went the writing samples for him to fix. I'm always happy to help former students—but only *after* they've done their best work. You need to adopt that same work ethic.

I used to tutor in a learning lab, and here's a distressing practice I saw often: Students would print a draft of an essay and bring it right over to the tutoring table, expecting me to go over it for them. Wrong! What they needed to do was sit down and read it over first. Taking that extra step shows respect for the tutor or instructor—and it also makes you a better writer.

Rule #2 is to *choose a stimulating topic.* You don't always have to solve a problem or take a for-or-against position about an earth-shaking topic. What you must do, however, is dig beneath the surface to uncover an unusual angle or conflict—or to explore complexities and multiple viewpoints. For example:

- Something unexpected: An adult who gets down on the floor to play with a child or won't let the telephone interrupt a visit with a child
- Something missing: A holiday celebration after a move, a death, or a divorce
- Something added: An unexpected guest shows up at a party, an extra person joins a family vacation, or a new person joins a class or club
- An outsider's viewpoint: A pediatrician talks about children who have been hurt or killed by a gun in the home
- A revelation: A surprising discovery about someone familiar—a boss, parent, teacher, or neighbor
- A topic related to a career (especially if you're doing a research paper)

Develop the habit of observing the people and places around you. *Think* about them—and watch yourself as you do it. What surprises you, annoys you, puzzles you? Keep a journal—nothing fancy, just a place where you practice digging into your ideas. Read a newspaper. Watch public TV and listen to public radio. Expose yourself to points of view and experiences different from your own.

And remember that even everyday experiences can stimulate good writing if you take a second look at them. I recall reading an excellent student paper about a topic that didn't look promising: Family life. The student told me that he'd been walking his dog one Saturday morning when he spotted two young children cheerfully helping their father clean up their yard. And he remembered how he had balked when his parents used to ask him to spend a precious Saturday working at home. *That family is different*, he thought—and he wondered why. Could he rear his future children to value that kind of cooperation? Those ideas sparked a marvelous paper.

Rule #3 is to work from a plan. Think about how you'll organize a writing task before you start your first draft. Chapters 6 and 13 taught you how to plan an essay, and Chapter 12 taught you how to write an introduction. Modes of development (such as classification, comparison/contrast, cause/effect) are explained in the next chapter; a discussion of research papers begins in Chapter 19 on p. 137. *Never* start a writing task with a blank piece of paper or an empty computer screen: Always start with a plan.

Sadly, some students never spend a single minute thinking about the advice in this chapter. Working with the principles you've just read automatically sets you apart and starts you on the road to success. You're on your way!

Chapter 18

Modes of Development

Modes of development are ways to organize ideas and information for a writing task. The terminology sometimes intimidates students, so you should know that you've been using these thinking tools all your life.

Comparison and *contrast* are useful when you're shopping. You might *contrast* two products, discover that one is much better than other, and decide to pay a little more. Or you might do a *comparison* and realize that the item with the higher price is no better than the cheaper item.

Classifications are useful when you need to sort a lot of information into simpler categories. If you walk into an appliance store to buy a refrigerator, chances are you're going to feel overwhelmed. A good salesperson will immediately start you thinking about categories: Price range? Size? Two doors or one? Freezer on top or on the side? Do you want an icemaker or a water dispenser? Thinking about those classifications will help you feel more comfortable about making a choice.

We think about *processes* any time we're trying to complete a task. How can I wash my car without contaminating the water supply hidden beneath the soil? What's the best way to teach manners to a child? What's the least painful way to end a relationship?

Cause and effect are vital to solving problems.

Narratives (stories) are so versatile that we'll probably never run out of ways to use them. A good story can help you teach values to a child, develop a point during a meeting, and clarify an idea or a problem.

Making Meaning

When I was a full-time professor, sales reps would often stop by my office to show me their latest English textbooks (hoping, of course, that I'd choose one and ask my students to buy it.) I'd always open the book they were offering to the section on modes of development. After about two minutes I'd give the book either a thumbs-up for further consideration (rare) or a thumbs-down (frequently). The sales reps who didn't know me well were always bewildered (and probably a little annoyed): How could I make a judgment by reading just a few pages?

The answer is that I was checking to see if the book emphasized *making meaning*. (Many textbooks don't.) I'd open the book to the section on Modes of Development and read a sample essay or two with one question in mind: Was it a list, or did it make a point? Unfortunately, most of the sample essays were lists that had been dressed up to look like essays. (Did you notice that I just used a *narrative*—a story—to make my point?)

Modes of development are problem-solving tools, and essays should always address a problem. Most—alas—don't. So, for example, I've read endless student essays contrasting sports cars with SUV's. Who, I ask you, ever walked into a car dealership wondering whether to buy a sports car or an SUV? No one.

In this chapter I'm going to emphasize *thinking* and *problem solving*. If you're assigned an essay using one of the modes of development, start by thinking about a problem you want to solve, and *then* match it with the mode (or thinking tool) that will do the job for you. Result: An excellent essay.

Making Meaning

Let's begin by clarifying the difference between *making a list* and *making meaning*. Here are two student paragraphs. Can you tell which one is just a list of facts, and which one *makes meaning*? (Hint: Look for the paragraph that makes a point.)

Learning Online

When I started college, I refused to take online classes. I thought online classes were too impersonal, and I was afraid the course content would be watered down. But this semester all the face-to-face algebra sections were closed, so I reluctantly signed up for an online class. To my surprise, I'm enjoying the online experience. The instructor encourages us to use Skype during her office hours, so I'm still getting face-to-face time with her. She's posted explanatory videos to help us understand course content, and I can watch them as many times as I need to. In my face-to-face classes last year, most instructor explained new concepts only once, and sometimes I felt lost. What I like best is my flexible schedule. Last semester I had conflicts with my boss when he wanted me to miss a class to work overtime. That's not a problem with the online class. Next semester I'm planning to take more online classes, and I'm encouraging friends to try an online course as well.

Job Hunting

Before you look for a job, it's important to know the differences between full-time and part-time jobs. Full-time jobs are usually more desirable because they pay better and tend to have more prestige. Full-time jobs often include benefits like health insurance and retirement plans. Another advantage is that you're likely to be covered for unemployment insurance if you're laid off later on. Part-time jobs, on the other hand, tend to pay less, and you probably won't get benefits. On the other hand, part-time jobs give you more flexibility, and you may even be able to choose what hours you want to work. Another plus is that many part-time jobs don't require a college degree or years of experience. In fact a part-time job can be a great way to gain experience and explore a career field before you commit to it. Both part-time and full-time jobs have advantages and decisions. Just make sure you know what kind of job you want before you start answering ads.

Which paragraph did you choose as the one that "makes meaning"? It's the one about 18. The paragraph about job hunting, on the other hand, is just a list of ideas that aren't likely to help anyone make a decision about a job. Most people already know whether they want to work full-time or part-time.

How to Use the Modes as Thinking Tools

1. Comparison

A comparison essay should show that two things that seem different are actually alike. In everyday life you frequently use comparisons when you shop. For example, brand-name bleach is identical to generic bleach: Chemically speaking, there's no such thing as "better" bleach. The same is true of sugar. No matter what package it's in, sugar is...sugar. (I can guarantee you've never seen an ad that promises that a certain brand of bleach or sugar is better!) Similarly most bottled water is the same as the water that comes out of a tap.

Of course you're not going to write an entire essay about bleach! But comparisons can be the basis for an excellent essay. I remember one comparison essay written by a parent who decided to send his child to public school rather than a private one. He reasoned that the teachers at both schools attended similar colleges, the textbooks are the same, and both schools teach the same skills—for example, in fifth grade everyone learns long division. (If you wanted to show that a private school was better, you would write a *contrast* paper. See below.)

You could use a comparison essay to show that an inexpensive vacation can be just as much fun as a costly one, a used car can be just as reliable as a new one, and so on.

2. Contrast

Many students find that contrast papers (which focus on differences) are easier to write than comparisons. Usually your point will be that one thing is better than another. You might contrast two political candidates (which one would you vote for?), a credit union and a traditional bank (which is a better place for your money?), living in a dorm and sharing an apartment (which would work better for you?), a small college and a large one (which meets your needs better?), and so on.

3. Combining comparison and contrast

Sometimes an essay will include both comparisons and contrasts. For example, the paragraph about online learning on p. 126 is mostly about similarities, so it seems to fall into the comparison category. But the paragraph also mentions two features of the online course that the student liked better: He could watch the instructor's explanatory videos as many times as he wanted, and his schedule was more flexible.

4. Classification

There are two ways to write a classification paper: You can emphasize either *sorting* or *possibilities*. Sorting transforms a heap of random information into meaningful categories. One of the best classification papers I ever read was about (of all things) disposable diapers! A young mother explained which various sizes and absorbencies were best for various situations. For example, she used super-absorbent diapers at night, and she switched brands, sizes, and absorbencies as her child grew bigger and became more active.

Classifications can also open up possibilities. Many times people think in narrow either-or categories. Classification can sometimes reveal additional choices and unexpected ways to solve problems.

I came across an excellent example of classification as a thinking tool in a recent *Car Talk* column in my local newspaper. Auto expert Ray Magliozzi heard from a reader who needed a second car for a temporary job that would probably last only a year. Should he rent a car or lease one? Instead of restricting himself to those choices, Magliozzi expanded the possibilities.

One was purchasing a good used car and then selling it at the end of the year, getting back most of the purchase price. Another was buying a new car with an efficient engine. At the end of the year, when the job was over and his family needed only one car, they could sell the old one and keep the new, fuel-efficient hybrid. That *Car Talk* column was a perfect example of how to use classification as a thinking tool: Magliozzi used *categories* to expand the reader's choices.

Here's a common example of either-or thinking: How to get money for college. Many students think in just two categories: Your parents pay for college, or you apply for a student loan. But if you look for other possibilities, you may be able to find another way to pay for college. Is a scholarship available? If you're employed, some corporations will pay for college if you agree to stay with the job after graduation. Another way to save on tuition is to study on your own and earn credits through CLAST exams. Some public colleges waive tuition for high-school students who want to earn college credits. Another possibility is to join the military and have the federal government pay for your college education.

Here are three more examples of narrow, either-or thinking that could be expanded in a classification paper.

- Disciplining children: Some parents think the only alternative to spanking is letting children misbehave. Can you think of other discipline methods?
- Getting away from home after high school: I've known teens who got married right after graduation because they didn't like living with their parents. Can you think of other choices they could make?
- Saving money to travel around the world: Are there other ways to travel to faraway places?

Classification is the most sophisticated thinking tool in this chapter. It plays a vital role in the sciences, for example. The average homeowner may not know the difference between a palm and a cycad, but the differences are important to any gardener who wants to grow healthy and beautiful plants. Physicians want their patients to understand the difference between bacterial infections (which can be treated with antibiotics) and viruses (which don't respond to antibiotics).

But the uses of classification go far beyond the sciences. Sorting things into groups is an essential task in organizing our personal lives—and it can also have huge consequences on a much larger scale.

Here's a political example: In World War II, American leaders lumped many Japanese-Americans into the "enemy" category. More than 100,000 Japanese-Americans living on the West Coast were imprisoned in government camps, losing their homes, jobs, property, and freedom. The reason? Our government didn't stop to think that citizens with a Japanese heritage could fall into many categories (such as business owner, Cub Scout, community leader) rather than just one (enemy).

Almost any subject or event you think or write about involves sorting and grouping into various categories. Classification is a basic thinking tool for anyone who wants to become a serious thinker and writer. In fact much of what we call "education" involves teaching students more sophisticated ways to classify experiences and ideas.

5. Process

Process refers to something that happens the same way, step-by-step, over and over. (A narrative is different: It's the story of something that happened only once.)

Some of the textbooks I've looked at reserve the process mode for writing instructions. That's a useful skill that I'll have more to say about in a moment, but it also overlooks something important: Process writing can add interest and vitality to many topics.

Here's an example of how you might focus on a step-by-step process for a real-world writing task. Suppose you were running a prenatal clinic, and you wanted to convince your patients to avoid alcohol while they were pregnant. A conventional approach would be to create a poster or brochure with warnings about possible birth defects, brain damage, hyperactivity, delayed development, seizures, and other problems.

But your brochure or poster might be more convincing if you explained, step-by-step, what happens when a pregnant woman drinks an alcoholic beverage.

Alcohol (unlike most foods) passes directly from the stomach into the bloodstream, before it has a chance to break down. If a woman is pregnant, it quickly passes through the placenta into the baby's circulatory system. The newly formed liver of an unborn baby can't safely handle alcohol. Instead of breaking down, the alcohol makes its way to the baby's brain, where it immediately starts destroying the developing brain cells there.

This is an example of persuasive writing. You could use process writing for a number of other purposes. One is making an ordinary process more interesting by placing it in an unusual setting, such as explaining how to cook a meal at a remote campsite. You can expose a process that's cruel (slaughtering an animal) or teach someone how to get more mileage out of an everyday process (using a bedtime ritual to strengthen your relationship with your child).

Instructions

Instructions can be challenging to write. Everyday life is full of processes that we wish we could do more efficiently—or we may not know how to do at all. When I worked for a veterinarian, I learned how to medicate a cat—something I'd never been able to do before. You can write instructions for a recipe, a computer skill, a household chore, or a hobby technique. Here are some tips:

- Consider inserting helpful diagrams or pictures.
- Make the process special. What is different about your grandmother's potato salad? The way you pack a suitcase for a trip? Your dental hygiene routine?
- Ask a friend or family member to try your instructions.

6. Cause and Effect

Causes are "before" factors, and effects happen afterward. So, for example, texting while driving might *cause* an automobile accident. Broken ribs might be an *effect* of the accident.

Causes and effects are important persuasive tools. When you can connect a chain of events to a bad (or good) result, people might be willing to invest money in a program, change a bad habit, or vote for a new law. Here are some examples:

- Unsupervised teens get involved in criminal mischief
- Working after school lowers students' grades
- Working after school teaches students responsibility
- Switching to a more natural diet lowers cholesterol
- Watching exciting TV programs late at night interferes with sleep
- Getting sufficient rest results in greater productivity the next day

7. Narrative

You've heard me say this before: Narratives—stories—add interest and power to your writing. Here are some suggestions:

- Start collecting stories for future writing projects

- Avoid unnecessary descriptions and details
- Make sure each story has a point

Using the Modes as Thinking Tools

I said earlier that some writers underestimate the modes of development. After students complete a Comp I or Comp II class, they tend to forget about them. Throughout this chapter I've tried to show that modes of development aren't just organizational patterns: They're important thinking tools.

To show you how they work, we're going to apply the modes to a topic that's been in the news lately—punishing criminals. I'm going to give you two models you can use to explore any topic that interests you. (You can use this system for writing research papers, solving business problems, and performing a host of other tasks.)

Everyone agrees that there should be penalties for breaking the law. "Lock 'em up!" is a simple and straightforward solution favored by many people. Recently, however, both Democratic and Republican legislators have been questioning the American prison system. Are all lawbreakers alike? How much tax money are we investing in our prisons—and are the results worth it?

It's an emotional topic, of course, and that's why thinking tools are so useful: We can bypass some of the strong feelings associated with crime and punishment to raise some important questions and answer them objectively. Another advantage is that these Thinking Tool activities are private—"for your eyes only." They're a safe place for you to dig into an idea, find an issue that interests you, and start focusing your thoughts.

Plus – Minus – Interesting

Start with a blank piece of paper. Write your topic on top. Then write these three words across the top of your paper: "plus, minus, interesting." Now start listing positive factors under "plus," negative factors under "minus," and anything

133

left over under "interesting." Ideas will start to flow while you're making your lists—plus you'll have a paper full of ideas that you can refer to later, as you're working on your project, paper, or report.

Here's a "plus – minus – interesting" worksheet about American prisons done by a student as preparation for a criminology project. In the "plus" column she listed positive features of our prison system. Negative features are listed under "minus," and other facts and ideas are in the "interesting" column.

US Prisons		
plus	*minus*	*interesting*
Protect the public	High annual cost (equivalent to attending Harvard or taking a cruise)	The US crime rate has been dropping since 1993
Drug treatment		
Remove bad outside influences	Many inmates return to prison	Most inmates eventually return to society
Religious programs	Inmates don't do salaried work or pay taxes	Prisons provide jobs for many people (officers, staff, medical personnel, etc.)
Offenders experience consequences of their choices	Aging inmates require expensive healthcare	
Work programs		
Education programs	Offenders' families may go on welfare	
Respect rules	Children lose their parents	
Respect authority		

Thinking Tools Activity

This activity encourages you to use all the modes. Start with a blank sheet of paper. Write your topic on the top. Then list the thinking tools on the left: Comparison, Contrast, Process, Cause, Effect, Classification. Leave space to write ideas next to each one. Then start writing questions and ideas for each category. If you're working on a research paper, keep adding information as you learn more about your topic.

This activity encourages you to go deeply into a subject, and it also provides a place to record information that you'll need when you begin writing your paper or report. Here's a worksheet done by our criminology student as additional preparation for her project on US prisons:

Thinking about Punishing Criminals

Comparison:
- In what ways are lawbreakers similar to law-abiding citizens?
- What common needs do we all share (healthcare, food, shelter)?
- How should our correctional system meet those needs?
- Are criminals prepared to meet these needs when they're released from prison?

Contrast:
- In what ways are lawbreakers different from law-abiding citizens?
- Are these differences inborn or learned?
- Are there ways to erase these differences?
- How is a teen-aged lawbreaker different from an adult?

Process:
- What stages might a person go through to change from a law-abiding citizen to a criminal?
- Are there ways to interrupt this process?
- What stages might a criminal go through to change into a law-abiding citizen?

Causes:
- What factors cause people to become criminals?
- What factors might cause a criminal to decide to stop breaking the law?

Effects:
- How much does it cost to imprison a criminal per year?
- What are the additional costs for elderly inmates with health issues?
- What are the economic effects on society (inmates don't earn paychecks or pay taxes)?
- What are the economic, social, and psychological effects on an inmate's spouse and children?

Classification:
- Are all lawbreakers the same? For example, is a rapist the same as a reckless driver?
- Are all sex offenders the same? For example, is having sex with a teenaged girl the same as molesting a small child?
- Are all violent acts similar? For example, could a normally law-abiding person commit a violent act?

These Thinking Tools are extremely helpful in the planning stage of a complex writing task. Because they're for your eyes only, you don't have to worry about spelling, punctuation, or neatness. You don't need sentences at all!

Jotting down ideas freely this way helps you explore a topic and discover ideas for your project. Later on, when you're drafting a paper or article, you have a record of your ideas, so you don't have to worry that you've forgotten something important. I use these Thinking Tools often when I'm tackling a writing project—and you should too.

Chapter 19

Writing a Research Paper

(Suggestion: Go to www.ResearchPaperSteps.com to view *free* presentations—in both PowerPoint and video formats—about research papers.)

It's the assignment that many students dread—but it's also the one that can transform your brain into a world-class thinking machine. There's a reason why research papers are challenging: You're learning a whole new set of thinking skills that you'll be using for the rest of your life. The toil can seem pointless while you're doing it. (How well I remember my own weary hours with note cards and outlines!) When are you ever going to use your research about (say) the Emancipation Proclamation, Sleep Disorders, or Welsh Poetry Devices in Hopkins's Poems (to mention the topics of some of my own papers)?

According to the *New York Times*, even some instructors are questioning the value of research papers. In "Term Paper Blogging," Matt Ritchel notes that blogs have become a popular component in college courses: "Across the country, blog writing has become a basic requirement in everything from M.B.A. classes to literature courses. " It's not hard to see why, he says: A research paper is "a staid writing exercise," while a blog is...fun.

But Ritchel points out that research papers have an important purpose: Teaching sophisticated critical-thinking skills. Douglas B. Reeves, a columnist for the *American School Board Journal*, agrees. "Writing term papers is a dying art," Reeves says, "but those who do write them have a dramatic leg up in terms of critical thinking, argumentation, and the sort of expression required not only in college, but in the job market."

He's right: What research papers teach is world-class thinking. You learn how to answer questions like these: Which experts are worth paying attention to? How do you weigh evidence and make a decision? What are the best ways to organize and present complex information? You'll use those skills long after you've forgotten how to do in-text citations and bibliographic references.

Research papers teach you to go to beyond the obvious to explore the complexity of an issue. For example, most Americans know that Abraham Lincoln freed slaves when he issued the Emancipation Proclamation on January 1, 1863. What many people don't know, however, is that historians are still arguing about how many slaves were actually freed that day.

Some historians say Lincoln ended slavery only in the Confederate states that had withdrawn from the Union and no longer regarded Lincoln as their President. Why did Lincoln issue a proclamation that—in effect—changed nothing? They argue that Lincoln's motivations were political, not humanitarian—ensuring continuing support from England (which was strongly opposed to slavery) and from loyal states such as Maryland, Delaware, Missouri, and Kentucky, which were allowed to keep their slaves. But other historians have argued that the Emancipation did free many slaves even in the rebellious Confederacy.

That kind of pro-and-con controversy is typical of many issues in the sciences, education, history, the arts, and other areas. Many personal decisions require research skills: Voting, investigating treatments for a disease, and investing for your retirement are just a few examples. You'll be calling upon your research skills whenever your boss asks you—either by yourself or as part of a committee—to investigate an issue or opportunity related to your career and present a report about your findings. Best of all, you can use those skills to get noticed (and perhaps promoted) on the job.

Understanding Resources

Chances are your instructor is going to have a lot to say about *plagiarism* (copying someone else's work and passing it off as your own). Plagiarism is a serious violation of institutional rules, but students don't always understand why it's wrong. Perhaps the biggest problem with plagiarism is that it prevents you from developing the thinking skills you need to learn. (Plagiarizing a paper is like paying for a gym membership and then just watching everyone else work out instead of getting on the machines yourself.)

But all that emphasis on avoiding plagiarism also has a downside: You're learning what *not* to do—pass others' work off as your own—instead of what you *should* do—demonstrate mastery of mature research practices. So let's discuss how professionals use resources.

My "aha!" experience with research came when I submitted the manuscript for my book *Pygmalion's Wordplay* to a publisher. I had spent years reading about Bernard Shaw—the subject of my book—and his play *Pygmalion* (which you may be familiar with in its musical version, *My Fair Lady*). My manuscript had hundreds of citations and references. The bibliography at the end was over five pages long. I even mentioned a production of *Pygmalion* in Moscow. I was proud that I had covered every possible angle.

Until, that is, I received the publisher's evaluation. Every scholarly manuscript has to undergo an approval process called a *peer review*. This involves a panel of experts who evaluate a manuscript and decide whether it's worthy of publication. Often they'll approve a manuscript conditionally, requiring changes and corrections before final approval.

In the case of *Pygmalion's Wordplay*, a panel member complained that I hadn't mentioned a recent book that included a whole chapter on *Pygmalion*. Well, I had indeed read the book—and dismissed it because I thought the *Pygmalion* chapter was awful.

I lost that argument. The expert agreed with my opinion of that chapter. But he also pointed out something I hadn't considered: To show my readers that I was current in my field, I had to demonstrate that I'd read it. That meant I had to include the book in my bibliography (which, you will remember, was already more than five pages long). And to list it there, I had to quote from it.

So back I went to the college library, where I checked out the book again, took it home, and reread that chapter searching for a few decent sentences to put into my book. (Yes, the book went into my bibliography, and *Pygmalion's Wordplay* received the panel's seal of approval and was published.)

Here's my point: Plagiarism isn't a big issue for professional writers and researchers. (At least it shouldn't be: A number of famous writers, including Doris Kearns Goodwin, Stephen Ambrose, and Jane Goodall, have been exposed as plagiarists.) What professionals *do* think about are the names, facts, and other kinds of information that need to be included in a piece of writing.

Let's say, for example, that you were writing a magazine article about performer Michael Jackson. He had an amazing life that included childhood performances with the Jackson Five, Pepsi commercials, a chimp named Bubbles, a marriage to Elvis Presley's daughter, and a controversy about his Neverland ranch. Your article could focus on his upbringing, his legal problems, his dancing, his songs, his concerts, his untimely death—or any number of other things. But there are two words that you have to include no matter what angle you chose to write about. Do you know what they are?

Stop for a moment to think about Michael Jackson. What would those two words be? When you think you know what they are, read on.

The two words I would choose are *Thriller* (one of the most important pop musical albums of all time) and *Moonwalk* (the amazing dance move he invented). No matter what aspect of Jackson's life and career you're examining, somewhere you need to mention his *Thriller* album and his *Moonwalk* dance move. (The Thinking Tools activities on pp. 133-6 can be a big help here.)

One of your goals as a researcher is to find this kind of essential information about the topic you're studying and work it into your writing. Who are the authorities? What were the defining events? Then you have to figure out a way to work them into the piece you're writing.

Here are some examples. If you were writing about Florence Nightingale, the founder of modern nursing, you'd have to mention Cecil Woodham-Smith's groundbreaking biography in 1950, along with the Crimea (where she instituted the profession of nursing), her book *Notes on Nursing*, and the nursing school she established at St. Thomas' Hospital in London.

If you're writing about American composer Scott Joplin, you need to know that Edward Berlin has written the best biography (and you'd better mention

Joplin's "Maple Leaf Rag"). Abraham Lincoln is the subject of hundreds of excellent books, but the one biographer you *have* to mention is Carl Sandburg.

Now how would you figure this out if you were going to write a paper about, say, Lizzie Borden, a 19th century woman who was accused of murdering her father and stepmother? (You probably learned a rhyme about her as a child: "Lizzie Borden took an axe, and gave her father 40 whacks. And when the job was nicely done, she gave her mother 41.") If your answer is "ask a librarian," you win first prize. Librarians are specialists in discovering and evaluating sources.

But professional researchers already know what a librarian might do in these cases: Check an appropriate encyclopedia—something you can easily do yourself. Experts write the articles in encyclopedias, and the best of them usually include a short list of the best books on the subject.

For American topics (like Scott Joplin, Abraham Lincoln, and Lizzie Borden), researchers look in the *Encyclopedia Americana*. (It will recommend, for example, a book about Lizzie Borden written by Edward Radin.) For most topics outside the United States, the world's best encyclopedia is the *Britannica*, and you should probably start there. But you might also begin with a specialized encyclopedia, such as *The Catholic Encyclopedia* if you're researching the Papacy, or *The Encyclopedia of Science Fiction* if you're writing a paper about Ray Bradbury.

Notice that you're not *copying* the encyclopedia entry: You're looking for general knowledge about your subject so that you don't miss anything vital. (Here's an example of what *not* to do: A student of mine once wrote a paper about Eleanor Roosevelt that never mentioned her marriage to Franklin D. Roosevelt, the 32nd President of the United States. She earned an "F.") More important, the encyclopedia will direct you to the most important books about your subject—the ones that *must* be mentioned in your bibliography or Works Cited page.

Your library card probably gives you instant, free online access to the *Encyclopedia Britannica* and many other useful reference books. It will also allow you to read many books and magazine and newspaper articles, free of charge, online. These resources cost money—a lot of it. Your taxes (if you use a public library) underwrite those expenses, allowing you to read endlessly for free. If you're a student, your fees help support the library budget—and, again, you can read as much as you want, whenever you want, at no charge.

Why do the resources cost money? Because research costs money. Let's use Scott Joplin as an example. A gifted black composer born shortly after the Civil War, Joplin was never considered important enough for a biography in his lifetime. In the late 1940s two researchers (Rudi Blesh and Harriet Janis) finally decided to start looking into his life. Joplin had been dead for more than 20 years, so it took a lot of digging to get the basic facts. (People are still arguing about Joplin's date of birth, for example.)

More than 40 years later, another researcher—Edward Berlin—did even more digging and produced the best and most important book about Joplin: *King of Ragtime*, published by the Oxford University Press. Berlin astounded Joplin's fans by uncovering many forgotten facts, including a third marriage. (Until Berlin did his research, everyone thought Joplin had been married only twice.) Berlin accomplished this by visiting newspaper offices in every city where Joplin lived, spending days reading old newspapers stored in their basements to look for scraps of information about Joplin.

That kind of research is time-consuming and expensive (think of plane tickets, rental cars, hotel rooms, and time off from a regular paying job). Research costs money because a professional had to be paid to do it. Quality information is printed in a book or magazine that someone has to pay for.

You'll often hear English teachers say that writing is a form of communication, and that's absolutely correct. But writing is also a *performance*. You're putting on a little show for your readers: "These are the things I know. I'm an expert, and I know how to find information. You can trust me."

Quality Control

And that brings us to an even more important reason why the best information is usually found in books, magazines, newspapers, journals, and other publications you have to pay for: Those resources go through a *quality control* process. An expert or a panel of specialists does an evaluation for accurate and worthwhile content. As I mentioned on p. 139, this process is called a *peer review*, and it's an essential step for any topnotch publication.

The unfortunate truth is that anyone can post information on a website; there's no quality control at all. Publishers of quality books and magazines, on the other hand, won't publish a manuscript until it undergoes a peer review.

When I submitted my book *Pygmalion's Wordplay* to an academic publisher, they asked three Shaw scholars to read and evaluate my manuscript. After I made some changes and corrections that the scholars requested, *Pygmalion's Wordplay* was published. At that point I achieved expert status myself, and now I am sometimes asked (and paid!) to evaluate manuscripts for possible publication. First-class magazines and journals use the same process.

How to Evaluate Information

Information is all around us, thanks to the Internet and the news media. Much of what we read and hear is accurate and useful, but the opposite is also true, especially online. Computers have made life easier for all of us, but they also subject us to a constant stream of misinformation about everything from crime (such as made-up stories about kidnap victims) to cures for diseases (such as claims that vinegar, lemon juice, and honey can cure a host of deadly diseases).

Sorting out what's true and what's not, what's worthwhile and what's a waste of time, is vital—and requires intellectual tools. There's a specialized vocabulary for information analysis (*double-blind study, standard deviation, control group*) that includes some ordinary words that take on special meanings when you're discussing research (terms like *significant, mean,* and *noise*). One reason for attending high school and college is to master the vocabulary and thinking skills that can help us separate truths from falsehoods.

You should be familiar with websites that investigate stories circulating on the Web (Snopes.com and UrbanLegends.com are two good ones). Learn how to Google a string of words in an email or online posting that sounds fishy—a skill that can save you time, money, and embarrassment.

A friend once forwarded an email to me that recommended deleting a string of code from the operating system in a computer. I immediately Googled the message, found out it was a hoax, and called her. Unfortunately it was too late: She had already carried out the directions and crashed her computer—and sent it along to a dozen unsuspecting friends who suffered the same fate.

Another friend subscribed to a dubious health magazine that made bizarre claims about prescription medicine. She refused to follow doctor's orders after she was treated for glaucoma—she claimed there was gasoline in the eye drops! She is now permanently blind. These are just two of countless people who have been victimized by bad information. It doesn't have to happen to you.

Exploring a topic for a research paper can help you learn how to sift, sort, and evaluate information. For example, suppose you were assigned a paper about solitary confinement (the practice of keeping inmates isolated in small cells) for a criminology course. One expert thinks the practice is a good way to keep order in a prison, while another expert thinks it creates hostility and disorder, and still another thinks it's a waste of money. Which would you believe?

The answer is to talk to people who are experts in evaluating information, such as librarians and instructors. The research paper is an ideal tool to help you develop the reading and thinking skills needed for success in your personal life and your career.

How to Put Your Research Paper Together

Many instructors (but not all) have specific directions for organizing a research paper. If an instructor asks you to write a research paper a certain way, follow those directions *exactly*. If, however, your instructor does not provide directions, use the outline on p. 146. (It's also useful for most professional writing tasks!) I also encourage you to use some free online resources to learn more. Go to ResearchPapersteps.com to view four short (and free) videos about writing a research paper. Go to RagtimeResearchPaper.com to read (free) a sample research paper. Another free and extremely useful resource (one that I use myself) is the online writing lab from Purdue University: owl.english.purdue.edu.

Thesis

Your thesis is the most important sentence in your research paper. (You may remember my saying that the thesis does the "heavy lifting.") Unfortunately, students don't always understand this principle. Students used to bring a partial draft of a research paper to my office and ask me to look at it. "I've written most of it," they would say, "but I don't know where to put the thesis." Disaster! You have to write your thesis *first* and then build your research paper around it. Here are some guidelines:

1. Your thesis must be a *statement*, not a question or a title.

~~The problem of underage drinking~~ (title, not a thesis)
~~What are the effects of underage drinking?~~ (question, not a thesis)
Underage drinking is a serious problem on many college campuses. √ thesis

2. A thesis must not contain two contradictory ideas. (See p. 114).

~~Abraham Lincoln is widely venerated as the Great Emancipator, but his real goal during the Civil War was preserving the Union.~~ (two opposing ideas)
Abraham Lincoln's real goal during the Civil War was preserving the Union. √ thesis

3. A thesis must be an idea that you can develop, not a fact.

~~David Fairchild was responsible for the introduction of more than 200,000 exotic species and varieties into the United States.~~ (fact)
American plant explorer David Fairchild had enormous influence on the foods we eat today. √ thesis

4. Your thesis should have a keyword or phrase that you can explore and develop. For example:

"Underage drinking is a *serious problem* on many college campuses."

Abraham Lincoln's real goal during the Civil War was *preserving the Union.*

American plant explorer David Fairchild had enormous influence on the *foods we eat today.*

Organizing Your Research Paper

Often you can use the template from Chapter 6, Writing Paragraphs and Essays. (I still use that template for my own professional writing.) Your basic structure will be an introduction (including a thesis), the body, and a conclusion.

Research Paper Outline

Introduction (first one or two paragraphs)

- Attention-getter
- Background about your topic
- Quotation from an expert about the importance of your topic
- Thesis (your main point)

First supporting idea (several paragraphs or pages)

- An aspect of your thesis OR a reason your thesis is true
- Stories, facts, statistics to back up your supporting idea
- Quotation from an expert to back up your supporting idea

Second supporting idea (several paragraphs or pages)

- An aspect of your thesis OR a reason your thesis is true
- Stories, facts, statistics to back up your supporting idea
- Quotation from an expert to back up your supporting idea

Most important supporting idea (several paragraphs or pages)

- The most important aspect of your thesis OR the most convincing reason your thesis is true
- Stories, facts, statistics to back up your supporting idea
- Quotation from an expert to back up your supporting idea

Conclusion (one or two paragraphs)

- Restate your thesis
- Close with an example, fact, or quotation that wraps up your paper
- State why your topic will be important in the future, or call your readers to action.

Writing Your Research Paper

Let's see how you might use this plan to organize an actual research paper. Suppose you were interested in Pilates, a physical fitness system developed by Joseph Pilates (1883-1967) that is used by many dancers, athletes, and fitness enthusiasts.

One approach (the wrong one!) would be to write down a lot of information about Pilates: who Joseph Pilates was, how he developed his system, how it works, what the benefits are, and how it spread around the world. This type of research is simply a collection of facts that doesn't require critical thinking or a hierarchy of ideas. Write your paper this way, and very likely you will end up with something that resembles an encyclopedia article, as well as a low grade.

Most instructors prefer that you select a point of view or controversy to explore. Stated in one sentence called a thesis, this point of view will shape your entire research paper.

So let's choose a thesis and see how to build a paper around it. Instead of trying to cover everything that's known about the Pilates system, we'll focus on one idea: *Pilates is beneficial to athletes.* Notice that this isn't a question. (You can't support a question!) A thesis must be a statement that takes a stand on an issue. The keyword is *beneficial.* Already you can see your research paper taking shape: You're going to focus on three benefits of Pilates.

The next step is to read, read, and read some more. Take notes. Make sure you use books and periodicals that have been through a quality-control process. You'll find a great deal of information on the online databases at your library's website, and you can ask a librarian for help. (You should also be familiar with both the advantages and limitations of Wikipedia: See Chapter 20 on p. 152.)

Google Books is a free online resource that can be a great help when you're doing research. The Google corporation has an ongoing project of scanning books and putting excerpts online. Because of copyright issues, you usually can't read the whole book online. But you can do a word search that will allow you to read a few pages from a book, and that might save you a trip to the library. I used

Google Books several times when I was writing my sample research paper about ragtime. I needed more information about ragtime music in Europe. I typed *ragtime* and *Europe* into the search box at https://books.google.com and was able to read pages from several books that had the information I needed.

After you've gathered your information, you should be ready to create an outline. Think of three reasons why Pilates is beneficial to athletes. Then choose the most important reason and put it last:

Outline

Thesis: Pilates is beneficial to athletes.

1st supporting idea: First, Pilates improves breathing.

2nd supporting idea: Next, Pilates is a safe path to fitness.

Climax: Most important, Pilates can help prevent sports injuries.

Now you can start drafting your research paper. Here's how you might organize your information:

Pilates for Athletes

Introduction (You'll probably need two paragraphs to fit all this information in):

- Attention-getter (a brief story about a successful athlete who's used Pilates)
- Background about your topic (what Pilates is, and how it got started)
- Quotation from an expert about the importance of your topic (Quotations from one or two athletes about how Pilates has helped them)
- Thesis (Pilates is beneficial to athletes.)

First supporting idea (several paragraphs or pages)

- Pilates helps athletes breathe more efficiently
- Oxygen intake is an important factor in athletic performance
- Details about how Pilates encourages better breathing
- Quotations from experts and successful athletes about Pilates and oxygen

Second supporting idea (several paragraphs or pages)

- Pilates is a safe pathway to better fitness for athletes
- Information about what makes Pilates so safe (trainers have a thorough background in how the body works, Pilates is a low impact approach to fitness, exercises are carefully designed for safety)
- Quotations from experts and athletes about Pilates and safety

Most important supporting idea (several paragraphs or pages)

- Pilates helps athletes avoid injuries
- Stories and quotations from athletes who credit Pilates with helping them avoid injuries
- Information about how Pilates prevents injuries (proper alignment of the body, core strength, protecting the back, flexibility)

Conclusion (one or two paragraphs)

- Restate your thesis
- Close with a quotation from an athlete or coach who recommends Pilates
- State why Pilates will continue to be beneficial to future athletes

Finding Topics for Research

Avoid topics that have been done again and again, such as capital punishment, gun control, and abortion. You can find provocative topics just by turning the pages in a newspaper and scanning the stories there. What issues are coming before the Supreme Court? What are the latest trends in law enforcement? What political issues are Americans debating? What's going on in the economy, families, schools, sports, science, medicine, and the entertainment world? Your instructor or a librarian can also help you choose a topic.

Another approach is to dig into something that already interests you. When I became interested in Wales and the Welsh language while I was in college, I had an endless supply of topics. When I enrolled in a history course, I wrote about a historical event in Wales. In my literature courses I researched Welsh poets. Often you can do the same for almost any topic that interests you: basketball, yoga, ballroom dancing, golf...the possibilities are endless.

Or consider researching a topic related to a career that interests you. Spend a few minutes asking an instructor or a librarian what new trends are emerging in a field that interests you, and build your research paper around one of those topics.

In years to come you'll be able to cite your research during job interviews, giving you a distinct advantage over other candidates who don't know as much about the field you've chosen. You might even be able to publish your findings in a newsletter or journal related to your career field—a sure way to get noticed.

It's true that research papers are demanding assignments, requiring a great deal of time, energy, skill, and concentration. But it's also true that your efforts will pay off handsomely again and again.

Where Students Get into Trouble

In the past couple of weeks I've been grading research papers as part of a collaborative project with a friend who's a college instructor. It has not been a happy experience for me (and I know the students receiving grades from me haven't been happy either). Here are some tips for student researchers based on the papers I've been reading:

1. Find out what documentation system your institution uses. Buy the handbook (or camp out in the library, which surely owns a copy) and follow it *exactly*.

2. Most English and humanities courses require MLA. Science courses generally use APA. But perhaps your institution uses Turabian, the *Chicago Manual of Style*, or some other system. Ask your instructor ahead of time.

3. Consider using an online documentation tool, such as the Son of Citation Machine. Warning: These tools aren't human, so you need to use your own brain

to double-check the results. Some online citation tools insert extra periods, for example.

4. Use capital letters correctly. I shouldn't even have to say this, but I'm noticing more and more problems with missing capital letters in the papers I read.

5. Write a first paragraph that includes a catchy opening (an interesting quotation or a story), background about your topic, a statement by an expert about the importance of your topic, and your thesis statement. If there's a lot of background, your introduction can be two paragraphs long.

6. No matter what—even if you're writing a book—put the thesis on the first page. (Not sure if you have a thesis? Get help *immediately* from your instructor or the learning center at your school or college. Consider this an emergency!)

7. Begin every paragraph with a topic sentence that relates to your thesis *and* predicts what the paragraph will be about.

8. Wrap up your paper in the last paragraph. Don't introduce anything new.

9. Find out the big names in your field and include them in your paper.

10. Be emphatic. Recently I read two research papers that started with "not" statements, explaining what something or somebody *wasn't*. Bad idea.

11. Don't stray from your topic. I'm on the editorial board for an important journal about playwright Bernard Shaw. This week someone submitted an article about Shaw with several paragraphs that didn't mention Shaw at all. I rejected it, and so did the other board members.

12. Remember that librarians are research experts. You'd be surprised how often I go to librarians for help with my research projects. If I'm a professional, and I rely on librarians for help, shouldn't you be doing the same? If you run into a research question or problem, ask. They'll be happy to help.

Chapter 20

Should You Use Wikipedia?

It's almost a pointless question, because chances are you already do use Wikipedia. It is, of course, a free online encyclopedia that accepts information from anyone. If you want to add information or make a correction, you don't even have to identify yourself. (This kind of open-to-all document is called a "wiki," so you can see where the name *Wikipedia* comes from.) Because a wiki is not a strict peer review process, most instructors won't allow students to use Wikipedia for a research assignment. (See p. 143 for a discussion of "peer review.")

The fact is, however, that Wikipedia is remarkably reliable. A panel of dedicated volunteers verifies the information submitted to Wikipedia. Mistakes do creep in, but they're rare. I've submitted corrections to Wikipedia several times, and I've always been asked to submit sources so that my information could be verified. For example, I noticed that the entry for David Fairchild (an important American botanist) omitted the title of one of his books. I supplied the title and, as a source, provided a link to the Library of Congress listing.

Another time I noticed a mistake in the Wikipedia entry for Richard Burton, my favorite actor. I corrected the mistake and cited the page number of a book about Burton that had the right information.

Why, then, shouldn't you use Wikipedia? The answer is that there's nothing wrong with Wikipedia *if* (and it's a big *if*) you use it properly. Wikipedia is an excellent (though not perfect) resource when you need quick facts about a subject. I use Wikipedia so often that I always contribute a few dollars when Wikipedia is hosting an online fundraiser. But encyclopedias (including Wikipedia) aren't intended for critical thinking and in-depth analysis.

The good news is that most of the information you find on Wikipedia doesn't require a source, so you don't have to worry about documenting it. Remember the basic rule that documentation is needed only for controversial information. Nobody is going to challenge the kinds of facts found on Wikipedia (names, dates, and locations). If you look up the scientific name for, say, the popular plant called Virginia creeper, you don't have to state your source. Scientists all over the world agree on the name *Parthenocissus quinquefolia*. No source is needed.

Where you will need documentation—and where Wikipedia is inappropriate—is for anything controversial or uncertain. For example, something as simple as a birthdate can be a problem for a famous person who was born during a tumultuous period.

American composer Scott Joplin was the son of a former slave and born shortly after the Civil War, when local governments didn't always bother with accurate recordkeeping for African-Americans. An additional problem was that some of Joplin's official records were stored in government buildings that suffered destructive fires. So Joplin scholars still disagree about Joplin's actual birthdate. It's an issue that ragtime scholars talk about, but you won't find it covered in Wikipedia.

Other controversies that Wikipedia doesn't cover include personal relationships (for example, was Abraham Lincoln happily married?) and judgments (for example, does the Watergate scandal negate the positive achievements from Richard Nixon's Presidential administration?). No encyclopedia will attempt to address these and similar issues. An encyclopedia is strictly a collection of facts.

Here's the bottom line: When you undertake a research project, get to know your subject thoroughly. Make sure you can tell the difference between accepted facts and information that's controversial. For example, because I'm a Shaw scholar, I know that experts are still arguing about who Bernard Shaw's father was. (Although Shaw's parents were legally married, their marriage was an unhappy one, and Shaw's mother had a close friendship with an attractive voice teacher. Was there an affair?) You won't find pros and cons of those issues in a

Wikipedia entry. On the other hand, there are no disagreements about Shaw 's birthdate and other facts about his life and career.

Links and Sources

If you use Wikipedia often, you'll notice that most entries include sources and external links that many people (like me) find useful. But you should remember that Wikipedia does not evaluate sources or make recommendations. It just posts whatever links and sources apply to the information that has been posted.

There are other encyclopedias, however, that provide reading lists of the most important books about a subject. Remember too that there are specialized encyclopedias in many fields: sports, religion, literature, science, entertainment, the arts, and so on. They too feature articles written by experts that may include sources for further reading and research.

Part Five

Solving Sentence Problems

Chapter 21

Avoiding Fragments

The first requirement for a sentence is also the most important one: Completeness. English grammar is full of obscure rules that you might be able to break without getting caught. But writing an incomplete sentence (also called a fragment) is a serious error that most good readers will notice immediately—to your detriment. (You were already introduced to fragments on p. 106 in Chapter 14, when you learned about "extra ideas"—another name for *fragment*.)

Fortunately there's an easy way to ensure that your sentences will probably meet this **completeness** requirement: Start every sentence with a person, place, or thing. (To put it differently: If you're unsure of your writing skills, take the safe route. Avoid writing complicated sentences that can get you into trouble.)

A Closer Look at Fragments

The following tips will help you avoid fragments (incomplete sentences):

- Remember that most fragments appear at the start of a paragraph. Be especially careful with sentences beginning with *first*, *next*, and *finally*.
  First, an outrageous estimate. INCORRECT
  First, he gave us an outrageous estimate. CORRECT

- Double-check every sentence that begins with an *–ing* word. (But an *–ing* word doesn't always mean that you have a fragment—just make sure the sentence is complete.)
  Driving with an expired license. INCORRECT
  Driving with an expired license is against the law. CORRECT

- If fragments are a consistent problem for you, start each sentence with a person, place, or thing.

- Avoid starting a sentence with a "red flag" word or phrase: *like, who, which, such as.*

He couldn't make any friends in the dorm where he was living. Which might mean that he needs to work on his social skills INCORRECT

He couldn't make any friends in the dorm where he was living, which might mean that he needs to work on his social skills. CORRECT

He was impressed with the activities offered at the recreation complex. Like folk dancing, swimming lessons, and cooking classes. INCORRECT

He was impressed with the activities offered at the recreation complex, like folk dancing, swimming lessons, and cooking classes. CORRECT

What Do Fragments Look Like?

Here is a paragraph containing several fragments:

Aiko signed up for modern dance this semester. Dancing has always interested her. First, making new friends. Because she lives off campus. She hasn't been meeting many other students. Also, a fun way to stay in shape. She has always loved moving to music. Hoping to become more flexible and have more energy. She can't wait for the class to begin. Looking forward to learning new ways to respond to music.

And here is the same paragraph with the fragments corrected:

Aiko signed up for modern dance this semester. Dancing has always interested her. First, she thinks it will be a good way to make new friends. Because she lives off campus, she hasn't been meeting many other students. The dance class will change that. Also, it will be a fun way to stay in shape. She has always loved moving to music. She hopes to become more flexible and have more energy. She can't wait for the class to begin. She's looking forward to learning new ways to respond to music.

Practice Activity: Fragments

Instructions: Mark each sentence **S** and each fragment **F**. Reminder: The first word will help you identify sentences and fragments. When you're finished, check your answers below.

1. ____Linda is taking her algebra final at 9:30 tomorrow morning.

2. ____Worried about tomorrow's test and her final grade.

3. ____Although, she's done well in algebra all semester.

4. ____Noticing that she tends to get nervous before finals week every semester.

5. ____Other friends have noticed the same thing.

6. ____They're trying to help Linda develop more confidence.

7. ____Several of us have discussed it with her.

8. ____Trying to teach her some relaxation techniques.

9. ____Which will pay off for her again and again.

10. ____Jeffrey and I also suggested a visit to the Counseling Center.

ANSWERS Practice Activity: Fragments

The beginning of each sentence is highlighted for you.

1. S Linda is taking her algebra final at 9:30 tomorrow morning.

2. F Worried about tomorrow's test and her final grade.

3. F Although, she's done well in algebra all semester.

4. F Noticing that she tends to get nervous before finals week every semester.

5. S Other friends have noticed the same thing.

6. S They're trying to help Linda develop more confidence.

7. S Several of us have discussed it with her.

8. F Trying to teach her some relaxation techniques.

9. F Which will pay off for her again and again.

10. S Jeffrey and I also suggested a visit to the Counseling Center.

Chapter 22

Avoiding Run-on Sentences

Of all the mistakes a writer can make, run-on sentences are among the most serious. So what's a run-on sentence, and how can you avoid making this error?

A "run-on" is two sentences joined together without a period. Sometimes this mistake is also called a "fused sentence" or a "comma splice." No matter what it's called, the mistake is the same: A missing period.

The dog barked loudly, Wilson looked out the window. RUN-ON
The dog barked loudly. Wilson looked out the window. CORRECT

A fight broke in the parking lot, Joan and Kay were arguing about a chicken sandwich. RUN-ON
A fight broke out in the parking lot. Joan and Kay were arguing about a chicken sandwich. CORRECT

The problem with a run-on is that it doesn't stop when it's supposed to. (Think of a car engine that "runs on": It's the same problem—not stopping when it's supposed to.)

Some writers mistakenly think that any long sentence is a "run-on." Not true! Long sentences are perfectly correct *as long as* there's a period in the right place. Here's a long sentence from Thomas Jefferson's first Inaugural Address. It's grammatically correct and doesn't need any corrections:

And let us reflect that, having banished from our land that religious intolerance under which mankind so long bled and suffered, we have yet gained little if we countenance a political intolerance as despotic, as wicked, and capable of as bitter and bloody persecutions.

Actually some run-ons are quite short. They're still wrong if the period is missing.

Jane was frightened, she hid in the closet. RUN-ON
Jane was frightened. She hid in the closet. CORRECT

I pushed, the door opened. RUN-ON
I pushed. The door opened. CORRECT

Avoiding Run-on Sentences

Here are a few suggestions to help you avoid run-ons:

Remember that "it" often starts a new sentence. (You've heard this before!) Use a period and a capital letter.

I stopped by the classroom, it was empty. RUN-ON
I stopped by the classroom. It was empty. CORRECT

Practice distinguishing between "extra ideas" (which end in commas) and sentences (which require periods or semicolons):

When the alarm went off, **we ran to the back door**. CORRECT ("When the alarm went off" is an extra idea)

The alarm went off, we ran to the back door. RUN-ON
The alarm went off. We ran to the back door.

Remember that there are only seven words that you can use with a comma to join two sentences (*for, and, nor, but, or, yet, so*). (They're often called the FANBOYS.) You can't use *however* or *then* (or similar words) to join sentences. (See Chapter 25 on p. 168 to learn more.)

I wanted some pizza, however the restaurant was closed. RUN-ON
I wanted some pizza. However, the restaurant was closed. CORRECT

My mother kissed me good-bye, then she left. RUN-ON
My mother kissed me good-bye. Then she left. CORRECT

Practice Activity Identifying and Correcting Run-on Sentences

Instructions: Insert periods or semicolons where they're needed. Some sentences don't need corrections. When you're finished, check your answers below.

:1. Mrs. Knudsen thought she saw someone in her backyard, no one was there.

2. When I dropped by the student lounge, I saw a party going on.

3. The lunchroom was crowded I couldn't find a seat.

4. The shop owner said the shoplifter had a heart tattoo, gold hoop earrings, and short brown hair.

5. Because Jessie just turned eighteen, she thinks she can do what she wants.

6. I saw the dog on the porch, it growled at me.

7. Lindsay returned the book, she borrowed two more by the same author.

8. One car had a dented fender, the other car was undamaged.

9. No one enjoys working holidays, however some jobs require it.

10. I did my workout, then I went straight to work.

ANSWERS Practice Activity: Identifying and Correcting Run-on Sentences

1. Mrs. Knudsen thought she saw someone in her backyard. No one was there.

2. When I dropped by the student lounge, I saw a party going on.

3. The lunchroom was crowded. I couldn't find a seat.

4. The shop owner said the shoplifter had a heart tattoo, gold hoop earrings, and short brown hair. d

5. Because Jessie just turned eighteen, she thinks she can do what she wants.

6. I saw the dog on the porch. It growled at me.

7. Lindsay returned the book. She borrowed two more by the same author.

8. One car had a dented fender. The other car was undamaged.

9. No one enjoys working holidays. However, some jobs require it.

10. I did my workout. Then I went straight to work.

Part Six

English Usage

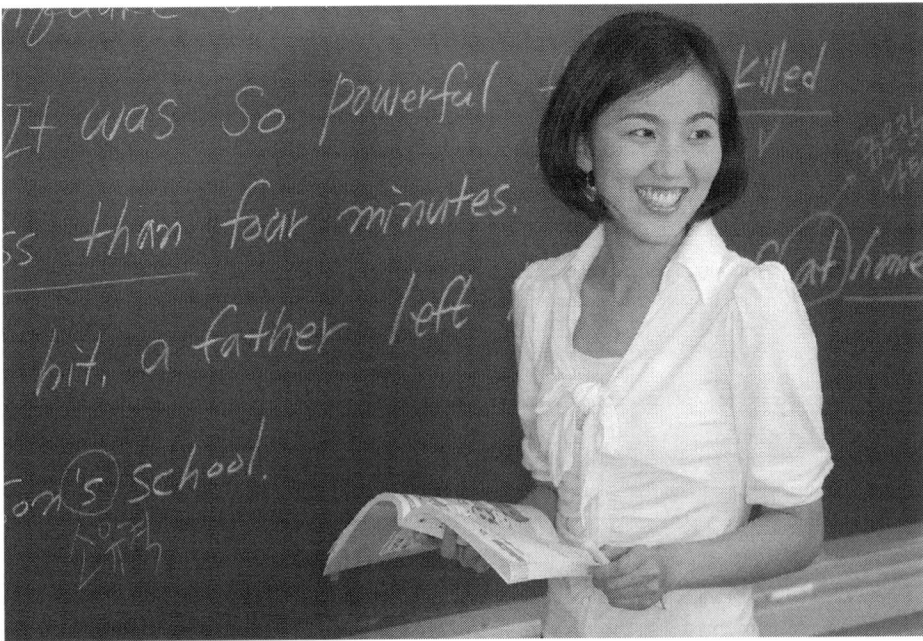

Chapter 23

Understanding Commas

Just three basic rules will cover most of the commas you will use in your writing. In the next three chapters you'll be taking a close look at each rule.

Rule 1

Use a comma whenever a sentence begins with an extra idea. (The real sentence is in **bold**).

Because we had a larger order to fill, **I asked Parker to come in an hour early.**

If the extra idea is at the back, omit the comma:

I asked Parker to come in an hour early because we had a large order to fill.

If the extra idea at the beginning is very short, you may omit the comma:

Late last night **we finished the store inventory.**

Rule 2

Use a comma when two sentences are joined by *and* or *but*.

First I sent the tenant a warning letter, and then I called him.
Wilson remembered making the inspection, but she didn't recall the date.

If you don't have two complete sentences, omit the comma. (In the examples below, the complete sentence is in **bold**.)

I called Jennings and wrote him a letter.
Wilson remembered the inspection but not the date.

Comma Rule 2 can also be used with five additional words: *for, nor, or, yet, so*. **For** in this context means "because": *Betsy suddenly turned around, for she sensed that someone was approaching.* (These seven words are often called the FANBOYS.) Usually, however, you need to focus only on two words: *and/but*.

Rule 3

Use a comma in front and another one in back when a sentence contains an *interrupter* (a word group that disrupts the sentence flow). And here's an easier way to think about it: Use a pair of commas when you drop your voice and raise it again.

Superman, who was disguised as Clark Kent, could bend steel with his bare hands.

Your mission, should you choose to accept it, is to find the hidden drugs.

Park Street, which is closed to traffic today, will reopen tomorrow.

Our new headquarters, scheduled to open in March, will be much more comfortable.

Omit the commas for essential information:

Inspectors who earned certifications will be honored in the ceremony.

> Tip: Reading the sentence aloud is a big help with Comma Rule 3 commas. You'll hear your voice drop and then go up again. Try it!

Chapter 24

Comma Rule 1

Professional Sentence Patterns		
Type of Pattern	**Special Words**	**Typical Sentence**
subordinate conjunction (Comma Rule 1)	*if, when, because, although*, **and similar words**	**Because we expect a large turnout, we're meeting in the auditorium.**
coordinate conjunction (Comma Rule 2)	FANBOYS words: *for, and, nor, but, or, yet, so*	I tried to talk Karen into running for treasurer, but she thinks Lois will do a better job.
interrupter (Comma Rule 3)	*who, which*	Mikki Yonker, who was program chair last year, is running again this year.
Semicolon	none required	We're electing officers today; be sure to come to the meeting.

Comma Rule 1 covers subordinate clauses (word groups beginning with *subordinate conjunctions* such as **if, when, because, although**) as well as prepositional phrases (word groups beginning with *prepositions* such as **of, in, by, for, with, to**). (These constructions are called "complex sentences.")

Using Comma Rule 1 Effectively

Here are a few suggestions for using Comma Rule 1 effectively:

- Never place a comma after a subordinate conjunction (*if, when, because, although*, and similar words).

  The street was closed because, we were getting ready for the parade.
  INCORRECT

  The street was closed because we were getting ready for the parade.
  CORRECT

- Don't confuse "extra ideas" with sentences. (Sentences are **in bold**.)

  I'd like to go back to college. Although, this might not be a good time.
  INCORRECT

  I'd like to go back to college although this might not be a good time.

- Use a comma if the "extra idea" is at the front of the sentence (*not* the back).

  I saw the driver toss something out the window, when he spotted me.
  INCORRECT

  I saw the driver toss something out the window when he spotted me.
  CORRECT

  When he spotted me, **I saw the driver toss something out the window.**
  CORRECT

Practice Activity Comma Rule 1

Instructions: Use Comma Rule 1 to insert commas where needed. Not every sentence needs commas. When you're finished, check your answers below.

1. While Professor Sibelius was setting up the projector I distributed handouts.

2. The party ended before we were ready to go home.

3. Ahmad played his violin solo well although he was nervous about the concert.

4. Because no shrubbery was broken the detective knew the burglar hadn't

jumped from an upstairs window.

5. If you vacuum the bedroom I will load the dishwasher.

6. He has been in business since January of last year.

7. Because I suspected he was lying I didn't sign the contract.

8. We take the children out for ice cream after the yard work is finished.

9. When the limb fell across our driveway my father started calling tree services.

10. Although the surveillance camera wasn't working the police found two eyewitnesses who saw the incident.

ANSWERS Practice Activity Comma Rule 1

1. While Professor Sibelius was setting up the projector, I distributed handouts.

2. The party ended before we were ready to go home.

3. Ahmad played his violin solo well although he was nervous about the concert.

4. Because no shrubbery was broken, the detective knew the burglar hadn't jumped from an upstairs window.

5. If you vacuum the bedroom, I will load the dishwasher.

6. He has been in business since January of last year.

7. Because I suspected he was lying, I didn't sign the contract.

8. We take the children out for ice cream after the yard work is finished.

9. When the limb fell across our driveway, my father started calling tree services.

10. Although the surveillance camera wasn't working, the police found two eyewitnesses who saw the incident.

Chapter 25

Comma Rule 2

Professional Sentence Patterns		
Type of Pattern	**Special Words**	**Typical Sentence**
subordinate conjunction (Comma Rule 1)	*if, when, because, although, and similar words*	Because we expect a large turnout, we're meeting in the auditorium.
coordinate conjunction (Comma Rule 2)	**FANBOYS words:** *for, and, nor, but, or, yet, so*	I tried to talk Karen into running for treasurer, but she thinks Lois will do a better job.
relative pronoun (Comma Rule 3)	*who, which*	Mikki Yonker, who was program chair last year, is running again this year.
Semicolon	none required	We're electing officers today; be sure to come to the meeting.

Comma Rule 2 covers sentences combined with the words **and** or **but**. Formally these are called "compound sentences."

Actually there are seven words for Comma Rule 2: **and/but** are by far the most common. The word FANBOYS is a good memory device to remember all seven Comma Rule 2 words: **For And Nor But Or Yet So**.

For has a special meaning in a Comma Rule 2 sentence: It's much like *because.*

We've been expecting you, for Helena said you'd be visiting us soon. CORRECT

Using Comma Rule 2 Effectively

Here are some tips for using Comma Rule 2:

- Never use a comma directly after a coordinate conjunction.

  I was nervous at first but, I soon got over my fears. INCORRECT
  I was nervous at first, but I soon got over my fears. CORRECT

- The seven coordinate conjunctions (FANBOYS words) are the only words you can use with a comma to join two sentences. Use periods or semicolons with other words.

  Dr. Casey checked my blood pressure, then she listened to my lungs.
  INCORRECT
  Dr. Casey checked my blood pressure. Then she listened to my lungs.
  CORRECT
  Dr. Casey checked my blood pressure; then she listened to my lungs.
  CORRECT

  The promotion that interests me pays well, therefore, I expect a lot of
  competition. INCORRECT
  The promotion that interests me pays well. Therefore, I expect a lot of
  competition. CORRECT
  The promotion that interests me pays well; therefore, I expect a lot of
  competition. CORRECT

- *And/But* are the most common Comma Rule 2 words. You'll rarely need to think about the other five FANBOYS words.

Practice Activity: Comma Rule 2

Instructions: Insert commas where they're needed. Not every sentence needs a comma. When you're finished, check your answers below.

Reminder: The key to Comma Rule 2 is thinking about the words *and* and *but*.

Check to see if there's a sentence before and after *and/but*. If that's the case, insert a comma.

1. Bill Asplund submitted his proposal and Jan Bernsen accepted it.

2. I took Sue to the playground and my brother took Joe to the Lego store.

3. Cashin found the right key but couldn't open the door.

4. The policy makes sense but we can't implement it this year.

5. The shoulders are puckered and the wristbands are loose.

6. The house the realtor showed us this morning is too small and has an outdated kitchen.

7. The shelter is overcrowded and does not provide enough services for displaced families.

8. I got into my car and immediately dialed 911.

9. We questioned the neighbors but no one heard anything unusual.

10. I looked for a leak but didn't see any.

ANSWERS Practice Activity: Comma Rule 2

1. Bill Asplund submitted his proposal, and Jan Bernsen accepted it.

2. I took Sue to the playground, and my brother took Joe to the Lego store.

3. Cashin found the right key but couldn't open the door.

4. The policy makes sense, but we can't implement it this year.

5. The shoulders are puckered, and the wristbands are loose.

6. The house the realtor showed us this morning is too small and has an outdated kitchen.

7. The shelter is overcrowded and does not provide enough services for displaced families.

8. I got into my car and immediately dialed 911.

9. We questioned the neighbors, but no one heard anything unusual.

10. I looked for a leak but didn't see any.

Chapter 26

Comma Rule 3

Professional Sentence Patterns		
Type of Pattern	**Special Words**	**Typical Sentence**
subordinate conjunction (Comma Rule 1)	*if*, *when*, *because*, *although*, and similar words	Because we expect a large turnout, we're meeting in the auditorium.
coordinate conjunction (Comma Rule 2)	FANBOYS words: *for, and, nor, but, or, yet, so*	I tried to talk Karen into running for treasurer, but she thinks Lois will do a better job.
interrupter (Comma Rule 3)	*who, which*	**Mikki Yonker, who was program chair last year, is running again this year.**
semicolon	none required	We're electing officers today; be sure to come to the meeting.

Use Comma Rule 3 when a word or group of words interrupts a sentence. In most cases you'll use two commas, and changes in your voice will tell you where the commas go:

Your mission, Jim, is to chair tomorrow's meeting. CORRECT
Your next assignment, which you'll find challenging, is to evaluate the proposals and select the best one. CORRECT

Only two students, Gina and Naomi, signed up for the class in conversational Welsh. CORRECT

I spoke to Charlie Aker, from the help desk, who solved the software glitch in less than two minutes. CORRECT

Using Comma Rule 3 Effectively

Here are a few tips for using Comma Rule 3 effectively:

- Read sentences aloud, and listen to your voice. Use the commas when your voice changes.
- Use two commas, not one, in most sentences.
- Remember that often (but not always), Comma Rule 3 sentences include a *who* or *which* clause.

Mrs. Jones, who reported the fire, said she first noticed the smoke at about 10:30 this morning. CORRECT

The orientation session, which is usually held in the auditorium, has been moved to the cafeteria. CORRECT

Practice Activity: Comma Rule 3

Instructions: Read each sentence aloud, listening for a voice change. Insert commas where needed. Check your answers below.

1. The shirts that I bought for Jennie last spring are already too small for her.

2. Cara who teaches in the nursing program part-time has some good suggestions about preparing for the state certification exam.

3. Students who do well at a community college often excel when they transfer to a university.

4. Sally's Style Shop which opened last month attracts new customers every day.

5. Abigail Gleason who was our dean for three years was just promoted to provost.

ANSWERS Practice Activity: Comma Rule 3

1. The shirts that I bought for Jennie last spring are already too small for her.

2. Cara, who teaches in the nursing program part-time, has some good suggestions about preparing for the state certification exam.

3. Students who do well at a community college often excel when they transfer to a university.

4. Sally's Style Shop, which opened last month, attracts new customers every day.

5. Abigail Gleason, who was our dean for three years, was just promoted to provost.

Practice Activity: Comma Rules 1, 2, and 3

Instructions: Use all three rules to place commas in these sentences. Not every sentence needs commas. When you're finished, check your answers below.

1. As I approached the house I heard a dog barking.

2. Linda grabbed her son's hand and they ran down the street.

3. Linda grabbed her son's hand and ran down the street.

4. Paul who just graduated from the police academy is planning to go back for a degree.

5. I went back to Professor Smith's office because I had more questions about our algebra assignment.

6. Bailey's uniform which should have been soiled was suspiciously clean.

7. Menzies arrived at the meeting on time although traffic downtown was moving slowly.

8. The library is closed for the holiday weekend but it will reopen on Tuesday.

9. Glenn was nervous about dealing with customers for the first few days but he soon overcame his fears.

10. I went over the contract myself and asked Frank Kelly from the account office to check it too.

ANSWERS Practice Activity: Comma Rules 1, 2, and 3

1. As I approached the house, I heard a dog barking.

2. Linda grabbed her son's hand, and they ran down the street.

3. Linda grabbed her son's hand and ran down the street.

4. Paul, who just graduated from the police academy, is planning to go back for a degree.

5. I went back to Professor Smith's office because I had more questions about our algebra assignment.

6. Bailey's uniform, which should have been soiled, was suspiciously clean.

7. Menzies arrived at the meeting on time although traffic downtown was moving slowly.

8. The library is closed for the holiday weekend, but it will reopen on Tuesday.

9. Glenn was nervous about dealing with customers for the first few days, but he soon overcame his fears.

10. I went over the contract myself and asked Frank Kelly from the account office to check it too.

Chapter 27

Periods and Semicolons

Professional Sentence Patterns		
Type of Pattern	**Special Words**	**Typical Sentence**
subordinate conjunction (Comma Rule 1)	*if, when, because, although, and similar words*	Because we expect a large turnout, we're meeting in the auditorium.
coordinate conjunction (Comma Rule 2)	FANBOYS words: *for, and, nor, but, or, yet, so*	I tried to talk Karen into running for treasurer, but she thinks Lois will do a better job.
interrupter (Comma Rule 3)	*who, which*	Mikki Yonker, who was program chair last year, is running again this year.
Semicolon	**none required**	**We're electing officers today; be sure to come to the meeting.**

For most writers, periods are the easiest punctuation marks. You already know that sentences end with periods and that most abbreviations are followed by periods (although some organizations no longer use them).

When you're uncertain about an abbreviation, you can check the organization's website or look at its stationery to see whether periods are needed. UNICEF, IBM, and NASA are examples of organizations that do not use periods. Mr., Dr., Sgt., and similar titles do use periods. If you're uncertain, check the dictionary or visit Dictionary.com.

Here's one more important piece of information about periods: Space once (not twice) after a period when you're typing. Computers are sophisticated typography systems, and the old rules about typewriters no longer apply.

Semicolons

Once you know how to use a period at the end of a sentence, you also know how to use a semicolon: Just change a period to a semicolon, and lower-case the next letter (unless it's a name with a capital letter). Please note that you *don't* pick out a long sentence, find the midpoint, and stick a semicolon there.

Note these examples:

Gail broke up with Carl. She was tired of being taken for granted. PERIOD
Gail broke up with Carl; she was tired of being taken for granted. SEMICOLON

Mark tried hiding the car keys. Judy found them and took his car. PERIOD
Mark tried hiding the car keys; Judy found them and took his car. SEMICOLON

Semicolons are easy to use, and they give your writing a professional look that impresses readers. Forget elaborate rules you may have heard for using semicolons. All you need to do is find two sentences that seem to go together.

Take a look at these examples:

I'm worried about Aram. Carol said he wasn't in class today. CORRECT
I'm worried about Aram; Carol said he wasn't in class today. CORRECT

I arrived promptly at seven o'clock. No one else was there. CORRECT
I arrived promptly at seven o'clock; no one else was there. CORRECT

Using Semicolons Effectively

Here are a few tips for using semicolons effectively:

- Use semicolons sparingly—one semicolon per paragraph, or one per page in a short writing task.
- Never use semicolons to divide sentences. A semicolon is like a period, not a comma.

- Think of a semicolon as a way to join two sentences into a long one with one capital letter.
- Remember that semicolons are just like periods. You never *have* to use a semicolon between two sentences. A period will always work.
- Don't be intimidated by semicolons. Any time you have two sentences that are related in some way (and that's most of the time!) you can change a period to a semicolon.

Semicolon or Comma?

Don't try joining sentences with a comma unless you're using Comma Rule 2 (see p. 168). Use a semicolon instead (or a period with a capital letter). Here are a few helpful tips:

1. *It* often starts a new sentence and needs a semicolon (or a period and a capital letter). (You've heard this before!)

> I like my new laptop, it makes writing easier. INCORRECT
> I like my new laptop; it makes writing easier. CORRECT
> I like my new laptop. It makes writing easier. CORRECT

2. *However, then, therefore,* and similar words can't be used with a comma to join sentences. Again, use a semicolon (or a period and a capital letter). Only seven words in the English language—the FANBOYS—can be used with a comma to join sentences: *For, and, nor, but, or, yet, so.* (Go to p. 168 to learn more about Comma Rule 2 and these FANBOYS words.)

> Lister found the receipt, then he showed it to me. INCORRECT
> Lister found the receipt; then he showed it to me. CORRECT
> Lister found the receipt, and then he showed it to me. CORRECT
> Lister found a receipt, but it wasn't the right one. CORRECT

Practice Activity: Using Semicolons

Instructions: Read the paragraphs below. In each paragraph, choose two sentences to combine with a semicolon. Check your semicolon sentences below.

> Luther Shalit is a math tutor in the Learning Lab. He helps students learn

elementary algebra and geometry. I've seen positive changes since he became a tutor. Luther is proud of his knowledge and happy to be doing something useful. Luther has always been interested in mathematics.

Professor Fallon asked Linda Hammond to talk to us. She described her work as a counselor at Penny Lane Middle School. She feels she's making a positive difference there. Discipline at the school has improved since she was assigned there. Students trust her and come to her for advice. She discusses substance abuse, family problems, and conflict resolution with students and faculty.

ANSWERS Practice Activity: Using Semicolons

Here are some possible answers:

Luther Shalit is a math tutor in the Learning Lab; he helps students learn elementary algebra and geometry.

I've seen positive changes since he became a tutor; Luther is proud of his knowledge and happy to be doing something useful.

Luther is proud of his knowledge and happy to be doing something useful; he has always been interested in mathematics.

Professor Fallon asked Linda Hammond to talk to us; she described her work as a counselor at Penny Lane Middle School.

She feels she's making a positive difference there; discipline at the school has improved since she was assigned there.

Students trust her and come to her for advice; she discusses substance abuse, family problems, and conflict resolution with students and faculty.

Chapter 28

Apostrophes

You need to know two ways to use apostrophes: in **contractions** (*can't, didn't, won't*), and in **"of" ideas**: *Mary's uniform* (uniform of Mary), *an architect's office* (office of the architect), *Wednesday's meeting* (meeting of Wednesday).

Apostrophes DO NOT mean "more than one." (There's one exception: p. 182).

Neighbors called the police when they heard gunshots. NO APOSTROPHE

The Browns live on the next block. NO APOSTROPHE

The Browns' house has a swimming pool. APOSTROPHE: house of the Browns

Karen's notebook is on her desk. APOSTROPHE: book of Karen

There are two Karens in my chemistry class. NO APOSTROPHE

There's one exception to the "no plurals" rule: Apostrophes are used in the plurals of numerals and letters: *10's and 20's, p's and q's*. You'll learn more about these apostrophes later.

Where Does the Apostrophe Go?

Before the *s* or after the *s*? It depends on how the word is spelled. Apostrophes always go after the **last letter** of a word or name. If you know how to spell the word or name, you know where the apostrophe goes:

John	**John's** injuries aren't serious.
Louis	**Louis'** car was stolen. OR **Louis's** car was stolen.
Mr. Brown	Mr. **Brown's** story needs to be checked.
The Browns	The **Browns'** neighbors called 911.
baby	The **baby's** mother is bringing him today.
babies	We're collecting **babies'** clothing for the charity drive.
family	Inspector Clay is inspecting the **family's** new house.
families	Both **families'** houses were damaged.

woman I heard a **woman's** voice in the next room.

women Politicians need to address **women's** concerns.

boy A **boy's** bicycle was found in some shrubbery.

boys The **boys'** teacher is on paid leave.

Be especially careful with these special words: *men, women, children, people.* They're all plural but don't end in "s." The apostrophe rule still applies: Spell the word correctly, and put the apostrophe after the **last letter.**

men **a men's** clothing store women **women's** dresses

children **children's** toys people **people's** concerns

Sometimes apostrophes are needed in *time* expressions:

a day's pay (pay of a day)

two days' absence (absence of two days)

a good night's sleep (sleep of a good night)

three years' experience (experience of three years)

a week's vacation (vacation of a week)

If you don't have an "of" expression or a contraction, don't use an apostrophe:

The Johnsons sent me a birthday card.

The Johnsons' birthday card surprised me.

My family's vacation wasn't long enough.

Having fun together keeps families strong.

If a name ends in "s," you may add another "s" before the apostrophe:

Dolores's baby is due in November.

Dolores' baby is due in November.

Contractions

Apostrophes represent omitted letters in contractions: *don't, can't, won't.* Be careful with spelling. For example, in *don't* the apostrophe replaces the missing "o" in *not.*

I am getting ready for my trip to Cleveland.

I'm getting ready for my trip to Cleveland.

Joe is going with me.

Joe's going with me.

Possessive pronouns (like *his*) don't get apostrophes:

That book is hers, and this one is mine.

Florida is seeing a decline in its population.

The Acme Corporation doubled its profits last year.

Is that beautiful car yours?

It's has only one meaning, a contraction of *it is:*

I won't need a ride home unless it's raining.

It's difficult to find a suitable gift for my mother-in-law.

When *its* is possessive (like *his*), omit the apostrophe:

My favorite shirt is missing two of its buttons.

Our town got more than its share of rain last week.

There's one more way to use apostrophes. When you're writing the plural of a numeral or a letter, use an apostrophe:

Dot your i's and cross your t's.

The cashier gave me my change in 1's and 5's.

During the 60's, many young people protested the Vietnam War.

This is the only situation when apostrophes mean "more than one."

Practice Activity: Apostrophes 1

Instructions: Insert apostrophes where needed. Hint: Remember that apostrophes are used in "of" ideas. They don't signify "more than one." When you're finished, check your answers below.

1. The supervisors desk is cluttered with papers.

2. Her stepchildrens claims are unfounded.

3. The puppies were turned over to an animal shelter.

4. The puppies condition is expected to improve.

5. Miss Jones office is down the hall.

6. We all benefited from hearing James explain the new policy.

7. James explanation cleared up several misunderstandings.

8. Families need to set aside time to have fun together.

9. Both instructors did an excellent job.

10. After a weeks vacation, I was ready to return to work.

ANSWERS Practice Activity: Apostrophes 1

1. The supervisor's desk is cluttered with papers.

2. Her stepchildren's claims are unfounded.

3. The puppies were turned over to an animal shelter.

4. The puppies' condition is expected to improve.

5. Miss Jones' [OR Miss Jones's] office is down the hall.

6. We all benefited from hearing James explain the new policy.

7. James' [or James's] explanation cleared up several misunderstandings.

8. Families need to set aside time to have fun together.

9. Both instructors did an excellent job.

10. After a week's vacation, I was ready to return to work.

Practice Activity: Apostrophes 2

Instructions: Insert apostrophes where needed. Not every sentence needs an apostrophe. Check your answers below.

1. I dont understand how to use this calculator.

2. Once again, the repairs to the Smiths house didn't pass inspection.

3. Two days work was lost when the computer system went down.

4. Lieutenant Conner asked me to address the familys concerns.

5. Last months paychecks will be ready at nine o'clock.

6. I saw the "for sale" sign in the front yard of the Browns house.

7. Lewis report was thorough and efficient.

8. The Browns were out of town all weekend.

9. The smoke alarm in the childrens bedroom needs a battery.

10. Mrs. Hansens sister arrived on an early-morning flight.

ANSWERS Practice Activity: Apostrophes 2

1. I don't understand how to use this calculator.

2. Once again, the repairs to the Smiths' house didn't pass inspection.

3. Two days' work was lost when the computer system went down.

4. Lieutenant Conner asked me to address the family's concerns.

5. Last month's paychecks will be ready at nine o'clock.

6. I saw the "for sale" sign in the front yard of the Browns' house.

7. Lewis' [OR Lewis's] report was thorough and efficient.

8. The Browns were out of town all weekend.

9. The smoke alarm in the children's bedroom needs a battery.

10. Mrs. Hansen's sister arrived on an early-morning flight.

Chapter 29

Quotation Marks

In this chapter you'll learn how to use periods and commas with quotation marks. There are two basic principles to remember:

1. In the United States, periods and commas always go *inside* (before) quotation marks at the end of a sentence. There are no exceptions. (Canada and the United Kingdom use a different system.)

Note these examples, which are punctuated correctly:

Linda said, "I tried to find someone to babysit tonight. No one was available."

"Let's get the project done this weekend," I told Joe.

"When are you hoping to graduate?" Lewis asked.

"No matter what," Carl said, "I'm breaking up with her."

Patel tried to open the door marked "Emergencies only."

"Stop!" I shouted as the boy ran towards the busy street.

2. Use quotation marks only for a person's *exact* words. If you change the words in any way, omit the quotation marks.

"When are you hoping to graduate?" Lewis asked. QUOTATION MARKS

Lewis asked when I was hoping to graduate. NO QUOTATION MARKS

I asked Potter, "Are you ready to set up the room?" QUOTATION MARKS

I asked Potter if he was ready to set up the room. NO QUOTATION MARKS

Practice Activity: Using Quotation Marks

Instructions: Make any corrections that are needed in these sentences. Use the sentences above as models. (Some sentences may already be correct.) When you're finished, check your answers below.

1. Katherine said that "she never spoke to her landlord, and she mailed the rent check two days early."

2. Sarah told me, "I heard tango music and knew I had to dance".

3. Brent said, "I'm going to do an internship with a software company."

4. I asked Ernesto, did you request an estimate?

5. "Your son's Eagle Scout project is impressive." Joe told me.

6. "That air conditioner is too small for this bedroom", said Farrell.

7. The official warned Rogers, "not to stock the store before the inspection."

8. "When will you complete your research paper?" I asked Susan.

9. Officer West asked Linda Hamilton if she had heard any strange noises before the deck collapsed.

10. There's a problem. Hasan told me. With the backup system.

ANSWERS Practice Activity: Using Quotation Marks

X 1. Katherine said that she never spoke to her landlord, and she mailed the rent check two days early. OR Katherine said that "I never spoke to my landlord, and I mailed the rent check two days early."

X 2. Sarah told me, "I heard tango music and knew I had to dance."

√ 3. Brent said, "I'm going to do an internship with a software company."

X 4. I asked Ernesto, "Did you request an estimate first?" OR I asked Ernesto if he had requested an estimate.

X 5. "Your son's Eagle Scout project is impressive," Joe told me.

X 6. "That air conditioner is too small for this bedroom," said Farrell.

X 7. The official warned Rogers not to stock the store before the inspection.

√ 8. "When will you complete your research paper?" I asked Susan.

√ 9. Officer West asked Linda Hamilton if she had heard any strange noises before the deck collapsed.

X 10. "There's a problem," Hasan told me, "with the backup system."

Chapter 30

Pronouns

Pronouns are short, everyday words like *I, me, we, us, she, he, her, him, they, us, you,* and *it* that we use in place of other words. It would be clumsy to say something like "Mary said that Mary can't come to the meeting." Most of us prefer to say, "Mary said that she can't come to the meeting."

In most sentences it's easy to use pronouns correctly. But there are four pronoun issues that every writer should know. You'll be reviewing them in this chapter.

1. Singular Pronouns

Several commonly used pronouns are always singular: *any each every someone somebody everyone everybody anybody nobody*

> Every manager was on time for the meeting. SINGULAR
> Somebody needs to enter these statistics. SINGULAR
> Any employee is eligible for the program. SINGULAR

Here's where the confusion arises: In everyday conversation we think of these words as plural. Picture *every officer* in your mind, and you'll probably imagine a room full of men and women in uniform. But a closer look at these sentences indicates that these pronouns are singular:

> Every manager [not *managers*] was [not *were*] on time for the meeting.
> Somebody needs [not *need*] to enter these statistics.
> Any employee [not *employees*] **is** [not *are*] eligible for the program

Words containing *any, one,* or *body* are singular:

> Everyone uses a laptop to write reports.
> Everybody likes our new headquarters.

Use singular words with singular pronouns (*his, her, its*).

Everyone should have his or her reports completed. SINGULAR

Somebody needs to do his or her job better. SINGULAR

Any inspector can view his or her evaluation beginning on Monday. SINGULAR

Every employee is happy about his or her raise. SINGULAR

Many professional writers dislike "his or her," even though it's correct, and they find ways to avoid using it. (I dislike it myself!) Often you can revise a sentence to avoid "his or her." One strategy is to make the sentence plural. For example, here's a sentence you just read that requires "his or her":

Every employee is happy about his or her raise. AWKWARD

If you make the sentence plural, you can avoid "his or her":

Employees are happy about their raises. BETTER

Sometimes you can avoid "his or her" by substituting "a" or "the":

Each inspector will need three copies of his or her time sheet. AWKWARD

Each inspector will need three copies of the timesheet.   BETTER

2. Its or It's?

Use *its* (no apostrophe) as a possessive word (similar to *his*):

Every department is making adjustments to its proposed budget.

My uniform is missing one of its buttons.

Remember that **it's** (with an apostrophe) always means **it is**:

When the fire alarm sounds, it's time for the residents to evacuate.

Because it's late, I'll make the phone call tomorrow.

All possessive pronouns work the same way: *his, hers, ours, theirs, yours*: no apostrophe, ever. (Thinking about *his* will help you keep them straight.)

3. The "Thumb Rule"

Use the "thumb rule" when a name appears with a personal pronoun: *I, me, she, her, he, him, we, us, they, them.*

Here's how: Make the sentence shorter by covering the *and* phrase with your thumb. Then use your ear to choose the pronoun that sounds right.

Let Jane and (I, me) help you.
Think: Let ~~Jane and~~ me help you.
Let Jane and me help you. CORRECT
Yesterday Jane and (I, me) helped Greg.
Think: Yesterday Jane ~~and I~~ helped Greg.
Yesterday Jane and I helped Greg. CORRECT

4. Comparisons

In comparisons, "finish the sentence" by adding an extra word: Your ear will tell you which pronoun is correct. (Go to p. 201 to learn more about comparisons.)

Bill is older than (I, me).
Think: Bill is older than I [am].
Bill is older than I. CORRECT
Cheryl works faster than (he, him).
Think: Cheryl works faster than he [does].
Cheryl works faster than he. CORRECT
Joe speaks Spanish better than (I, me).
Think: Joe speaks Spanish better than I [do].
Joe speaks Spanish better than I. CORRECT
Carole has been with the agency almost as long as (we, us).
Carole has been with the agency almost as long as we [have].
Carole has been with the agency almost as long as we.

Practice Activity: Pronouns

Instructions: Make corrections in the sentences below. Not every sentence needs corrections. When you're finished, check your answers below.

1. Did everyone complete their paperwork for the field trip?

2. Its obvious that the academy needs to revise its curriculum.

3. Jill has more confidence taking tests than me.

4. Rewriting the regulations is going to be difficult for the captain and I.

5. Everyone in the agency has been talking about their upcoming evaluations.

6. Lois replied to this email before she forwarded it to Mr. Morris and he.

7. Ken understands the procedure better than her.

8. The agency is proud of its' safety record.

9. Someone didn't sign their timesheet for this month.

10. No one knows that part of town better than her.

ANSWERS Practice Activity: Pronouns

1. Did everyone complete ~~their~~ his or her paperwork for the field trip? OR Did all the students complete their paperwork for the field trip?

2. √ It's obvious that the academy needs to revise its curriculum.

3. Jill has more confidence taking tests than I [do].

4. Rewriting the regulations is going to be difficult for the captain and ~~I~~ me.

5. Everyone in the agency has been talking about ~~their~~ his or her upcoming evaluation. OR The entire staff has been talking about their upcoming evaluations.

6. Lois replied to this email before she forwarded it to Mr. Morris and ~~he~~ him.

7. Ken understands the procedure better than ~~her~~ she [does].

8. The agency is proud of its safety record.

9. Someone didn't sign ~~their~~ his or her timesheet for this month. OR Someone didn't sign a timesheet for this month.

10. No one knows that part of town better than ~~her~~ she [does].

Chapter 31

Verbs

Verbs are action words (words like *go, work, help,* and *run*). Most of the time verbs are easy to use correctly. You should be aware, though, of common verb mistakes that can mar your writing:

1. Using *seen* without a helper (*is, are, was, were, has, have, had*):

    Caruthers seen him with his sister several times. INCORRECT
    Caruthers had seen him with his sister several times. CORRECT
    Caruthers saw him with his sister several times. CORRECT

Using *done* without a helper:

    Gene done time for burglary in Tennessee. INCORRECT
    Gene had done time for burglary in Tennessee. CORRECT
    Gene did time for burglary in Tennessee. CORRECT

2. Using *snuck* (considered slang) instead of *sneaked*:

    Chan snuck outside to make a phone call. INCORRECT
    Chan sneaked outside to make a phone call. CORRECT

3. Placing the apostrophe in the wrong place in contractions: Remember that the apostrophe takes the place of a missing letter: For example, *do not* becomes *don't*; *is not* becomes *isn't*; *was not* becomes *wasn't*; *I am* becomes *I'm*.

    Inspector Farris was'nt on duty yesterday. INCORRECT
    Inspector Farris wasn't on duty yesterday. CORRECT

I'am thinking about getting a bachelor's degree in nursing. INCORRECT
I'm thinking about getting a bachelor's degree in nursing. CORRECT

If you're typing on a computer, the spellchecker or grammar checker may warn you that you've made an error. Always double-check what you've written, and–if possible–ask a friend or co-worker to read over it as well. It's much better to catch and correct errors yourself (rather than your instructor or boss).

Verb Endings

Many people have difficulty with *–s* and *–ed* verb endings, especially during conversation. When people talk, they naturally run sounds together, and we tend to omit letters. In most conversations, that's not a problem. But those omitted letters will detract from the professionalism of a report you're writing.

For example, listen to yourself read this sentence aloud:

Bill tried to find the glitch in the program.

Chances are you ran the *d* in *tried* together with the *t* in *to*—that's what most people do. Here's the problem, though: Are you going to remember to *write* that *-ed* ending, since you don't hear or say it? All too often, students write sentences like this:

Bill try to find the glitch in the program. INCORRECT

Here's another one. Again, listen to yourself read this sentence aloud:

The attachment lists the days and times for next month's meetings. CORRECT

Chances are you omitted the final "s" in "lists": It's a difficult word to pronounce correctly, especially when you're talking fast. As a result, the sentence may look like this when an officer writes it:

The attachment list the days and times for next month's meetings. INCORRECT

Memo is singular, so you should write *lists* in this sentence:

The attachment **lists** the days and times for next month's meetings. CORRECT

A similar problem arises with *supposed to* and *used to*: Many people omit the *–ed* ending.

I use to work every holiday. INCORRECT
I used to work every holiday. CORRECT

We're suppose to receive a raise next month. INCORRECT
We're supposed to receive a raise next month. CORRECT

Wilson use to fix cars before he decided to go back to school. INCORRECT
Wilson used to fix cars before he decided to go back to school. CORRECT

192

We're suppose to have a sunny weekend. INCORRECT
We're supposed to have a sunny weekend. CORRECT

Adding Verb Endings

Misspellings often creep in when writers add endings to verbs. You can avoid most errors by following a few simple rules:

1. In general, drop the silent *e* when you add a verb ending that starts with a vowel:

state   hope   care
statinghoping   caring

2. Keep the silent *e* when you add a verb ending that starts with a consonant:

state   hope   care
statement   hopeful   careless

3. When you're adding an ending to a word that ends with *y*, change the *y* to *i* when it is preceded by a consonant.

supply   worry
supplies   worries

4. *Don't* drop the final *y* when you're adding *-ing*.

study   carry
studying carrying

Practice Activity: Verbs

Instructions: Correct the verb errors in these sentences. Every sentence needs at least one correction. When you're finished, check your answers below.

1. We use to write all our reports by hand.

2. Sergeant Larsen did'nt see the memo about the new inspection procedure.

3. Pollard said she seen the social worker last Friday.

4. I snuck Catherine a piece of candy during the meeting.

5. The assignment consist of three research questions and a bibliography.

6. It's going to take a while for me to get use to the procedure.

7. Perkins is suppose to be graduating tomorrow.

8. Inmates from the vocational program done most of the carpentry.

9. The report list everyone who has a doctor's appointment today.

10. I've been studing so hard for this exam that I'am sure I'll pass.

ANSWERS Practice Activity: Verbs

1. We used to write all our reports by hand.

2. Sergeant Larsen didn't see the memo about the new inspection procedure.

3. Pollard said she ~~seen~~ saw the social worker last Friday.

4. I ~~snuck~~ sneaked Catherine a piece of candy during the meeting.

5. The assignment consists of three research questions and a bibliography.

6. It's going to take a while for me to get used to the procedure.

7. Perkins is supposed to be graduating tomorrow.

8. Inmates from the vocational program ~~done~~ did most of the carpentry.

9. The report lists everyone who has a doctor's appointment today.

10. I've been studying so hard for this exam that ~~I'am~~ I'm sure I'll pass.

Chapter 32

Subject-Verb Agreement

Subjects and verbs are the basic building blocks of sentences. These rules will help you avoid mistakes with subjects and verbs in any sentence you write.

1. When a sentence begins with *there* or *here*, reverse the sentence to get the verb right.

Here (is, are) your assignment.
THINK: Your assignment **is** here.
Here is your assignment. CORRECT

There (go, goes) two amazing women.
THINK: Two amazing women go there.
There go two amazing women. CORRECT

Here (come, comes) trouble.
THINK: Trouble comes here.
Here comes trouble. CORRECT

There (seem, seems) to be many possibilities.
THINK: Many possibilities **seem** to be there.
There seem to be many possibilities. CORRECT

2. Don't be fooled by numbers. A *unit* of time or measurement is always singular.

Twenty minutes is usually enough time for an interview.   (unit of time—singular)
Twenty students are taking exams. (twenty separate students —plural)
Two suspects are waiting to be interviewed. (two separate applicants —plural)
Two days is barely enough time to catch up on my sleep. (unit of time—singular)
Five feet is the average distance between the tables in the restaurant. (unit of measurement—singular)

Five cars **are** parked illegally on Main Street. (five separate cars—plural)

3. In *either/or, neither/nor* sentences, use the words near *or/nor* to choose your verb.

> Neither the associates nor **the manager likes** the new schedule.
> Neither the manager nor **the associates like** the new schedule.
> Neither your report nor **the newspaper articles have** the right information.
> Neither the newspaper articles nor **your report has** the right information.

4. Remember that prepositions (*in, by, for, with, to, of*) introduce phrases that must be crossed out before you choose the verb. (You can think of these cross-outs as "soft" parts of sentences. See p. 111.)

> **One** ~~of the lockers~~ **is** empty. (skip "of the lockers")
> **The box** ~~on the top shelf~~ **is** heavy. (skip "on the top shelf")
> **The inspectors** ~~in the Building Department~~ **are** getting new computers today.
> (skip "in the Building Department")

5. Words like *each, every, any, everybody, anybody* are always singular.

> **Each** of the witnesses **is** [not are] telling a different story. (*Each* means *Each one*—singular)
> **Every** programmer **has [not have]** a work assignment. (*Every programmer*—singular)
> **Everyone** from both departments **was [not were]** here for the meeting. (Look for the singular word "*one*" in "*everyone*")

Notice that *somebody* contains the singular word *body*—and so does *anybody*.

Practice Activity: Subject-Verb Agreement

Instructions: Choose the correct word in each sentence. When you're finished, check your answers below.

- Five minutes (isn't, aren't) long enough to fill out the form correctly.
- One of the windows (wasn't, weren't) locked.
- Neither the students nor their professor (was, were) familiar with the emergency procedure.

- Either the backup system or the locks (is, are) malfunctioning.
- Advertising for new positions (is, are) going to be posted tomorrow.
- Departmental policy about interviews (needs, need) to be reviewed by an attorney.
- Each of the witnesses (is, are) telling us a slightly different story.
- All of the witnesses (is, are) in agreement on some of the details, however.
- There (is, are) problems with Praeger's proposal.
- There (is, are) a good reason why the dean has doubts about this project.

ANSWERS Practice Activity: Subject-Verb Agreement

1. Five minutes (**isn't**, aren't) long enough to fill out the form correctly. [*Five minutes* is a single unit of time]

2. **One** of the windows (**wasn't**, weren't) locked.

3. Neither the students nor **their professor** (**was**, were) familiar with the emergency procedure.

4. Either the backup system or **the locks** (is, **are**) malfunctioning.

5. **Advertising** for new positions (**is**, are) going to be posted tomorrow.

6. **Departmental policy** about interviews (**needs**, need) to be reviewed by an attorney.

7. **Each** of the witnesses (**is**, are) telling us a slightly different story.

8. **All** of the witnesses (is, **are**) in agreement on some of the details, however.

9. There (is, **are**) **problems** with Praeger's proposal.

10. There (**is**, are) **a good reason** why the dean has doubts about this project.

Chapter 33

Prepositions

The grammatical term *preposition* sounds intimidating to many people. But it doesn't have to be. The simple truth is that you've been using prepositions ever since you learned how to speak...and you've probably used them correctly most of the time. As a serious writer you need to learn only a few usage rules about prepositions.

What are prepositions? They are small, ordinary words that indicate direction or purpose: *in, by, for, with, to, of, on, over, under, beside, near, along*...you can probably think of many more.

Prepositional phrases are small word groups that begin with prepositions: *in the garden, by the sea, for a year, with my sister, to the store*, and so on.

Here are the usage points you need to know:

1. Most of the time prepositional phrases are **extra** ("soft") parts of sentences (p. 111). When you're analyzing a sentence, you should usually skip over the prepositional phrase to get to the really important parts.

A change in city policies are causing headaches for construction inspectors.
INCORRECT

What is the sentence really about? Answer: A change. "City policies" aren't causing the headaches: The *change* is.

So the sentence needs to be corrected:

A change in city policies is causing headaches for construction inspectors.
CORRECT

(You can learn more by reading about Rule 4 on p. 196.)

2. You can use a comma when a sentence begins with a prepositional phrase. Note, though, that many good writers omit the comma if the prepositional phrase

is short. It's your choice.

On Tuesdays the building commissioner meets with the mayor. [No comma: *On Tuesdays* is a short prepositional phrase.]

Under the subflooring in the apartment next door, I found black mold on the joists. [Use a comma: *Under the subflooring in the apartment next door* is a long prepositional phrase.]

You can learn more about these commas by reading about Comma Rule 1 beginning on p. 165.

3. Shorten the sentence and use your ear when a pronoun (*he, she, him, her, I, me,* etc.) follows a preposition.

I gave the report to her for proofreading. CORRECT [not "to she"]

I gave the report to Fakir and her before I delivered it to the mayor. CORRECT [not "to Fakir and she"]

Joan Strang thanked me for the thoughtful gift. CORRECT

Joan Strang thanked Officer Brown and me for the thoughtful gift. CORRECT

You can learn more about sentences like these by reading about the "Thumb Rule" on p. 188.

4. Use prepositions with precision. Notice the different meanings in these two sentences:

Mr. McCaffrey walked in the room. [He spent time walking around the room.]

Mr. McCaffrey walked into the room. [He entered the room.] CORRECT

Practice Activity: Prepositions

Instructions: Correct the errors in the sentences below. Not all sentences contain errors. When you're finished, check your answers below.

1. In an apartment on the second floor I found two cross-connections.

2. An array of arc fault circuit interrupters, ground fault circuit interrupters, and tamper-resistant receptacles was displayed on a table at our booth at the fair.

3. A decision about criminal charges for the unlicensed contractors are

expected by tomorrow morning.

4. For now the new commissioner is trying to getting to know the inspectors.

5. By the end of next October we will be ready to discuss the new budget.

6. Under the sink in the kitchen I found a leaking trap.

7. Misuse of temporary heaters by contractors cause property loss.

8. Of all the applicants for the position Patricia Cooney seems most qualified.

9. An assortment of problems were found when we checked the report.

10. For the most part unlicensed contractors don't seem to understand the seriousness of what they've done.

ANSWERS Practice Activity: Prepositions

1. In an apartment on the second floor, I found two cross-connections.

2. An array of arc fault circuit interrupters, ground fault circuit interrupters, and tamper-resistant receptacles was displayed on a table at our booth at the fair.

3. A decision about criminal charges for the unlicensed contractors is expected by tomorrow morning.

4. For now the new commissioner is trying to get to know the inspectors.

5. By the end of next October, we will be ready to discuss the new budget.

6. Under the sink in the kitchen I found a leaking trap.

7. Misuse of temporary heaters by contractors causes property loss.

8. Of all the applicants for the position, Patricia Cooney seems most qualified.

9. An assortment of problems was found when checked the report.

10. For the most part, unlicensed contractors don't seem to understand the seriousness of what they've done.

Chapter 34

Comparisons

"Better than," "as good as," "rather than": These kinds of comparisons sometimes appear in essays, articles, and reports. Good writers know there are some pitfalls to watch for when you're using these and similar words to make comparisons.

1. Remember that our English language is often concerned with the numbers *two* and *three*:

- Use *-er* comparisons (*better*, *faster*, *older*, and similar words) when you're comparing **two** people or things. (The word *worse* and phrases beginning with *more* also fall into this category.)

- Use *-est* words when you're comparing **three or more** people or things. (The word *best* and phrases beginning with *most* also fall into this category.)

Gail is *more* experienced than Donald.   (comparing two people)
Gail is the *most* experienced writer in our office. (comparing three or more people)
If you'd spent some time riding with Larry and Tom, you'd know that Larry is the *better* driver.   (comparing two people)
Larry is the *best* driver in our fleet.   (comparing three or more people)

2. Be sure to use *than* (not *then*) in comparisons.

I'd rather work on Saturday than Sunday. CORRECT
The coffee from the staff canteen is better than the coffee in the mess hall. CORRECT
Alan is usually more thorough than she.   [she is]

3. When you're writing a comparison sentence, pay extra attention to pronouns (*he*, *she*, *I*, *we*, and so on). Take a look at the last example. Many people

would (incorrectly) write it this way:

Alan is usually more thorough than her. INCORRECT

If you add an extra word ("is," in this sentence), you can hear that **she** is needed:

Alan is usually more thorough than she is.
Alan is usually more thorough than she.

By keeping these pointers in mind, you can handle comparisons effectively every time. (To review using pronouns in comparisons, go to p. 189.)

Practice Activity: Comparisons

Instructions: Choose the correct word in each sentence below. When you're finished, check your answers below.

1. I'd rather stay home tonight (than, then) go to the party.

2. Margaret is nearly as good at carpentry as (he, him).

3. Brock is the (best, better) of the two drivers.

4. Out of all the places I've lived, I like Savannah (best, better).

5. Few people work as hard as (we, us) in the produce department.

6. Calvin is the (worse, worst) driver in the department.

7. I'm good at setting up spreadsheets in Excel, and Gary knows almost as much as (I, me).

8. I like outdoor work much more (than, then) sitting in an office cubicle.

9. I tried both laptops, and this one is definitely (better, best).

10. Which of the three applicants is (more, most) qualified?

ANSWERS Practice Activity: Comparisons

1. I'd rather stay home tonight (**than**, then) go to the party.

2. Margaret is nearly as good at carpentry as (**he**, him). [*he is*]

3. Brock is the (best, **better**) of the two drivers.

4. Out of all the places I've lived, I like Savannah (**best**, better).

5. Few people work as hard as (**we**, us) in the produce department. [*we do*]

6. Calvin is the (worse, **worst**) driver in the department.

7. I'm good at setting up spreadsheets in Excel, and Gary knows almost as much as (**I,** me). [*I do*]

8. I like outdoor work much more (**than**, then) sitting in an office cubicle.

9. I tried both laptops, and this one is definitely (**better**, best).

10. Which of the three applicants is (more, **most**) qualified?

Chapter 35

Capital Letters

Capital letters aren't difficult. Most people know about capitalizing personal names, months of the year, days of the week, and place names. A few special rules sometimes cause difficulty, however. This chapter will help you master those rules (they're simple, when you think about them).

Capital letters present special challenges today because texting is so popular. It's easy (and a serious mistake!) to fall into texting practices when you're typing a report. Always capitalize *I* and the names of people and places, and be sure to apply all the rules in this chapter in every job-related writing task.

Capital Letters Made Simple

1. Capitalize words like *North*, *South*, and so on only when they refer to specific parts of a nation: Midwest, Northeast, the South, the Deep South, and so on. Use lower case the rest of the time.

> I grew up in the Northeast but moved to the Midwest after I married.
> Several fires have occurred in the northeast section of town.

2. Capitalize anything that might appear on a sign. Otherwise, use lower case.

> My sister is away at college until November.
> My sister attends Florida Southern College.

> I think you need to go to the hospital.
> North Shore Hospital has an excellent reputation.

> The shop at the corner of First and Broadway was robbed last night.
> After my last class, I often have a snack at Sam's Snack Shop.

3. Capitalize days and months, but not seasons.

> Every winter our workload decreases as the pace of construction slows.

December usually sees an increase in frozen pipes.

Every Tuesday we have a staff meeting.

4. *Always* capitalize languages.

Inspector Perez grew up speaking both English and Spanish.

Does anyone here speak Arabic?

5. Don't capitalize other academic subjects unless they're part of the title of a course. Don't capitalize careers.

I enjoyed biology in high school, but I didn't like physics.

In Home Economics 101, I learned the science behind many common cooking practices.

Adam is planning to become a youth minister.

6. Capitalize words like *Mother, Father, Aunt,* and *Pastor* only when they're used as people's names. (*Doctor* becomes *Dr.* with a name.)

Did you talk to Mother about her plans for the weekend?

My mother is proud that I chose a career as a building inspector.

We invited Pastor Taylor and Rabbi Levine to the committee meeting about housing the homeless.

We invited both a rabbi and a priest to give invocations.

You should see a doctor about that mole.

I have a lot of faith in Dr. Parker.

7. Be careful with titles of books, articles, poems, movies, and so on. Capitalize every word except coordinating conjunctions, prepositions, and articles—but capitalize them as well if they're the first or last word in a title.

Every Way but Up

Climbing Your Way up the Ladder of Success

Gone with the Wind

All about Eve

Practice Activity: Capital Letters

Instructions: Make corrections where needed in the sentences below. When you're finished, check your answers below.

1. My mother, father, and grandfather proudly attended my graduation from north central police academy two years ago.

2. Although english and science have never been easy for me, I'm thinking of enrolling in college this fall.

3. The professor who teaches Art History has an excellent reputation.

4. You'll enjoy taking Creative Writing I and II with professor Henry.

5. The college is going to erect a new administration building in the northwest corner of the campus.

6. I'm seriously thinking about becoming an Engineer, and my sister plans to become an Architect.

7. I had many questions about gardening in the deep south when we moved from Michigan to Florida.

8. Our girl scout troop met weekly during the school year and did special projects in the Summer when school was out.

9. Although Mr. Gottlieb is retired, Tracy elementary school still displays the safety posters he made.

10. After working as a phlebotomist for two years, Will decided he wanted to become a registered nurse.

ANSWERS Practice Activity: Capital Letters

1. My mother, father, and grandfather proudly attended my graduation from North Central Police Academy two years ago.

2. Although English and science have never been easy for me, I'm thinking of enrolling in college this fall.

3. The professor who teaches art history has an excellent reputation.

4. You'll enjoy taking Creative Writing I and II with Professor Henry.

5. The college is going to erect a new administration building in the

northwest corner of the campus.

6. I'm seriously thinking about becoming an engineer, and my sister plans to become an architect.

7. I had many questions about gardening in the Deep South when we moved from Michigan to Florida.

8. Our Girl Scout troop met weekly during the school year and did special projects in the summer when school was out.

9. Although Mr. Gottlieb is retired, Tracy Elementary School still displays the safety posters he made.

10. After working as a phlebotomist for two years, Will decided he wanted to become a registered nurse.

Chapter 36

Confusing Words

A/An

When you're thinking about *a/an*, go by the sound, not the spelling. "A uniform" is like "a youthful offender." "A uniform" is not like "an uncle."

> He was wearing a uniform issued by the Red Robin Casino.
> He became an uncle when his sister's daughter was born.

Advice/Advise

Advice is a noun (a thing). *Advise* is an action.

> I often asked Inspector Jones for advice when I was new to the department.
> I would advise you to get medical attention for those bruises.

All ready/Already

All ready means "all prepared." *Already* means "by this time."

> The lunches are all ready and set up in the mess hall.
> We've already been to that apartment building twice.

All right, a lot

In the United States, *always* two words. There are no exceptions.

Between/Among

Use *between* for two people or things, *among* for three or more.

> The hiring committee is trying to decide between two qualified candidates.
> Cooper, Daniels, and Peterson divided the inspections among themselves.

Break/Brake

Break means "shatter" or "separate"; *brake* refers to stopping and the pedal in a car.

I had to break my appointment to talk with the mayor.

The brake pedal doesn't feel right.

Breath/Breathe

Breath is a noun (a thing). *Breathe* is an action.

I smelled an alcoholic beverage on his breath.

The medic asked her to breathe deeply while he listened to her lungs.

Complement/Compliment

Complement refers to completeness or making something complete. *Compliment* means "praise."

A full complement of officers attended the ceremony.

I want to compliment you on the way you handled that incident.

Comprise/Compose

Comprise means "include." *Compose* means "made up of."

The committee comprised all 15 department heads.

The committee is composed of representatives from every agency.

Eminent/Imminent

Eminent means "famous" or "respected." *Imminent* means "about to happen."

She is an eminent authority on DNA.

Although there's no imminent danger, you need to fix the brakes.

Good/Well

Use *good* with nouns; use *well* with actions. (*Good* is an adjective; *well* is a verb.) *Well* also can be an adjective meaning "healthy."

That was a good meal.

He did well on his certification exam.

Portia missed the party because she wasn't feeling well.

Imply/Infer

Imply means "to hint." *Infer* means "to deduce."

> Landers said she struck her husband because he implied she was having an affair.
> I inferred that Rogers would be out sick for at least a week.

Its/It's

Its is a possessive word (like *his*) and does not use an apostrophe. *It's* means *it is*. The apostrophe replaces the missing *i*. Never put an apostrophe after *its*.

> Her car is overdue for its oil change.
> I have to hurry because it's almost time for our meeting.

Less/Fewer

Use *less* when you're comparing amounts that can't be counted, like noise. You should also use *less* in expressions like *less than one*. Use *fewer* when you're comparing things you can count, like fasteners or victims.

> The storm left less damage than we were expecting. ["Damage" can't be counted.]
> She received fewer votes than Kay did. ["Votes" can be counted.]

Lay/Lie

Use *lay* when you place something. Use *lie* (not lay) to refer to resting, napping, and sleeping. (*Lay* is done to things; *lie* is something you do yourself.)

> Don't lay anything on that desk; it needs to be dusted first.
> Sanders was lying on the sofa watching a football game.

Lose/Loose

Lose means "misplace" or "get rid of." *Loose* means "not tight."

> When he realized he was going to lose the argument, Felder hit his wife.
> Now that I've lost 15 pounds, these pants are loose.

More/Most

Use *more* to compare two things or two persons; use *most* for three or more.

Phyllis is the more skillful of the twins.

He is the most disrespectful student in the class.

Of/Have

Don't substitute *of* for *have* when you need a helping verb.

Mattson could ~~of~~ have left through the bedroom window.

Passed/Past

Passed is an action that already happened. *Past* is an adjective referring to a previous time.

Karen said she passed out after taking a few breaths of the gas.

In the past, inspectors wrote their reports by hand or on a typewriter.

Be careful not to write *pasted* ("glued") when you mean *passed*.

Patients/Patience

Patients are people treated by a healthcare professional. *Patience* is the quality of waiting without complaint.

Many of Dr. Morrow's patients came to him for mood-altering prescriptions.

A successful police investigation requires patience and skill.

Personal/Personnel

Personal means "private" or "intimate." *Personnel* are employees.

Jackson kept his personal papers in a locked drawer.

All personnel were asked to stay in the office for a special meeting.

Pre-

This prefix is often unnecessary. There's no difference between *registration* and *pre-registration*, *paid* and *pre-paid*, and *existing* and *pre-existing*.

Principal/Principle

A *principal* is the director of a school; *principal* is also an amount of money that has been borrowed or invested, and it's an adjective meaning important. A *principle* is a truth, rule, or law.

The principal wants to expand the D.A.R.E. program in her school.

Our principal concern is the possibility of a fire.

Having high principles and sticking to them is vital to the code enforcement profession.

Quiet/Quite

Quiet means "not noisy." *Quite* means "rather" or "very."

It was two a.m. before the dorm was quiet again.

The evidence is quite clear.

Saw/Seen

Use *saw* by itself, and *seen* with a helping verb (*am, is, are, was, were, has, have, had*).

I saw the manager before he spotted me.

We have already seen good results from the new training program.

Stationary/Stationery

Stationary means "not moving." *Stationery* refers to paper products used for correspondence.

I spend 15 minutes on a stationary exercise bicycle every morning.

Please order a new box of our official department stationery.

Supposed to, Used to

Make sure you've inserted a "d" at the end:

We're supposed to meet Jamal at the library in half an hour.

Gino used to live in Detroit, so he's a huge Red Wings fan.

Than/Then

Than is a comparison word; *then* is a time word.

Sometimes a dog's nose is more sensitive than our sophisticated laboratory equipment.

If you're interested in advancement, then you should think about going back to college.

Their/There/They're

Their refers to ownership by two or more people. *There* is an adverb similar to "here." *They're* is a contraction of "they are."

The junk dealer took all their old parts.

Melissa saw a leak there and called a plumber.

There are two witnesses waiting to be interviewed about the incident.

They're all in agreement about what happened.

To/Too/Two

To indicates direction or purpose. *Too* means "excessive" or "also." *Two* is a number.

I'm going to the materials lab to submit concrete cores for analysis.

Chen and Wu said they were too frightened to call police.

Horvat is interested in a criminal career too.

I spent two hours searching the database.

Who/Whom

Whom is like "him" (notice the final *m* that they both share). *Who* is like "he."

We're trying to discover who had the combination to the safe. [like *he had the combination*]

The officer who did this should be commended. [like *he did this*]

The neighbor whom I talked to described the suspect. [like *talked to him*]

Note: *Whom* is disappearing. It's not needed unless you're writing formally.

Your/You're

Your means "belonging to you." *You're* is a contraction of "you are."

I'm impressed with the thoroughness of your report.

When you're finished, the data will go into our annual report.

Practice Activity: Words Often Confused

Instructions: Make any corrections needed in the sentence below. When you're finished, check your answers below.

1. Were assigned to the committee that's drawing up a policy about travel.

2. Not all agency personal travel to meetings and conferences, so its hard to be fair to everyone.

3. Your going to find that an uniform doesn't automatically earn you respect.

4. If its alright with the chief, we'll replace alot of the exercise equipment.

5. Safety should always be our principle concern.

6. If the report is to long, I'll help you cut it, and Mike can help us to.

7. 7. Janet's M.A. in psychology compliments her business experience.

8. That car just past me going sixty in a 30 mph zone.

9. The courtroom became quite when Caruso went to the stand to testify.

10. Whom is going to meet with the city council tomorrow?

ANSWERS Practice Activity: Words Often Confused

1. We're assigned to the committee that's drawing up a policy about travel.

2. Not all agency personnel travel to meetings and conferences, so it's hard to be fair to everyone.

3. You're going to find that a uniform doesn't automatically earn you respect.

4. If it's all right with the chief, we'll replace a lot of the exercise equipment.

5. Safety should always be our principal concern.

6. If the report is too long, I'll help you cut it, and Mike can help us too.

7. Janet's M.A. in psychology complements her business experience.

8. That car just passed me going sixty mph in a thirty mph zone.

9. The courtroom became quiet when Caruso went to the stand to testify.

10. Who is going to meet with the city council tomorrow?

Chapter 37

Avoiding Common Errors

This chapter is a refresher about usage points that cause problems for many writers. Take a look at these quick, easy-to-understand explanations. In just a few minutes you can clear up some of the most common mistakes found in code enforcement reports.

1. Not ending sentences with a period:

Here's a quick lesson: Extra ideas end with commas. Sentences end with periods. (See p. 102 for more help.)

When Carol asked to borrow my car, EXTRA IDEA
Carol asked to borrow my car. SENTENCE

Although the course was difficult, EXTRA IDEA
The course was difficult. SENTENCE

Here's how to put extra ideas and sentences together:

When Carol asked to borrow my car, I handed her the keys. CORRECT
Although the course was difficult, I managed to earn a B. CORRECT

2. Not knowing what a sentence is:

Here's another quick lesson: A sentence begins with a person, place, or thing.

He ran out the door. SENTENCE
After he ran out the door, EXTRA IDEA

After he ran out the door, Clara called 911. CORRECT

It's a sentence even if it's short or unclear:

I understand. SENTENCE
He did. SENTENCE
It is here. SENTENCE

215

Go to p. 176 for more help with periods, and to p. 165 for more help with commas.

3. Using a comma instead of a period to start a new sentence with *it*:

Good writers use a period to end a sentence before beginning a new one.

The rope broke, it wasn't strong enough. INCORRECT
The rope broke. It wasn't strong enough.   CORRECT

I rejected her explanation, it didn't make sense. INCORRECT
I rejected her explanation. It didn't make sense. CORRECT

4. Getting pronouns mixed up (*I/me, he/him, she/her, we/us, they/them*):

Jim and me attended the meeting. INCORRECT (Think: I attended the meeting.)
Jim and I inspected the warehouse. CORRECT

Professor Kovac gave Cynthia and I a special assignment. INCORRECT (Think: *Professor Kovac gave **me** a special assignment.*)
Professor Kovac gave Cynthia and **me** a special assignment. CORRECT

I spoke to he and his wife about the discount. INCORRECT. (Think: *I spoke to **him**.*)
I spoke to him and his wife about the discount. CORRECT

For more help with these pronouns, go to p. 188 and read about the Thumb Rule.

5. Using unnecessary apostrophes with the letter *s*:

Here's a refresher: Use apostrophes only in contractions (*don't, can't*) and "of" ideas (*Mary's car, Tom's schedule*). Apostrophes aren't decorations, and they don't mean "more than one."

The cars will be replaced in two years. (no "of" ideas, and no apostrophes) CORRECT
John's laptop isn't working properly. (laptop of John) CORRECT
The Browns are taking a vacation next month. (no "of" ideas, and no apostrophes) CORRECT
My uniform doesn't need to be dry cleaned until next week. (*doesn't* is a contraction) CORRECT

216

Go to p. 180 for a review of apostrophes.

6. Putting a comma after a subordinate or coordinate conjunction:

Sounds intimidating! But actually those conjunctions are words you use every day: *and*, *but*, *if*, *when*, *because*, *although*, and so on. Don't put commas after them. (If you need a comma, put it *before* the conjunction.)

I walked around the whole perimeter of the store but, I didn't see or hear anything. INCORRECT

I walked around the whole perimeter of the store, but I didn't see or hear anything. CORRECT

I walked around the whole perimeter of the store but didn't see or hear anything. CORRECT

Be especially careful with *although*. Anything that starts with *although* is an extra idea that has to be attached to a real sentence (and of course you'll never put a comma after *although*):

He insisted on driving his car home. Although, his friends tried to stop him. INCORRECT

He insisted on driving his car home although his friends tried to stop him. CORRECT

For more help with Comma Rule 1, go to p. 165.

7. Misspelling *all right* and *a lot*:

All right and *a lot* are always two words. Always. There are no exceptions. You can check the dictionary to verify this: It will tell you that the common one-word spellings are "nonstandard," meaning that professionals never use them.

Leon told me he was all right and didn't need medical attention.

Denise said she'd heard a lot of yelling coming from the Wrights' apartment.

8. Misusing quotation marks:

Use quotation marks *only* for a person's *exact* words. If you change the words, omit the quotation marks.

When you use quotation marks, always put commas and periods inside.

217

There are no exceptions in the United States. Go to p. 185 for more help.

Casey said, "I was afraid the wall would collapse, so I ordered the workers to evacuate."

Casey said she was afraid the wall would collapse, so she ordered the workers to evacuate.

9. Using texting style:

Because texting is so popular, many people have become careless about abbreviations and capital letters. Beware! If you text often, ask someone to check your reports to make sure you haven't slipped into texting style.

I will call u when i no the location for our September meeting. INCORRECT
I will call you when I know the location for our September meeting. CORRECT

10. Misusing verbs or forgetting to use "helping verbs" like *is, are, was, were, has, have,* and *had*:

Writing the way you speak can cause huge problems. Be especially careful with commonly misused verbs like *seen, went, did,* and *done.*

My partner and I seen her get into her car. INCORRECT
My partner and I saw her get into her car. CORRECT

After I had went to the parking garage, Thompson changed his story.
INCORRECT
After I had gone to the parking garage, Thompson changed his story.
CORRECT

Wilkes said he done everything by four o'clock. INCORRECT
Wilkes said he did everything by four o'clock. CORRECT
Wilkes said he had done everything by four o'clock. CORRECT

Practice Activity: Avoiding Common Errors

Instructions: Correct any errors in the sentences below. When you're finished, check your answers below.

1. When I seen smoke coming from the engine, I called the fire department.

2. The lock is sticking, it probably needs some graphite.

3. Alot of inspectors are watching the weather closely because, the US Weather Service is predicting a hurricane.

4. I don't no the answer to that question but i will find the answer for you.

5. Many people think that crime rates go up every year but, in many places crime rates have gone down.

6. Although I gave the data to Mary Alice was the one who entered it into the database.

7. When I questioned Fischer about the missing batteries', he said, "he didn't know what happened to them."

8. Later his boss said "I don't allow no workers to remove batteries from the shop".

9. We done everything we could to prepare our headquarters for the open house next Saturday.

10. I'm signing up for a Spanish course next month although, French might be more useful in some neighborhoods.

ANSWERS Practice Activity: Avoiding Common Errors

1. When I ~~seen~~ saw smoke coming from the engine, I called the fire department.

2. The lock is sticking. It probably needs some graphite. OR The lock is sticking; it probably needs some graphite.

3. ~~Alot~~ A lot of inspectors are watching the weather closely because the US Weather Service is predicting a hurricane.

4. I don't ~~no~~ know the answer to that question, but ~~i~~ I will find the answer for you.

5. Many people think that crime rates go up every year, but in many places

219

crime rates have gone down.

6. Although I gave the data to Mary, Alice was the one who entered it into the database.

7. When I questioned Fischer about the missing batteries, he said he didn't know what happened to them.

8. Later his boss said, "I don't allow ~~no~~ any workers to remove batteries from the shop."

9. We ~~done~~ did everything we could to prepare our headquarters for the open house next Saturday.

10. I'm signing up for a Spanish course next month although French might be more useful in some neighborhoods.

Part Seven

Write Like a Pro

Chapter 38

Mistakes Pros Make

Over the years I've worked on both sides of the editorial desk. When I write an article or book that's accepted for publication, an editor gets in touch with me with suggestions (sometimes demands!) for changes and corrections. I've also worked as an editor myself, so sometimes I'm the one who decides whether to accept (or reject) a submission, and I'm also the one who recommends changes and requests corrections.

My experience with correcting both my own work and the work of other writers has taught me a lot about writing. There are errors and problems that occur again and again in the writing that I edit. I also see them in the reading I do for pleasure.

This chapter is aimed primarily at writers who want to publish their work. But if you're a student, you can start learning these advanced principles now, so that you're ready for the professional world later on. As a bonus, you'll be able to solve writing problems that confuse many students.

Indefinite Pronoun Reference

A pronoun is a word that takes the place of a noun. Some common pronouns are *he, him, she, her, they, them, that, which, these, those, and it.* If you're a strict grammarian, you make sure that each pronoun stands for something definite. This is a sticky problem that some writers struggle to solve. The pronoun and the person or thing it refers to (which grammarians call an *antecedent*) have to match *perfectly.*

Take a look at this example:

He never returned my call, which made it impossible to solve the problem.

INCORRECT

What made it impossible to solve the problem? *Ignoring your call*—but you don't see those exact words in the sentence. What you see in the sentence is something slightly different: *He never returned my call.* That's not close enough for someone who's strict about grammar! As a result, *which* is an indefinite pronoun reference.

Most professional writers would find a way to avoid that vague *which*:

> He never returned my call, making it impossible to solve the problem.
> CORRECT

> Because he never returned my call, I couldn't solve the problem. CORRECT

Here's an example of an indefinite pronoun reference from a professional writer. What's interesting is that she's an editor herself! The author is Mary Norris, a well-known stickler for good usage, and the book is *Between You & Me: Confessions of a Comma Queen.* (By the way, "danglers" will be our next topic.)

> For many danglers, there is no perfect fix, which can make the writer, and sometimes the editor, want to retain the original, even if it's technically flawed.

What makes writers and editors "want to retain the original"? *The lack of a perfect fix.* But those exact words don't appear in the sentence. As a result, "which" is an indefinite pronoun reference. Here's how you could rewrite the sentence to eliminate the problem:

> For many danglers, there is no perfect fix. Consequently the writer, and sometimes the editor, may want to retain the original, even if it's technically flawed. CORRECT

Often the solution to a usage problem is to break the sentence in two. The less complicated your structure is, the less likely you to run into trouble.

A more common problem is a pronoun (*he, she, him, her*) that could refer to two people:

> Aunt Betty suggested that she and Aunt Peggy spend the weekend at her condo in Port Charlotte. INCORRECT

Who owns the condo? You can't be sure. Never use *she/her* in a sentence about two females. This version is clear:

> Aunt Betty suggested that she and Aunt Peggy spend the weekend at Aunt Betty's condo in Port Charlotte. CORRECT

Similarly, don't use *he/him* in a sentence about two males:

> Carl asked David what was causing the fruit to drop from his apple tree. INCORRECT

Whose apple tree? Again, you can't be sure. This version is clear:

> Carl asked David what was causing the fruit to drop from David's apple tree. CORRECT

Misplaced ("Dangling") Modifiers

The term "misplaced modifier" may sound like English teachers' jargon, but it points to a real-world writing problem you should avoid in your reports. (Another name for this problem is "dangler" or "dangling modifier.")

"Misplaced" means *hanging*, and a "modifier" is a *description*. So a "misplaced modifier" is a description in the wrong place. Most misplaced modifiers are easy to spot because they sound ridiculous. Take a look at these examples, and *think* about what is said:

> Leaking in several places, Othmar knew the radiator needed replacement. MISPLACED MODIFIER
> The officer spotted the bloodstained shirt searching for evidence. MISPLACED MODIFIER
> I heard a scream walking into the living room. MISPLACED MODIFIER

Here are the corrected sentences:

> Because the radiator was leaking in several places, Othmar knew it needed replacement. CORRECT
> Searching for evidence, the officer spotted the bloodstained shirt. CORRECT
> Walking into the living room, I heard a scream. CORRECT

Sometimes misplaced modifiers are harder to spot. To many people, this sentence probably looks correct on first reading—but it isn't:

Stepping on the gas pedal, the car roared down the highway. MISPLACED MODIFIER

There are two problems with the sentence. First, the car didn't step on the gas pedal! Second, the sentence doesn't specify *who* did. Here's the corrected sentence:

When Wilson stepped on the gas pedal, the car roared down the highway
CORRECT

Did you notice that misplaced modifiers tend to start with an *-ing* word? Of course you can start sentences that way—but you need to be careful that you don't slip into a misplaced modifier. Here again are two *correct* sentences that start with *–ing* words:

Searching for evidence, the officer spotted the bloodstained shirt. CORRECT
Walking into the living room, I heard a scream. CORRECT

Parallel Construction

Even professional writers with many years of experience sometimes make parallelism errors when they write sentences with three parts. Knowing how to use parallel construction correctly will make your writing stand out! Here's an example of a sentence *without* parallelism:

The room had mold on the ceiling, the walls, and the floor was buckling.
INCORRECT

Here are two ways to correct it:

The room had mold on the ceiling and the walls. The floor was buckling.
CORRECT
The room had mold on the ceiling and the walls, and the floor was buckling.
CORRECT

Here are some suggestions for fixing parallelism problems:

- Pay special attention to sentences with three parts
- Remember that the third part is usually the problem
- Try thinking of the sentence as a little poem

Let's try that "little poem" strategy with the previous example so you can see how it works:

The room had mold on

- the ceiling

- the walls

- the floor was buckling

You can quickly see that "the floor was buckling" doesn't match the other two parts. The easiest solution is to make two sentences: *The room had mold on the ceiling and walls. The floor was buckling.*

This sentence about mold would work if there were three items that matched "had mold on":

The room had mold on

- the ceiling

- the walls

- the floor

Here's how the corrected sentence would read: *The room had mold on the ceiling, walls, and the floor.*

Let's try another example:

Aidan and I approved the menu, checked the guest list, and inspected the rest rooms.

To check this sentence for correctness, think of it as a little poem:

Aidan and I

- approved

- checked

- inspected

You can see that all parts match: *approved, checked, inspected*. The sentence is correct:

Aidan and I approved the menu, checked the guest list, and inspected the rest rooms. CORRECT

Overloaded Sentences

Sometimes professional writers try to cram too much information into a sentence. Here's an overloaded sentence from *The New Yorker*:

Her mother, Rachel Faucette, the daughter of an Englishwoman and a Frenchman, inherited her father's Nevis plantation at sixteen, and was married off, very young, to Johann Michael Lavien, an older Danish man with aspirations to be a planter.

Notice how many facts have been included in this one sentence. Rachel Faucette:

- was someone's mother
- was the daughter of an Englishwoman and a Frenchman
- inherited his Nevis plantation when she was sixteen
- married Johann Michael Lavien
- was young when she married

Oh, and there are three more pieces of information: Her husband was older and Danish, and he aspired to be a planter. Too much! I once had a professor whose motto was "One idea per sentence." That's good advice.

Problems with Sources

If you're working on a writing project that includes sources such as endnotes, footnotes, works cited lists and bibliographies, make sure they're easy for readers to use. Suppose, for example, you include a quotation from American philosopher

Ralph Waldo Emerson. When you document the quotation, be sure to give the title of the work as well as the page number.

I often come across endnotes that refer to, say, p. 54 of Volume I of *The Collected Works of Ralph Waldo Emerson*. How likely is the average reader to have the complete set? It's ten volumes, and each one costs over $100. If, however, the author mentions that the quotation comes from Emerson's essay "The American Scholar," I can find it in another collection of Emerson's work.

Another helpful practice is to include the chapter titles if you're listing endnotes in the back of a book. When endnotes are listed with a minimum of information—"Chapter 1"—readers looking for a particular endnote have to thumb through the book to find out which chapter they're reading. Including the chapter title—"Shaw's Childhood" or "Voter Suppression"—would make the search easier.

Getting the Details Right

One trademark of true professionals is their insistence on getting the details right. They're careful with spelling, punctuation, and capital letters. Because the average human brain can hold only a limited amount of information, pros don't rely on their memories. Instead, they make frequent use of resources, such as asking a librarian for help with sticky questions.

For example, a professional will never guess at the spelling of someone's name. Is it *Katherine, Catherine, Katharine,* or *Kathryn*? Jody or Jodie? O'Brien or O'Brian? You might also be working with someone whose name has an unusual spelling: *Barbra* instead of *Barbara*, or *Soozie* instead of *Susie*. What to do? Check. If the person you're writing to works for a company with an online directory, you can find the correct spelling there. If not, a phone call is in order.

Company names can be just as tricky. *Walgreens* does not have an apostrophe, but *Macy's* does. There's no "wagon" in *Volkswagen*. *Walmart* no longer has an apostrophe. There's no "u" in *Qantas*, and *Super Bowl* is two words, not one.

The Internet makes it easy to verify spelling and punctuation. If you're really stuck, a phone call to the library will usually clear things up. (Remember that reference librarians are paid to answer questions—they'll be happy to help you!)

Another problem you should be careful to avoid is using British spellings (unless you're writing for a publication in the UK). There's one exception, though: *theater*, which is often spelled British style (*theatre*), even in the very American city of New York.

Style guides (often available on the Internet) can help find answers to thorny questions. If the company you're working for has a style guide, you can find out which spelling of ok is preferred (OK? Okay? o.k.?) and how a.m. and p.m. should be written. (AM? PM? By the way, *always* insert a space first: it's 7:30 p.m.) A style guide will also tell you whether to use the final comma in a series (commonly known as an Oxford comma—p. 64) and whether you're supposed to capitalize the first word after a colon.

If your company, agency, or organization doesn't have a style guide, the *Chicago Manual of Style* is a widely accepted usage guide. The *American Heritage Dictionary* employs a prestigious Usage Panel to weigh in on controversies about words. For example, writers today disagree about whether *snuck* is acceptable; some writers still insist on the more traditional *sneaked*. If you check the *American Heritage Dictionary*, you'll learn that the most recent Usage Panel voted 75% in favor of *snuck*. If you get involved in an argument about usage, it's helpful to have some heavy hitters on your side.

The Associated Press also has a useful style guide, but remember that newspapers do things differently, and their practices don't always transfer well to business usage. For example, I'm a strong advocate for capitalizing titles when you're referring to a specific person: the President, the Manager, the Director. Most people work hard to earn those titles, and I like to honor them. But newspapers lower-case all of those terms unless they're followed by a name: the *queen, Queen Elizabeth II, the president, President Roosevelt.* I don't like it, and I'm glad I don't work for a newspaper!

Organizing Your Ideas

Because I'm an editor as well as an author, I've read a large number of submissions from writers hoping to be published. Here are two major mistakes you should avoid:

1. Delaying your main point until the end

You've heard this advice before: State your main point (thesis) on the first page. Disconnected facts and ideas leave readers struggling to figure out where the article is going. Give them a destination right away.

2. Taking detours

This is another problem that's worth mentioning again: Straying from your subject. I've read submissions to the *Shaw Journal* that wander for a page or more without a single mention of Shaw! The remedy for this is to make sure that the first sentence in every paragraph has a relationship to both your thesis and the content of the paragraph. A good way to check for effective organization is to read the thesis and the first paragraph of every paragraph. If they flow naturally, chances are you have a well-organized article.

Another useful trick is to choose a keyword—"Shaw," for example—and make sure it appears often. Sometimes I use the Find function to ensure that my article or book doesn't stray from my main point. If the finder highlights my chosen word many times on each page, there's a good chance that I'm on track. In this book, for example, I've been careful to use the words *write* and *writing* many times.

Advanced Punctuation Marks

1. The colon

A colon is two dots stacked on top of each other: This is an example. There are two principles to keep in mind when you use a colon. The sentence must come to a complete stop, and the second part of the sentence should explain the first. Professional writers have a number of uses for colons:

- introducing a bullet list (like this one)

- writing the greeting of a business letter
- adding a touch of formality to correspondence and reports

Be careful not to interrupt a sentence with a colon: The sentence *must* come to a complete stop.

> The meeting agenda includes: a budget report, a discussion about the vacation policy, and a review of last month's marketing data. INCORRECT

Here are two ways to fix the problem:

> The meeting agenda includes the following: a budget report, a discussion about the vacation policy, and a review of last month's marketing data. CORRECT
> The meeting agenda includes a budget report, a discussion about the vacation policy, and a review of last month's marketing data. CORRECT

Should you use a capital letter after a colon? Practices vary. If you're writing for an organization or a publication, you should ask if there's a style guide (p. 229). If there are no guidelines in place, you can make your own decision about what to do. In this book, I decided to use upper case if a sentence follows the colon, and lower-case the rest of the time.

2. The hyphen

Hyphens are little dashes that join two related words. Here's an example:

> For years Johnny Carson was the king of late-night television. CORRECT

On p. 18 I told you that I used to worry about using hyphens. In fact they made me so nervous that I was afraid to become an editor. Over time, however, I learned that they're not scary at all.

The basic rule is that you should use a hyphen when two or more words meet these criteria: They relate to each other, and they're followed by a noun (a person, place or thing). So, for example, the phrase *back-door key* requires a hyphen. It's not a *back key*; it's a *back-door* key.

> I locked the back door. NO HYPHEN
> I lost my back-door key. HYPHEN

231

Here's another example:

I had a fried-egg sandwich for lunch. HYPHEN

I had a fried egg for breakfast. NO HYPHEN

If the two words don't relate to each other, use a comma rather than a hyphen:

We adopted a fat, playful puppy from the animal shelter. COMMA

And here's a second rule: Don't use a hyphen with an adverb ending with *–ly*:

It always cheers me up to meet a happily married couple CORRECT

The fire department insists that we have clearly marked signs at each exit.
CORRECT

There are two more complications. *Well* is an adverb, but it doesn't end with *–ly*. Should you use a hyphen? An honest answer is...maybe. If you go online to check style guides for various organizations, you'll see that some of them use hyphens with *well*, but others don't.

He's a well known advocate for abused children.

My heart leaps when a student submits a well-written essay.

What should you do? If a style guide is available, follow its guidelines. If not, you can make your own decision. (My own practice is to use a hyphen with *well* most of the time.) Consider asking your organization to appoint a committee to put together a style guide. The suggestion might be appreciated!

Hyphens tend to disappear over time. If you read business reports regularly, you'll notice that some companies are still using hyphens for *life-style, child-care* and *health-care*; other companies write *lifestyle, childcare* and *healthcare* as one word. Many organizations create style guides so that every employee knows the company policy for these words.

3. Semicolons in a list

In Chapter 27 you learned that a semicolon is just like a period, but it's followed by a lower-case letter:

Rain pounded the pavement. We ran for shelter. CORRECT

Rain pounded the pavement; we ran for shelter. CORRECT

There's another way to use semicolons that I'm often asked about when I do workshops for businesses and agencies. Here's the rule: If a list contains an item with a comma, you should separate *all* the items with semicolons.

Here's an ordinary list:

I bought a bunch of bananas, a jar of grapefruit sections, and two apples. COMMAS

But watch what happens if you add an item with a comma—*a big, juicy orange.*

I bought a bunch of bananas; a jar of grapefruit sections; a big, juicy orange; and two apples. SEMICOLONS

Practice Activity: Misplaced Modifiers

Instructions: Make any corrections that are needed in these sentences. Not all sentences need corrections. When you're finished, check your answers below. (Answers may vary.)

1. Holding the tray unsteadily, the platter slid off and crashed to the floor.

2. We spotted Aimee's truck driving down Parker Avenue.

3. After questioning Li, I left my card and asked him to call me.

4. Scattered around the room we saw clothing, jewelry, and cosmetics.

5. Hiding under a rosebush in the back yard, I found the kitten.

ANSWERS Practice Activity: Misplaced Modifiers

(Sentences with misplaced modifiers have been rewritten.)

X 1. Because the server was holding the tray unsteadily, the platter slid off and crashed to the floor.

√ 2. We spotted Aimee's truck driving down Parker Avenue.

√ 3. After questioning Li, I left my card and asked him to call me.

X 4. We saw clothing, jewelry, and cosmetics scattered around the room.

X 5. I found the kitten hiding under a rosebush in the back yard.

Practice Activity: Parallelism

Instructions: Make any corrections needed in the sentences below. Not all sentences need corrections. Check your answers below. (Answers may vary.)

1. For safety Sonia always locked the door, turned on the alarm, and a neighbor had the alarm code.

2. We spent the evening roasting marshmallows, singing camp songs, and one of the counselors told us ghost stories.

3. Each applicant must submit a birth certificate, take a physical examination, and they must come in for an interview.

4. In recent years we've been recruiting more women, minorities, and taking a harder line on racism and sexism.

5. Always check your reports for accuracy, spelling, and completeness.

ANSWERS Practice Activity: Parallelism

1. For safety Sonia always locked the door and turned on the alarm. A neighbor had the alarm code.

2. We spent the evening roasting marshmallows and singing camp songs. One of the counselors told us ghost stories.

3. Each applicant must submit a birth certificate, take a physical examination, and come in for an interview.

4. In recent years we've been recruiting more women and minorities and taking a harder line on racism and sexism.

5. Always check your reports for accuracy, spelling, and completeness.

Practice Activity: Semicolons in a List

Instructions: Arrange the following items in a list. Start your sentence with "I went shopping and bought." The items include:

1. a thick, fluffy rug
2. a reading lamp
3. a small, exquisite vase
4. an alarm clock

Check your answers below.

ANSWER Practice Activity: Semicolons in a List

I went shopping and bought a thick, fluffy rug; a reading lamp; a small, exquisite vase; and an alarm clock.

Chapter 39

Self-Publishing

Everyone should self-publish! If you have word-processing skills and you're willing to learn how the process works, the cost is low—and few projects will give you as much satisfaction as creating your own book. You can publish a 6" x 9" black-and-white paperback book for around five dollars a copy, including shipping. Whether you buy one copy or a thousand, the cost per book is the same.

A book you write can become a gift, memento, or showcase for your imagination—a children's story or collection of your poetry, for example. A memoir can become a cherished family heirloom. You can share your expertise, promote an idea, earn extra money, or stir up support for a favorite cause. You can publish a book about a family reunion (complete with photos), your gardening skills, or your service club's history. You can honor a grandchild, record memories of a beloved pet, or create a cookbook to raise funds for your church.

What Is Self-Publishing?

The technical term is Publishing on Demand (often abbreviated as POD). You write a book, format it, and design a cover. If you deal with a free publisher, your ISBN, cover design, and cover art are free. You can even download a free proof copy to review before your book is finally published. The total cost for all of this is...not a penny. You pay only for books you actually buy (to put under the Christmas tree, for example, or to sell at book signings).

If you use CreateSpace.com, you'll even get a free marketing page on Amazon.com, which will ship the books to your customers for you and deposit your royalties directly into your checking account every month. (If the book is a very personal one, you don't have to put it up for sale to the public.)

Aren't there hidden costs? Not necessarily. I've self-published five paperbacks, and three of them cost me absolutely nothing. The book you're reading cost me a few extra dollars because I purchased some photographs (for a dollar each) from DollarPhotoClub.com (see p. 244). For my book *Gretel's Story* I commissioned original cover art work from an artist. Those have been my only expenses. (Reminder: There are NO paid endorsements in this book. I mention companies only when I've used them extensively as a paid customer and been happy with the results.)

Advice for Self-Publishers

1. Develop your word-processing skills. Learn how to use styles and insert pictures (p. 243). You can pay someone to format your book for you, but it will drive up the price significantly. It's wise to take a couple of classes in word-processing and to invest in a good instructional book.

2. Be meticulous. Double-check any facts in the book. Use the spellchecker and grammar checker that come with your word-processing software, but don't stop there. Reread frequently to make sure you don't miss any errors. Use consistent styles for headings and lists. Ask a friend to help with the proofreading.

3. Respect copyright laws (p. 254).

4. If you're writing a memoir, respect the privacy of others. Ask for a signed release from anyone you're going to write about. Even if you're gracious when you discuss friends and family members, they may not appreciate having their names out in public. Ask first. (The same policy applies to pictures.)

5. Be professional. Take yourself and your project seriously.

6. Consider including extra features to make your book more appealing to buyers. How about adding a section in the back for book clubs, with questions to answer and topics to discuss? If you've written a book for children or young adults, consider creating a teacher's guide with activities and topics for classroom discussions.

7. If the screen name for your personal email account is cute or complicated, set up a professional email account just for book-related emails.

8. Have a professional headshot done by a photographer, put it on the back cover of your book, and use it for marketing (see below).

9. If you're going public with your book, invest some time and thought in your marketing page on Amazon.com. Provide all the information that the author's page asks for. Write a short autobiography, and post your headshot there (and replace it with a new one every five years).

10. Ask friends (and strangers, if you're brave enough) for short endorsements. Put at least one endorsement on the back cover of your book. Save the others for marketing activities (see below).

11. Include an Acknowledgments page where you thank everyone who has helped you (but first make sure they don't mind having their names in print).

12. Don't pressure friends to buy your book. (No one has enough friends to make a book profitable.)

13. Don't rely on word-of-mouth to sell your book. That's your job (see below).

14. Learn how to do marketing.

15. Choose a professional-sounding name for your publishing company. I'm the Maple Leaf Press (in honor of Scott Joplin's "Maple Leaf Rag").

How Much Money Will You Make?

Probably not much. Most self-publishers sell only a few books. Even if you put the squeeze on friends, relatives, college pals, and business associates to buy your book (I'm cringing), you're going to run out of customers very quickly. Free publicity doesn't help much either. The local newspaper printed a lovely article about my *Gretel's Story*, and I did a radio interview that people enjoyed listening to—but I sold only a handful of books as a result.

It's possible to make money, but it isn't easy. Even if your book is marvelous, few people are ever going to hear about it unless you work hard at reaching a national audience. Advertising is astronomically expensive, and there's no guarantee that it will work. (Some of my attempts at paid advertising were disappointing.)

Are you still hoping to earn some cash for your writing? It's possible—and you may even surprise yourself if you handle your writing career in a professional way. Two years ago an educational company discovered my report-writing book online and hired me as a consultant to design three online courses for them. I earned more money through that project than from all the books I sold that year. More recently an educational company hired me as a free-lance blogger on the strength of one of my self-published books.

Here are some suggestions that can help you achieve writing success:

1. Find a need and fill it.

While I was teaching in a police academy, I noticed that report writing was a persistent problem—and there were few books available. Bingo! I started writing *Criminal Justice Report Writing*, self-published it, and have been making money ever since.

2. Produce a quality book.

You don't want a piece of junk that looks like it was dashed off over a long weekend. Think "meticulous" and "professional." Remember that readers are likely to post reviews on Amazon.com. A mediocre book is going to get negative reviews.

3. Study the competition.

Before I wrote *Criminal Justice Report Writing*, I purchased a copy of every competing book to make sure I didn't overlook any information that police officers would be looking for.

4. Learn as much as you can about marketing. (See below.)

5. Promote your book *daily*.

6. Get involved with LinkedIn.

Anyone who's thinking about hiring you in a professional capacity will go to LinkedIn.com (a free social media website for professionals) to check your background. Make sure you've filled out a profile there (p. 242).

7. Consider honing your speaking skills.

Many writers make extra cash by hosting workshops and selling their books afterward to participants. Libraries and service clubs might be happy to feature you and your book. If public speaking makes you nervous, consider joining Toastmasters, a volunteer organization that has changed many lives (Toastmasters.org).

To Market, To Market

Marketing requires time, effort, and imagination—especially if you're doing it on a budget. If you're publishing through CreateSpace, post a carefully written description of your book on the marketing page and Amazon.com, and fill out the author's page. Bear in mind that approximately the first 10% of your book will be posted on your marketing page (the free "Look Inside" feature): Those pages need to *sparkle*. Get at least one endorsement (it doesn't have to be a famous person).

Your second step is to study the free marketing guide available at Smashwords.com (even if you're not publishing an e-book). You'll find many useful strategies there. (But don't forget about the 80-20 Rule I discussed in Chapter 11: Be choosy about how you invest your time, energy, and marketing dollars. Eighty percent of the potential lies in twenty percent of the possibilities.)

Here are some marketing strategies I've used myself:

Blogging

I sell most of my books for police officers through YourPoliceWrite.com, a blog I created that features book covers, descriptions, tables of contents, and a short sales video. Links on my blog send customers to my book page on Amazon.

I'm always looking for fresh content for my blog. I use Google Alerts to keep up with news stories about police reports that I comment on. I also post links to my videos and PowerPoints there, along with many other resources I've developed. I decided to pay for hosting because I had a bad experience with an experiment with a free blog: Some days it would load, while other days it wouldn't—and there was no customer service.

Everything on my blog (except, of course, for the books I'm selling) is free. It seems counterintuitive: Why would anyone pay for my books if I post quality information free? The reality, though, is that the more visitors I get, the more books I sell.

I've invested some time learning about SEO (search engine optimization), and I choose search terms for my blog posts carefully. I subscribe to a daily newsletter about WordPress (my publishing platform). Although most of the suggestions don't interest me, occasionally a newsletter will contain an idea that's solid gold. (Some of the free plugins available for Wordpress users are amazing!)

E-Books

My self-published paperback books are also available as e-books in both Kindle and Smashwords editions. The advantage of Smashwords is that readers can download them onto any device—or just onto their desktops if they don't own an e-book device. The Smashwords coupon service allows me to give my e-books away at no cost (useful when I'm seeking reviews).

Be sure to take advantage of the free formatting and marketing guides available at Smashwords. They're invaluable even if you're not planning to publish an e-book.

One unusual marketing strategy I've tried successfully is to publish a short (and free) e-book on Smashwords that includes an ad in the back for a book I'm selling, along with a sample chapter. Total cost: Nothing.

Videos

The easiest way to make a video is through PowerPoint. (See below for tips about finding free and inexpensive pictures and images.) I've also used my ASUS Transformer tablet to make videos in my home office (my husband pushes the *on* and *off* button for me). I've used an easel and poster board purchased at Staples for visuals. Although the videos are low tech, they've been popular and help me sell books (I always hold up a book and talk briefly about it at the end).

I have a playlist of all my police-report videos on YouTube, and I bought a domain name through GoDaddy so that users can find them easily (CJVideos.com). Recently I bought a subscription to a video software service that creates videos right on my PC.

Free Articles

I write articles at no charge for a police news website and for a service called EzineArticles.com (there's no "www"). They return the favor by posting a paragraph at the end of each article that links back to my books and website. EzineArticles.com also offers my articles free to any newspaper, magazine, newsletter or magazine that wants to republish them—with the condition that they include the links I've provided. That's free publicity for me and another way to market my books.

LinkedIn

I mentioned LinkedIn earlier—it's a free social media website just for professionals. All my writing activities (videos, PowerPoints, articles, blog posts) are reposted on LinkedIn, and I'm active in groups related to criminal justice, writing, and teaching English. When I write a new book, I post a notice on an appropriate group page asking for reviewers—I've received some good reviews and endorsements that way.

Facebook

In addition to my personal Facebook page, I have a page about writing (called "Write with Jean") and another one about police reports ("The Language Police"). I repost all my videos and articles on Facebook.

Electronic Newsletters

Twice a month I email a free e-newsletter about police reports. Subscribers come from a link on my blog at YourPoliceWrite.com. (I offer a free handout called "Ten Days to Better Police Reports" as an incentive to subscribe.)

I use a paid service called Constant Contact (MailChimp offers a similar service). Every issue of my newsletter contains one or two news stories related to criminal justice, a link to a video or PowerPoint I've made, and a quickie grammar quiz with the correct answer and an explanation.

Most important, there are links to my police report website and the Amazon marketing page for *Criminal Justice Report Writing*. Warning: Don't try to use a regular email account to send an e-newsletter to a large number of subscribers. The newsletter might be considered bulk mail, and your email account could be shut down.

Professional Relationships

Over the years I've made some good friends through my books and writing activities. Professionals I've never met have sent me suggestions about topics to cover and ways to publicize my books.

I try to nurture those relationships by responding promptly to messages and remembering to say "thank you" to everyone who is helpful. On holidays I like to send economical Jacquie Lawson musical e-cards or special pop-up holiday cards (Graphics3inc.com—pricey but worth the cost).

Sources for Pictures and Graphics

Pictures and graphics add interest and a professional touch to your books and marketing materials. But because of copyright laws, you can't simply copy pictures into your book, blog, or marketing materials (p. 254). Sometimes you can find excellent free pictures at the websites below.

Caution: Don't assume that everything posted at these websites is free. Be sure to click through to the source for each picture to see if there's a fee or restriction. For example, you might be required to give credit to the person who took a particular picture. Sometimes there are limitations on reusing a particular picture.

1. Commons.wikimedia.org

This website is especially good for pictures related to real people and historical events.

2. Wikipedia.org

Most (but not all!) pictures on Wikipedia are "fair use" (p. 254).

3. Google.com

Click on Images, Search Tools, Usage Rights, and Labeled for Noncommercial Use. Many (but not all) the pictures you will find are "fair use"—but click through to the source to make sure. "Noncommercial use" means you can't sell the image as a poster or make money by putting it on a poster, t-shirt, mug, or calendar.

4. Microsoft Word

If you have some computer skills and patience, you can make some of your own graphics. I used the SmartArt feature in Word to make the "Writing Process" graphic on p. 42 and the "A+" on p. 122. (I used Jing to convert each graphic into a .jpg.)

5. Wordle.net

You can see a "word cloud" that I made (free) on p. 117. (You'll need to have free Java software installed.)

6. Jing

Go to Techsmith.com to download free Jing software. It will allow you to take a picture of *anything* on a computer screen and turn it into a .jpg in less than a minute. I use Jing almost every day.

And...

At Dollar Photo Club you can find professional-quality pictures for almost any purpose—and you'll pay only a dollar for each picture. The basic subscription is $10 a month for 10 pictures. Any unused credits carry over to the next month.

Chapter 40

Writing for Pleasure and Publication

Writing is miraculous. That is not an overstatement! Most human endeavors require a huge investment in resources, energy, and time. But writing is something you can do anywhere, anytime. You don't even need writing materials: I do some of my writing—the thinking and organizing parts—in my car when I'm driving to and from dance lessons.

You don't need a graduate degree in English or creative writing. Here are the essential items: A brain (check) and lots of language practice (check—you've been doing that since infancy). You also need to log many, many hours of reading. For most writers that's no problem: We love to read.

In this chapter I'm going to offer some suggestions for various kinds of writing. For more in-depth information, visit your local library or spend some time browsing at an online bookstore.

I encourage you to experiment with as many types of writing as you can. You'll learn a lot that way, and your confidence will grow.

Writing for Publication

Here are a few more tips:

1. Invest in the latest edition of *Writer's Market* by Robert Lee Brewer. (Your library probably has a copy.) It features markets, writing tips, and step-by-step instructions for submitting your work. Years ago my husband used to write stories for children's magazines. *Writer's Market* was invaluable.

2. Know the competition. Book publishers always ask authors to fill out a form comparing their manuscript to competing books. How is your book different? What niche are you filling, or what makes your book stand out? Think about those questions while you're writing your book, and keep a record of the answers—it will come in handy later.

3. Follow trends, controversies, and experts in your subject. (LinkedIn groups are a great way to keep up with current issues in your field.)

A friend learned this lesson the hard way. She invested a great deal of time and brainpower writing a marvelous children's story about an adoption. Her theme was "the chosen child," and she worked the "chosen" idea into an imaginative story. But when she submitted the story to several children's magazines, she learned that child psychologists no longer subscribe to "the chosen child" as a way of explaining adoption.

Librarians are great resources for learning what's going on in the publishing world. Be sure to check with them before you embark on an ambitious writing project that you hope to publish. (My friend could have talked with a children's librarian, for example.)

4. Perfect your manuscript.

You already know that I'm on the editorial board for a journal that publishes scholarly articles. Occasionally submissions come in that haven't been proofread. Careless mistakes cast you in a poor light when an editor is evaluating your work.

Here are some tips for specific types of publishing:

Letters to the Editor

They're a wonderful way to build your critical thinking skills. Get into the habit of reading and evaluating the letters to the daily newspaper. You'll notice that some writers sound off without supporting their ideas at all. Others try to provide evidence but don't manage to sound convincing. There's usually just a small group of people who can make and support a point in an interesting and engaging way. Your goal, of course, is to become part of this group.

Letters to the editor can also teach you how to find writing topics in unexpected places. You'll be astonished at the range of subjects that arouse strong emotions in your fellow citizens—and the unexpected angles and viewpoints that they express.

I strongly encourage you to try your hand at writing a few letters. You'll see an improvement in your writing skills, and you'll enjoy seeing your name in print and hearing feedback from friends and family members. Letters to the editor are a wonderful (and free) education for anyone who wants to be a writer.

Memoirs

A good memoir is a gift that keeps on giving. How I wish that my parents and great-grandparents had written their life stories! Even details that probably seemed commonplace at the time would make fascinating reading now.

Example: The house where my mother grew up had a cold-water faucet in the kitchen—and no other plumbing. Hot water came from a kettle on the stove. My mind boggles. How did the family do laundry? What about going to the bathroom on a cold winter night—or in a storm? And how do you keep a baby clean and healthy under those conditions?

Don't be discouraged if your children aren't interested in your memoirs (especially if they're teenagers). They'll come around later on. If they don't, your grandchildren may be fascinated by what you've written.

Make it a priority to organize your thoughts, emotions, and memories around a theme. Avoid—like the plague—lapsing into lists of what happened and who was there. Beverly Lerner, a member of my Write Like a Pro group, organized her memoir around life-changing words. As a result, her book *That That Was, Was* is lively and engaging. By focusing on transitional moments in her life, she "made meaning," as Ann E. Berthoff recommends, about the events in her life.

Recommendation: *Naked, Drunk and Writing* by Adair Lara is my favorite book for writers interested in vignettes, personal essays, and memoirs.

Fiction

Friends tell me that there's nothing quite like the thrill of creating characters, putting them into an intriguing story, and then seeing your work in print. You can also write a story to use as a holiday card, birthday gift, or holiday present. (One year my husband and I used a story he'd written about a stray kitten as our Christmas card.)

But you need to know what you're doing! I've worked with a number of aspiring fiction writers who, alas, failed to understand the special requirements of fiction.

There isn't room in this book to teach you everything you need to know about writing fiction, but your library will have many resources. Joining a writing group can be a tremendous help. In the next few pages I'll share some lessons about fiction that friends and I have found especially useful.

Avoiding Common Mistakes with Fiction

Here are some typical comments I've heard from fiction writers that always signal problems ahead:

1. "My story builds slowly."

You won't sell books that way. You need to hook readers by the middle of the first page. Amazon.com is going to make the first chapter or so of your book available free on their website. If readers aren't engaged, they won't buy.

I always advise fiction writers to read a novel or two by John Grisham. A few months ago I came across a Grisham thriller in the library and wasn't sure I'd read it before, so I brought it home. By the end of the first chapter I realized I'd read it a few years ago—but by then I was so hooked that I read it all the way through a second time. *That's* the feeling you want to create in your own writing.

2. "I'm letting readers make up their own minds about my characters."

What you're really saying is that you haven't yet *worked* your material, and that means your story or novel isn't very good. Sorry.

Advice: Read some Hemingway short stories and notice that he barely describes his characters—and yet they seem alive and interesting. Your job is to do the same with *your* story and *your* characters.

3. "I'll start telling my story after I introduce the characters and setting."

This approach seems to make sense (it's called *exposition*), but there's a problem: Exposition has to be combined with action. Trying to introduce characters and get your story moving at the same time is the biggest challenge in fiction writing. Nobody finds it easy, but you have to do it.

To see an example of effective exposition, turn to p. 95, where you can read the first 121 words in Louisa May Alcott's timeless novel *Little Women*. In just a few sentences you will meet the characters and discover the challenges they're facing—and the story takes off.

Wisdom from Successful Novelists

Here are six excellent tips for fiction writers.

1. Don't let any characters get lost. If there are several people in a scene, make sure each one has something to say or do. If two people are arguing, for example, let the other characters react or interrupt.

2. Give the reader at least one character to root for. (This advice comes from Kurt Vonnegut.) I've often had friends tell me they stopped reading a book because they didn't like any of the characters.

3. Make every character react to everything that happens.

4. Every sentence must do one of two things—reveal character or advance the action. This is also from Kurt Vonnegut, and it's probably the best fiction writing advice I've ever heard. You don't want readers skipping parts of your story or novel.

5. Don't do your readers' thinking for them. This advice, from William Zinsser, is solid gold. Don't slow down your story by pointing out what should be obvious.

6. "Arrive, leave early." Avoid going into great detail to set up situations for your readers. Try to bring your readers in after the situation is already in motion—and cut it off before it's over. As I mentioned on p. 93, you can learn how to do this from good fiction and from movies and TV shows. Notice how often you're plunged into a developing situation—and pulled out before it's over.

The following excerpt is from Ernest Hemingway's short story "The Killers." Two tough-looking men have just walked into a diner to kill a man named Ole Anderson. They've heard that Ole comes to the diner every evening at six. George, who waits on customers, sends young Nick Adams to find Ole and warn him. Notice that Hemingway follows all of the advice you've just read.

---

from Ernest Hemingway's "The Killers"

"Mixing up in this ain't going to get you anywhere," the cook said. "You stay out of it."

"I'll go see him," Nick said to George. "Where does he live?"

The cook turned away.

Perhaps you're thinking, "That's it? What am I supposed to learn from just five sentences?" A lot.

Read the selection again. Did you notice that Hemingway had the cook turn away when Nick talked to George? Even though Nick is leaving on an urgent errand—trying to save Ole Anderson's life—Hemingway made sure we didn't forget that the cook was there. (Advice #1: "Don't let any character get lost.")

And did you notice that Hemingway didn't over-explain what was going on? He didn't need to say that Nick responded "eagerly," or that the cook was "cynical." Hemingway allowed readers to figure things out for themselves. (Advice #5: "Don't do your readers' thinking for them.)

Most important, did you notice that all three characters *reacted* to what was happening? George sent Nick to warn Ole, Nick agreed to go, and the cook turned away. You know exactly what each person was thinking and feeling. (Advice #3: "Make every character react to everything that happens."

Outlining

Emma Donoghue is the author of *Room*, probably the most gripping novel I've ever read. She says that she does a lot of outlining before she writes a novel from an unusual angle: the reader's viewpoint. Most writers focus on how the plot if unfolding. But Donoghue says, "I write down what revelations the reader is getting at each point, so I can see whether I'm giving away a lot in chapter one and then there's really no new important information until chapter five." Donoghue's approach makes sense when you remember that your primary goal as a writer is to please your readers.

Marilyn Durham's Story

In 1969 a woman named Marilyn Durham decided that she wanted to write a novel. Durham was a college dropout who described herself as "a frumpy housewife." Nothing about her background suggested that she could become a successful writer, and she didn't sign up for writing courses or join a support group. But in 1972 her novel *The Man Who Loved Cat Dancing* became a bestseller, and in 1973 it became a Hollywood movie. Later Durham went on to write two more novels: *Dutch Uncle* and *Flambard's Confession*.

She learned to write fiction at her town library. Every day she piled novels on a library table and studied how they were put together. For example, she read the first page in thirty novels and then went home to write *her* first page. (She never checked anything out.) Every day she went through the same ritual to try to figure out how professional writers develop characters, handle chapter transitions, and create plots.

Another problem was finding background information. Because her novel was set in the Civil War, she had to do research. She went to the children's library and read books that covered Civil War topics (weapons, for example—she was writing an adventure story) in simple language with lots of pictures.

Fiction for Children and Teens

Charles Warren is the author of *Address Unknown*, a novel for children ages eight and up and one of the best books for young people that I've ever read. The themes are homelessness and bullying, and it's such an absorbing story that I read the whole book in one afternoon.

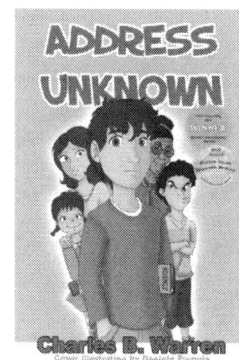

Charles Warren is (obviously!) a gifted writer who knows his craft. Here's his advice for authors who want to write for children and teens:

- Never lecture. Your story may teach, but the lesson must be a natural outcome of the storyline.
- The protagonist should grow and change in some way by the end of the story.
- The protagonist should be the age of the readers you are writing for, or perhaps a little older—never an adult.
- Spend some time with the age group you are writing for so you'll get the dialogue right. Volunteering at a school or Boys and Girls Club is a great way to get a feel for how kids talk.
- Write every day, even if you don't know what to write or don't feel like writing.

Blogging

A blog is an online log—kind of a diary. You can set up a free blog with a number of online providers (Google, for example). Blogs are useful for writing practice, exploring a topic, recording your progress with a goal, publicizing a book, and numerous other writing goals.

Blogging has many benefits. You'll make friends, expand your knowledge, and grow significantly as a writer. You'll gain an audience (one of the biggest thrills for a blogger). Most important, you'll find your writer's voice. Blogging has helped me develop my own personality as a writer, making this book much more fun to write (and, I hope, to read).

I have four websites, and keeping up with them has given me many opportunities to grow as a writer:

Soulspace.us: This is a blog about my personal life. I discuss issues related to my book *Gretel's Story*, and I reflect on time-management issues related to my book *Five Minutes a Day*.

WritewithJean.com: This blog is about writing, and it's helping me publicize the book you're reading right now.

YourPoliceWrite.com: This blog is about writing police reports, and it helps publicize my books *Criminal Justice Report Writing* and *Police Talk*.

DancewithJean.com: This blog is about ballroom dancing. I record thoughts, experiences, and pointers about dancing in the hope that they will stick with me, at least until my next lesson.

Finding Blog Content

The first rule for successful blogging is to post as often as you can. Fresh material attracts visitors to your blog and encourages them to keep coming back.

If you're writing about an ongoing experience, finding content probably won't be a problem. I find it easy to write blog posts for DancewithJean.com: Every ballroom lesson produces plenty of ideas. Julie Powell, working her way through Julia Child's *Mastering the Art of French Cooking* in just a year, never had to worry about content (and she ended up with a bestselling book and movie contract—*Julie and Julia*).

Unfortunately finding content isn't always that easy. I know a great deal about writing (as you can tell from the heft of this book), but I want my WritewithJean blog to be fresh and different—more about the *life* of a writer than *how* to write. So I have to move past what I know well in order to find quirks, gaps, and oddities to write about.

That struggle turns out to be an advantage! Why? It forces me to go beyond conventional ideas about writing to find something interesting for a post. And that's one of the big advantages of a blog: You learn how to find content in unexpected places. Soon you find yourself developing a voice that's uniquely yours—and that's the key to all successful writing.

Google Alerts (google.com/alerts) is a wonderful free resource. Every day (or every week, if you prefer) you'll get a list of links to new content about any subject (or subjects) you request. For example, Google Alerts sends me steady stream of news articles about police reports for my blog for police officers.

Copyright Issues ©

If you hope to publish your writing, you need to be familiar with copyright law. Please note that I'm not an attorney! When in doubt, consult a legal expert with a background in copyright law. What I can give you here is some basic information about what copyright is and how it works.

The United States has laws to protect the rights of authors and artists. If you create a work of art, no one else may copy it without your permission. Copyright protection lasts for 70 years after the author or artist's death. A person who copies your work without permission may face severe penalties. Good intentions or ignorance of copyright law do not constitute a legal defense.

1. Registration

You can go online to register your work with the US Copyright Office. Go to http://copyright.gov/fls/sl35.pdf to learn more. The process involves filling out a form, paying a fee, and sending in non-returnable copies of your work.

But you don't have to register your work. You can simply insert a copyright symbol, the year, and your name (or the name of your company or organization) into your writing project. You can find the copyright symbol in the Symbols menu in your word processor. Registration is useful if you need to go to court to prove that the work is yours, but many writers choose not to register their work.

2. Fair use

Certain kinds of copying—called "fair use"—are allowed. In general, you may copy a small portion of a copyrighted work. (Suggestion: Go to the Wikipedia entry for US Copyright and read the "fair use" section there.) There is no formula for what constitutes "fair use," and a court challenge is possible. A popular rule of thumb of 5% or 450 words or so (whichever is less), but there is no guarantee that this rule of thumb will apply in a particular case.

3. Public domain

In general, works published before 1923 are in the public domain. This is why you see the full text of many older books published online—and why publishers keep bringing out new editions of older books. It's also why you sometimes see classic books rewritten with a modern twist. (*Little Vampire Women* and *Pride and Prejudice and Zombies* are examples.) Once a work goes into the public domain, anything goes.

4. Protecting yourself

Copyright covers books, magazines, journals, newspapers, essays, letters, poems, pictures, photos, cartoons, and *any* creative work. Do not copy anything without considering possible copyright issues. If you want to use something created by another person, seek permission (sometimes called "licensing") first. Expect to pay a fee. Often you can go to the publisher's website, fill out a form there, and then send in your payment.

I've often sought copyright permission to include the work of other writers in my books. Sometimes I've dealt directly with the author or artist. (I once talked to Sidney Poitier on the telephone to ask for permission to copy a story from his autobiography, *This Life*. He was wonderful!) Be sure to allow plenty of time for copyright requests to be processed. (On p. 243 I offer sources for free and inexpensive artwork that does not violate copyright law.)

Copyright can be complicated. For example, did you know that the popular "Happy Birthday" song used to be copyrighted? Every time it was used in a movie, audiences saw a permissions notice in the closing credits. The song was estimated to be worth five million dollars. Recently there was a legal dispute about the song's copyright, and there's even been a documentary about the case. It is now in the public domain, and anyone can use it free for any purpose.

Other famous court cases involved George Harrison's song "My Sweet Lord" (Harrison lost the case when a court found that he had copied many elements from the Chiffons' hit "He's So Fine") and the Shepard Fairey *Hope* poster, which was based on an Associated Press portrait of Barack Obama (the case was decided out of court).

Here's the bottom line: Respect copyright law, and be careful.

Chapter 41

Business Writing

Imagine this situation: A talented young woman is just beginning her career at a large organization with many opportunities for advancement. Her first morning on the job begins with two tasks. One is filling out a form for a parking tag in the employee lot. The second is asking her boss what to do about three binders she found in a desk drawer—they seem to be incomplete reports about a project that a former employee was doing.

Question: How can she dress up these tasks to impress her boss?

The answer is that she can't. There is no fancy way to fill out a parking lot form. The same principle applies to her question about the three binders. She is going to have to wait for other opportunities to show her boss what she knows and what she can do.

Perhaps you're puzzled by this example. Obviously nobody would try to make a big deal out of filling out a parking form or asking what to do with a few binders. But many people really do try to dress up ordinary tasks in a mistaken attempt to impress others. The results are ridiculous—but it's a practice that's hard to stop.

Take a look at this email sent to a professor from the financial aid office at a college:

> Due to the need to monitor academic progress for students enrolled in college and receiving financial aid, regular progress reports are necessary from faculty actively providing instruction. Such reports enable the financial aid office to determine whether additional support (i.e. tutoring in various academic subjects) will be beneficial to individual students.
>
> A progress form for the abovementioned student is attached herewith. A release form signed by said student is on file. Faculty cooperation in this matter is highly valued.

Now read this alternative version (same request, different wording):

Because Anthony Ratto is on financial aid, our office needs regular reports about his grades in your class. (He has already signed a release form.) Please fill out the progress form I've attached and return it to me. Your responses will help us ensure that Anthony is on track academically. We can arrange for him to receive tutoring if it's needed. Thank you for your help.

If you were the official in the financial office, which version would you send? Whenever I ask this question at a business writing workshop, participants invariably choose the first version. When I ask why, they say something vague like "It has more information."

But that's nonsense: Both versions have the same information. The first version is a time-waster bogged down with empty and repetitious verbiage. The second version is much better because it gets to the point quickly and sounds like a real person making a friendly request.

So why doesn't every business person use that warm and direct approach to writing?

There are two answers. One is that many business people are trying to impress their bosses and co-workers with big words and fancy sentences. As I pointed out on the previous page, this kind of overwriting doesn't work, and it makes the writer look ridiculous. (It also wastes time.)

The second reason is tradition. Most working people don't sign up for business writing courses in high school or college. (In fact I've never taken a course in business writing.) The average person acquires work-related writing skills on the job, the way I did. (I learned how to write prison reports while I was teaching in a prison school.) Often there's an informal training process that consists of simply imitating the way their co-workers write. As a result, many businesses are still using outdated practices going back more than a hundred years: Long-winded, machine-like gobbledygook.

Writing to a Business or Organization

I sometimes hear business people say there's no point in using a friendly tone because they're writing to a company, not a person. If you think about that statement for a moment, you'll see how ridiculous it is. Companies can't read! Your emails, letters, and reports are always read by a real human being.

And here's another point that's often overlooked: Writing with warmth and humanity can go a long way toward forging goodwill—always a valuable commodity in the professional world.

Here's an example of what I'm talking about. After a court case that accused the New York Police Department of some illegal searches, Peter Zimroth was appointed federal monitor to ensure that the NYPD obeyed the law. (Before you read on, stop and think about how the police leadership felt about this situation. Were they happy to have an outsider monitoring their practices? Did they look forward to Zimroth's findings? The likely answer to both questions is *no*.)

In July 2015, Zimroth submitted his first report and a cover letter. Here's the first sentence of the letter:

> I am pleased to submit my first report describing the work done under the court orders in *Floyd v. City of New York, Ligon v. City of New York* and *Davis v. City of New York*.

Question: How do you think the police leadership felt when they read that sentence? The answer is obvious: They breathed a huge sigh of relief. That word "pleased" conveyed the message that all was well—Zimroth was aiming to support the agency, not condemn it.

Now I want you to think about this: How would the NYPD leadership have felt if Zimroth had begun his letter with an old-fashioned and impersonal opening? Here's what how he might have written it:

> Enclosed herewith is my first report describing the work done under the court orders in *Floyd v. City of New York, Ligon v. City of New York* and *Davis v. City of New York*.

The answer is that they probably would have felt apprehensive—because that opening doesn't give them a single clue about whether Zimroth's findings were positive or negative. Nor would that sentence help forge a trusting relationship between the two sides. (And there's another disadvantage to writing that way: Zimroth would have sounded old-fashioned and out of touch.)

Now imagine *you* were in Zimroth's position—submitting a report to an organization that wasn't looking forward to hearing from you. What tone would *you* adopt? Would you make yourself sound modern, progressive, and human—or cold, stuffy, and out of date? I hope the answer is obvious.

The Plain Language Act

In 2010, concerns about inefficient and confusing writing practices in government led to the passage of the Plain Language Act. Congress passed it, the President signed it, and now federal employees are required by law to use plain English in government documents.

The law doesn't cover state and local agencies, and of course it doesn't apply to writing outside the government sector. But plain writing makes sense, and its popularity is growing. Business and government leaders are beginning to understand the importance of clear, direct communication, and they're recommending the pleasant tone you would use if you were talking to someone face-to-face. In-house writing workshops have become popular. (I've conducted quite a few of them myself.)

There are some excellent resources posted online, free, at PlainLanguage.gov. (As you would expect, the information is easy to read, understand, and apply.)

The Golden Rule of Business Writing

Always state your main point early. Always. If you're broadcasting bad news (such as an announcement that there won't be a raise this year), you can write an introductory sentence or two to soften the blow. If you're writing a major report, you might have a preliminary paragraph where you describe the situation you're dealing with and thank everyone who helped you. But the Golden Rule still applies: Get to your main point early.

In a long report, you can state your main point in a summary on the first page that briefly states your findings and recommendations. Emails and correspondence don't begin with a formal summary, of course. But you should still put your main point as close to the beginning as you can—in the first sentence, if possible.

If you're thinking that this is common sense, think again. After many years of consulting with businesses and agencies, I can testify that very few business writers begin with the point they're trying to make.

A story: Some years ago I was called in to help a government agency that did land acquisitions for highway projects. Agents were wasting time revisiting the same homeowners to do the same preliminary investigations.

The reason? There was a lot of turnover in the agency, and that was causing time-wasting repetition. When a new employee—call him Harry Paolucci—took over a project, he was handed a report describing a visit to an elderly woman who had a piece of property the government wanted to buy. The report rambled on about the visit—tea and cookies, a walk around her property, a description of the new highway that was coming, and—finally—the problem of the doghouse in the northeast corner.

Rather than wading through pages of descriptions of the property, the cookies, and the dog, Harry decided to visit the homeowner herself. He then generated a new report.

A month later, when Harry was transferred (as frequently happened), a new agent would arrive—Sandra Cooprider. Now there were *two* reports—the first one and Harry's. Rather than wade through them, Sandra made *another* visit to the homeowner, who by now was getting very tired of serving tea and giving mini-tours to agents from the highway department.

My suggestion was simple: Redesign the report form with a summary box on the top of the first page. If an agent was transferred, all the new agent had to do was read what was in the box. If there were questions, answers could probably be found in the rest of the report. But most of the time there was no need to go through all that material about the tea, cookies, and doghouse. Whatever the agent really needed to know was in that summary.

Don't Start at the Beginning

It's human nature: We want to start our stories at the beginning. "On Tuesday evening at 7 PM I rang Mrs. Watson's doorbell. She greeted me and took me into her kitchen, where we sat down and talked over tea and cookies. I told her about the new highway ramp and showed her the construction plans...."

Most people handle writing tasks that way. But it's a big time waster, and confusing to boot. Readers plod on and on, wondering what point you're trying to make. Get there quickly! If you doubt me, take a look at your own email inbox. I'm predicting you'll find messages organized like this:

> To: Department Heads
> From: Joanna Caffrey, Human Resources Director
> As you know, every employee is entitled to two weeks of paid vacation each year. Paul Oates, our payroll director, will begin his vacation on July 15. That means he will be out of the office on July 20, the normal date for department heads to submit their payroll forms. Accordingly, we're asking you to submit them by Monday, July 10. Thank you for your cooperation in this matter.

What you're reading is Joanna Caffrey's thinking process: *Let's see...Paul is going on vacation, and he's in charge of payroll, and everyone needs to get paid, but he won't be around when the reports come in on the 20th—I'd better send an email asking for them on the 10th.*

But those busy department heads don't care when Paul takes his vacation. What part of the message concerns them? *The early date for payroll reports.* That information should come first. Often you can even omit some of the other information:

> To: Department Heads
> From: Joanna Caffrey, Human Resources Director
> Please submit your payroll reports on July 10 this month so that Paul Oates, our payroll director, can process them before his vacation beginning July 15.

It's efficient, professional, and courteous—an example of good business writing!

More Tips for Effective Business Writing

- Don't repeat numbers in parentheses, like this:

    The project will be implemented in three (3) steps. WRONG

    This is an old-fashioned military practice that never made sense in the first place, and it doesn't belong in modern business writing.

- Use bullets to simplify lists of information (as I'm doing here).

- Set up an informal buddy system for double-checking important documents. My husband and I do this for each other to eliminate the slippery mistakes that find their way into most writing projects.

Emails

Here's the most important rule for workplace emails: Never write anything that you wouldn't want the entire workplace to read. Emails go astray. All it takes is one person who accidentally forwards a message, or clicks "reply to all" instead of "reply," and you could have a disaster on your hands.

One weekend the email system at my college went crazy and spewed emails everywhere—including to the college president's inbox. Chaos and embarrassment ensued. Luckily no incriminating emails from my own correspondence went astray—but the truth is that no luck was involved. My work-related emails were always squeaky-clean: No opinions, no gossip, no secrets. I highly recommend the same policy to you.

Another tip: *Always* update the subject line when you reply. Emails often get linked into chains, so that a message about Monday afternoon's meeting is still circulating two weeks later, with other subjects tacked on.

What if you need a detail from one of those later emails—say, the phone number from a vendor who's coming to do a presentation? You're stuck scrolling through fifteen or twenty emails with the same subject line: *Monday Afternoon's Meeting*. Changing the subject line to *Acme Supply's Presentation* might save someone (perhaps you!) a great deal of time down the road.

Business Letters

- Be warm, professional, and efficient. Never begin a letter with "This is in reference to...." Often it will be obvious what you're writing about. If you do need to provide an order number or product code, use a subject line.
- Never repeat what the customer told you: "On July 13, you wrote us to inquire whether the Fisherman's Sweater can be shipped overseas." Your letter should begin, "Yes, we'll be happy to ship the Fisherman's Sweater overseas."
- Soften negative information with a friendly sentence or two. Here's a useful rule of thumb: "Say *yes* quickly; say *no* slowly."

Writing a Report

Professional reports give you an opportunity to showcase your writing, thinking, and problem-solving skills. Because they're often the product of a task force or a committee, you can also demonstrate your ability to work as a team—and your leadership skills, if you're the person in charge of a report.

To make the most of these opportunities, you need to produce an impressive final product. Make it readable and well organized, and proofread it carefully. Here are some tips:

- Make your main point early—in the first paragraph if possible, and no later than the bottom of the first page.
- Ensure that the first sentence of every paragraph supports your main point and predicts what the paragraph will be about.
- Don't get bogged down when you're presenting background information. Move it to an Appendix at the back.
- Use the Appendix to store supporting data you've collected. If questions arise after you've submitted your report and moved on to another project, you'll know where to find the answers.

Be sure to review Chapter 6, Writing Paragraphs and Essays (p. 46). If you're doing research in connection with your report, review Chapter 19 as well.

Chapter 42

Using a Word Processor

If you're serious about writing, you need to become a word processing expert. These tips are especially valuable if you're self-publishing a book.

1. Make sure your formatting is compatible with other publishing systems. I recommend using Microsoft Word, not an open-source system.

2. You can often Google a problem to find out how to fix it. I've learned a lot about word processing that way. YouTube has instructional videos for almost anything you want to do.

3. Never right-justify a document unless you're told to format it that way. (Many books are right-justified.)

4. Respect your computer. It's a sophisticated typesetting instrument that can do things that were impossible on a typewriter. Use the word wrap feature rather than hitting the Enter key at the end of each line. And use only one space after a period. (If you still need convincing, go to this link: adamsdrafting.com/one-space-or-two/).

5. Underlining is ugly, and you should never use it. Professionals use underlining only for specialized printing jobs (it tells the printing company to use italics). If you want to emphasize a word or phrase, use bold formatting, a different color, a larger typeface size, or a contrasting typeface.

Styles

Do not touch the space bar EVER except to hit it once after a sentence. (The same goes for the Tab key.) For centering and other formatting, use Styles (found in the Format pull-down menu). That means setting a style for each formatting feature in your document.

Here are some of the settings I used for the Styles in this book:

Styles in Microsoft Word

Document:

Mirror margins, no right justification, gutter .5"

Top .8"; Bottom, Inside, and Outside .75"

Header .4"; Footer .6"

Normal:

Georgia 12 pt., line spacing exactly 18 pt., spacing 6 pt. before and after

First line indented .3"

Heading 1:

Bold, centered, Calibri 20 pt., spacing 12 pt. after, no indentation for the first line

Heading 2:

Bold, flush left, Calibri 14 pt., spacing 6 pt. before and after, no indentation for the first line.

Formatting an E-book

For an e-book, use the same typeface for everything. Different e-readers have different formats, so a mix of styles that looks great on one person's e-reader can look *horrible* on someone else's—some words oversized and others tiny, for example. You can download a wonderful formatting guide for e-books at Smashwords.com. It will also teach you a lot about general word processing.

Inserting Images, Graphics, and Pictures

Use the Format Pictures option. First, insert your picture. It may look weird—in fact you may barely be able to see your picture at all. Right-click on it, and a menu will appear. Choose Format Picture. Experiment to find out what commands work best for you.

Page Numbers, Headers, and Footers

Microsoft Word can give you headaches when you're working with headers and footers. Page numbers go into "headers" (the top margin) or "footers" (the bottom of the page). Section breaks are required if you want to switch from one numbering system to another (from Roman to Arabic numerals, for example, or to have some pages without numbers). The magic trick is to get into the header/footer menu or toolbar and unclick "Same as Previous." I couldn't find the command at first, and then a short video on YouTube saved the day.

You may also run into have difficulty if you want a different header for each chapter. I did my *Criminal Justice Report Writing* book that way. I pulled it off— but it was so labor intensive that I will never do a book that way again.

More about Section Breaks

Once you insert a section break, you may have difficulty removing it if you change your mind. Here's a trick: Hit the Enter key right in front of the section break, so that the section break is on a separate line. Insert any key in front of the section break. (I usually type an *x*). Now you should be able to delete the Section Break.

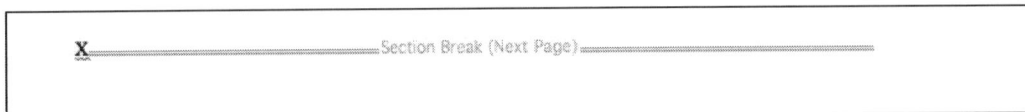

Show All Nonprinting Characters

This feature will help you find formatting mistakes. Click on the symbol.

Solving Stubborn Problems

I ran into some huge problems when I was formatting a collection of essays for a publisher. Some authors didn't know the rule about using Styles consistently. I had to clean up a mixture of double-spacing and single spacing, a variety of typeface sizes, and several other messes. Some essays had hidden commands that I couldn't find and couldn't delete. Every time I fixed a paragraph and hit the Enter key, the corrections I'd made in the *previous* paragraph would disappear. I went crazy until I learned two important tricks for using Word:

1. Sometimes Word hides formatting commands in the paragraph symbol at the end of a paragraph. You're tearing your hair out because you keep typing commands, but Word ignores them. Word may be obeying a command that it secretly stuck in the paragraph symbol when you hit the Enter key earlier.

Solution: Click on "Show all nonprinting characters" on your toolbar (it looks like a paragraph mark) and delete the paragraph symbol at the end of the paragraph with the problems. Fix your formatting, and then hit the Enter key again. Here's an example. The arrow points to the paragraph mark to delete:

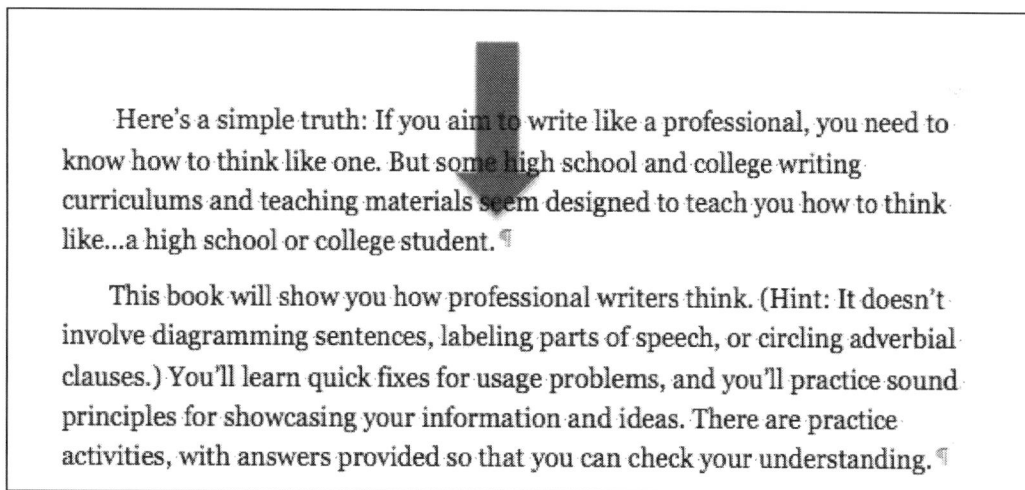

Here's a simple truth: If you aim to write like a professional, you need to know how to think like one. But some high school and college writing curriculums and teaching materials seem designed to teach you how to think like...a high school or college student. ¶

This book will show you how professional writers think. (Hint: It doesn't involve diagramming sentences, labeling parts of speech, or circling adverbial clauses.) You'll learn quick fixes for usage problems, and you'll practice sound principles for showcasing your information and ideas. There are practice activities, with answers provided so that you can check your understanding. ¶

Deleting the paragraph mark will cause both paragraphs to run together. Just hit the Enter key to separate the paragraphs again.

2. The other way to solve stubborn problems is to save your document as a .txt file. (This is the same as saving it in Notepad.) All the old formatting (good and bad) will be stripped away, and you can start over. Yes, it's tedious! But you'll end up with a document that's formatted correctly. (A word to the wise: When you start over, be sure to use Styles for everything, so that you don't create a new set of problems.)

Appendix

Print and Online Resources

Books

John McWhorter is a professor of linguistics who writes about a wide range of language issues. I recommend anything (and everything) he's written.

Theodore Bernstein was the assistant managing editor of the *New York Times*. His books about writing are fun to read and right on target. I learned more about English usage from him than from any other writer.

The *American Heritage Dictionary* has a Usage Panel that votes on trends in language. It's a great resource when you're dealing with a usage controversy: Is *snuck* acceptable? What about using *their* with a singular pronoun?

The Elements of Style by William Strunk, Jr., and E.B. White is a classic book that every writer should read.

Adair Lara's *Naked, Drunk and Writing* is one of the best books on writing I've ever read. She teaches practical strategies for discovering ideas, bringing them to life, and presenting them with an impressive and professional polish.

Websites

Dictionary.com

Besides offering definitions, this website compares what various dictionaries say about a particular word or phrase, and it sometimes offers usage notes.

PlainLanguage.gov

Jargon and gobbledygook waste time, create confusion, and make a bad impression on your readers. This government-sponsored website provides many easy-to-use resources to help you write more clearly and efficiently.

WritewithJean.com

My own website provides ongoing instruction and my personal take on a wide variety of writing issues.

owl.English.Purdue.edu/owl

(Note that there's no "www.") Purdue University's online writing lab is an indispensable resource for students, especially when you're working on a research project. I'm a frequent visitor when I'm working on a scholarly project and need help with documentation. This website also offers advice about technical writing, including engineering reports.

Evernote.com

Say good-bye to Post-It notes—although they're handy, they're also easily lost. This free, privacy-protected website sorts and stores any information you want to save. You can access the information from any computer with Internet access. Evernote allows you to clean out your desk and set up a quick, reliable system to find important information.

Passpack.com

This isn't really a writers' website, but it's a lifesaver for many professionals. You can securely store passwords here, free of charge, and access them from any computer with Internet access. This is a great resource if you have accounts with many websites, and it's especially useful if you travel often: You don't have to worry about carrying (and possibly losing) a list of passwords.

Jing at Techsmith.com

Jing is a free app that allows you to turn anything on a computer screen into a .jpeg. You can also use Jing to make videos. Rarely does a day go by that I don't use Jing.

wpbeginner.com

A great resource for bloggers who want to improve their WordPress skills. I've subscribed to the daily newsletter and picked up many useful tips for my websites.

ImageOptim for Mac

This free app compresses images so that they load more quickly online. Indispensable for bloggers. Unfortunately it's not available for PC's.

CreateSpace.com

A terrific one-stop website for self-publishers. The free services are amazing, and the technical support is fabulous.

Smashwords.com

A terrific one-stop website for anyone who wants to publish e-books. You should visit Smashwords even if you're not planning to publish an e-book because you can learn a lot about formatting and marketing from the free instructional books.

LinkedIn.com

Every serious writer needs to get involved with LinkedIn. You can network with other professionals and showcase your writing.

DollarPhotoClub.com

You can subscribe for only ten dollars a month and receive the rights to high-quality photos for only a dollar each. If you purchase fewer than ten photos in a month, the unused ones carry over to the next month.

EzineAarticles.com (There's no "www")

Submit articles you've written to this free website, and it will evaluate them and make them available for possible publication. (There's no payment and no guarantee that a newsletter or magazine will pick them up.) If your articles are published, they'll include a paragraph at the end directing visitors to your website or book. Ezine Articles offers free writing instruction and some paid resources that are highly useful if you're just starting out.

Commons.Wikimedia.org

This is usually my first stop when I need a picture of a famous person, a historical event, or a location. Most pictures can be reused at no charge (but check carefully—sometimes you're required to give credit).

Wordle.net

You can make word clouds at this free website (you can see one of mine on p. 118). You'll need to have the latest version of Java installed—also free.

http://Graphics3inc.com.

Graphics3 sells 3-D popup cards for the winter holidays and other occasions. They are expensive—but they make treasured keepsakes for the recipients. I use them as thank-you gifts for colleagues who go out of their way to help me with my writing projects.

JacquieLawson.com

On holidays I like to send Jacquie Lawson musical e-cards. A subscription is inexpensive and covers unlimited cards, and recipients always say they enjoy them.

GoDaddy.com (there's no "www")

You can purchase a domain name that will send Internet visitors directly to a video, PowerPoint, book, or article so that potential customers don't have to search a website or online store.

www.PlanMyPaper.com

This link features short (and free) PowerPoints and videos I've made that explain how to organize an essay.ResearchPaperSteps.com

This link will take you to my instructional PowerPoints and videos for writing a research paper.

RagtimeResearchPaper.com

I've written a sample research paper and posted it at this link.

https://Books.Google.com

Google has scanned countless books and posted them here. For copyright reasons, you can't read most books online. But you can do word searches—a great timesaver for anyone doing academic work.

Toastmasters.org

Public speaking (in person, or via videos that you make yourself) is a great way to showcase yourself and market your writing. Toastmasters is a nonprofit organization that has helped countless people overcome their fears and develop skill in public speaking.

Index

About Jean Reynolds

Dr. Jean Reynolds is Professor Emerita at Polk State College in Winter Haven, Florida, where she taught English for over 30 years. She is the author of *Succeeding in College, Sentence Power, Introduction to College Writing, Criminal Justice Report Writing, Gretel's Story: Finding the Way Home*, and *Five Minutes a Day: Time Management for People who Love to Put Things Off*. She is co-author (with the late Mary Mariani) of *Police Talk*.

   Other publications include articles and reviews in a variety of magazines, newspapers, and journals. She has served as a writing consultant to numerous businesses and agencies, including Health and Rehabilitative Services and the Florida Department of Corrections.

   Jean holds a doctorate in English from the University of South Florida and is an internationally recognized Shaw scholar. She is the author of *Pygmalion's Wordplay: The Postmodern Shaw* and co-editor, with D. A. Hadfield, of *Shaw and Feminisms: Onstage and Off*. She serves on the Editorial Board for the *Shaw Journal*.

   She is an accomplished ballroom dancer. She and her husband, garden writer Charles Reynolds, live in Florida and enjoy reading and traveling.

   Visit Jean's website at WritewithJean.com for more writing instruction and practice. You can email her at jreynoldswrite@aol.com.